CW00344281

Being Irish in Liverpool

© Tommy Walsh 2011

Published by St. Michael's Irish Centre, Liverpool
Book design by March Design, Liverpool
Printed by W&G Baird, Antrim

Acknowledgements
I must say many, many thanks, go raibh mile maith agaibh in fact to Maureen
Morrison and Moira Callaghan. The only way I know how to write is with pen
and paper, so I have been totally dependent on them for all the typing and
electronic assistance. It is certainly true to say that this book would not have
been printed without their help. Thanks also to Michael March for his
professional advice and help with the design and preparation for printing.

Being Irish in Liverpool

Tommy Walsh

CONTENTS

Tommy Walsh attending a Gaelic
football game in Navan, County
Meath, John Mitchels v Moynalvey
11 January 2009.

Tommy Walsh

Sadly, Tommy Walsh passed away in October, 2010, after a short illness, while in the process of finishing this book. His loving family have attempted to ensure his words are presented here as he would have intended. This introduction has been taken from Colum's eulogy at his father's funeral.

Tommy Walsh was born on 14th September 1930, in Blundell Street, Liverpool, to Irish parents, Colum from Carraroe, and Mary, a Liverpool girl of Carlow parents. He was the youngest of four children – baby brother to May, Sadie and Colum. While growing up he helped to run the family grocers' shop, a talent which was to serve him well in later life. In 1963 he was appointed Manager of the Liverpool Irish Centre in Mount Pleasant, which officially opened 1 February 1965. The Centre became regarded as the best-run Irish Centre in Britain, and Tommy was invited to advise and assist committees, up and down the country, that wanted to open their own Irish Centre. This he did willingly, as he was passionate, that all Irish people should remember and promote their heritage.

In 1973 Tommy became the first Chairman of the Federation of Irish Societies. This society created a very powerful voice of the Irish in Britain in many topics, including lobbying Irish governments for grants for various groups, including, Youth, Community Care and Welfare. Significantly being awarded their first grant in 1979 for Community Care. Charles Haughey doubled the grant whilst in office and the then Minister of Labour, Bertie Ahern, became a regular visitor to the Irish community in Britain, presumably on the way to Old Trafford!

In 1974 Tommy was awarded the accolade 'Irishman of the Year', voted for by readers of the *Irish Post* in Britain, in recognition of his work with the Federation of Irish Societies and the Liverpool Irish Centre. He won the award, beating jockey, Pat Eddery into second place, with Terry Wogan in third, Johnny Giles in fourth and Danny La Rue way down the list in ninth place.

After his retirement from the Irish Centre, he was offered jobs, two of which he took, both of which were Irish based companies, Cocina Kitchens and Dunloe Menswear. But it was his appointment as Shop Manager at Liverpool Football Club that caused great consternation. His very good friend Jim Kennefick, who was a commercial manager at LFC, approached Tommy to oversee the move into the new shop as it is now, and enhance the mail-order catalogue purchasing system. The consternation was due to Colum, his brother, being such a staunch Evertonian. Tommy was too, along with his sons Colum and Nick, always quoting 1949/50 team, including Peter Farrell, Tommy Eglington and others. When Tommy's children, Mary, Nick, Kathleen and Colum, were growing up Uncle Colum would call LFC the redskins, that of course was before bad language. The success of the LFC shop is a clear indication that his time there was successful.

Tommy was passionate about the welfare of Irish people in Britain, including prisoners. This was a very difficult and nervous time, particularly during the 1970s and 1980s, with the Prevention of Terrorism Act. He was a member of the Irish Commission for Prisoners Overseas and visited many irish prisoners since he first became involved in 1969. He tells the story of visiting Martina Shanahan, one of the so-called Winchester Three, a victim of a dubious conviction, sentenced to serve 25 years in Category A, Durham Prison. This particular visit there were three prisoners only in Cat A, Martina, a 2nd girl, a girl from East Germany as it was then,

7

when Tommy said goodbye to her through the bars she replied 'Tiocfaidh ár lá,' which set him smiling all the way home.

Hugh Callaghan, of the Birmingham Six, in his book *Cruel Fate* quotes, "Tommy Walsh wrote endlessly to us in prison, as well as visiting." At a meeting in the House of Commons, Tommy reminded the audience he could have been talking about six corpses, if the death penalty was still on the statutes.

Over the years, hundreds of men and woman were detained off the boats from Dublin and Belfast by the Special Branch and held for up to seven days without acknowledging that they were being detained. Tommy would visit the Bridewell in the hope that he could let worried relatives know at least they were alive, although often they would be deported back to Ireland. He took many a phone-call from Rita Mullen of the Association of Legal Justice in Belfast, Cardinal Tomas O'Fiaich, and Fr Denis Faul with names of people who had gone missing.

Along with Fr Paddy Sheridan and Fr Frank Ryan, they took the *Daily Express* to the Press Council, and won, after the paper reported that Irish men and woman were involved in multi-million-pound racket, sending their Social Security money home to fund the IRA.

Tommy has been involved with the Irish Community Care Merseyside and Irish Youth Federation in the UK. His involvement in other groups also included St Margaret Mary's, serving as a Governor to the schools.

GAA has played a huge part in Tommy's life, and in 1961 was elected Vice President of the Provincial Council of Great Britain, becoming President in 1964 at the age of 33, serving for three years, and remained on Central Council for a further nine years as a elected delegate. Tommy always took his family on an extra holiday to Ireland during Easter-time, when he attended the annual convention. He was involved in a number of sub-committees at this time, but one in particular stood out for him. That was when he was invited by Croke Park to be part of the Crossmaglen Rangers National GAA Committee to lobby Britain to get the troops out of the club grounds that they had occupied. This eventually proving successful. He made wonderful friends there including Gene Duffy, Donal Duck Whelan, Gene Larkin, and also hooked up again with his old friend the Cardinal.

He served as an officer Lancashire Co Board starting in

1953, aged 23, and serving in each role, as well as playing and serving as officer with his club, John Mitchels. Together with his best friend Chris Johnston, they would 'catch' new players that came into the Irish Centre. Between himself and Chris it often seemed they kept the Club going, but sadly in early 2000, Mitchels could not field a team. In 2006 Barry Morris and Danny McDonough re-formed the club, and re-affiliated it to the Lancs County Board, subsequently they have become a very strong and succesful club, also forming a Ladies club. In 2008 Mitchels won the championship of Great Britain, and since travelled to Navan to play Moynalvey, the Leinster champions, and winning. Thus becoming the first club from the UK to win a game in the All Ireland series, then going on to beat Killala in Carrick on Shannon, and finally to Croke Park for the All Ireland Junior Football Final v Skellig Rangers from Kerry, losing by a single point.

Tommy, Chris and Jim Morrin were guests on each trip courtesy of Danny and Barry. His son, Colum, sat next to him in Carrick on Shannon v Killala, and says that Tommy kicked and caught every ball through the match, with the odd elbow into his ribs, all fair of course. He was so proud of Danny and Barry and the panel, and all they have achieved since 2005. The picture on the frontispiece was taken in Navan during the quarter final, and shows how happy he was. He said of the GAA, 'it generates lasting friendships',

Of course behind this busy lifestyle was his wife, Kathleen, until she passed away in 1994, leaving him heartbroken. Kathleen was very like Tommy, quiet, not liking a fuss. She often joined him on trips that he was invited to for dinners or other events, but just as happy to stay at home. Over the years at Irish Centre. Tommy used to take Monday nights off. That was when his children and Kathleen had to find things to do. Kathleen took up a keep-fit programme with her good friend Irene Bradley, just to get out of the house, as he had control of the TV. His schedule was *World in Action* at 8.30, *News* at 9.00, followed by *Panorama*, hosted by Ludovic Kennedy. He appeared on the programme too. Any requirements for knowledge of Irish history Tommy Walsh was contacted, therefore appearing regularly on local TV or radio in both Ireland and UK. Although, a year or two ago, he was filmed for three hours by Japanese TV, leaving all that knew him wondering, how he went down in Tokyo.

X

Being Irish in Liverpool

Childhood

BEING IRISH IN LIVERPOOL was easy for me. I didn't have to make any decisions ... they came much later. I was born 'over the shop' in Blundell Street on the south side of Liverpool city centre. I was to learn later in life that Scotland Road on the north side was the Irish side of town.

My father, Colum, was a native of Carraroe, Co. Galway. Like so many others from Carraroe, he made his way to Huddersfield. It had to be there or Boston, where his two sisters went: Mary in 1912 and Sarah (Sala) in 1916. He came to England in 1922, working first shovelling coke in Huddersfield. Even then, automation was around, though the word didn't come in to great use for many more years. An automatic shovel came on the scene and the men were dispensed with. My father headed for Liverpool. He became a lodger in my grandmother's house at 37, Blundell Street, and found work as a docker. He remained at the docks until he retired about fifty years later.

After my mother and father married, they moved into a shop and house higher up the street at 13/15 Blundell Street. I was born in 1930, the youngest of four children, two girls and a boy, then me.

My mother's name was Mary. Her mother was Bridget Murphy, a lady I remember well. My grandfather died before I was born. His name was Tommy Murphy. He came from his home in County Carlow, with his two brothers, James and Jack. They were from Railway Cottages, Bagenalstown, County Carlow. My grandfather joined the Army 'to see the world', after coming to Liverpool, and fought in India. When he returned, he worked at Levers, Port Sunlight, making soap. He died of pneumonia in 1920, ten years before I was born. One of his brothers, Jack, was killed at the bottom of Blundell Street, by a goods train, on the Dock Road. His other brother, James, married in Liverpool and lived in nearby Fisher Street.

Tommy Walsh was born on the corner of Blundell Street and Jamaica Street, marked with an x. The black roof running from left to the centre of the picture was the LMS Railway goods yard which was built on the site of Crosbie Street. John Denvir, in his book *Life of an Old Rebel* said that, "Nearly all in Crosbie Street were from the West of Ireland and amongst them there was scarcely anything but Irish spoken".

Pictures from the family album. Tommy's father, in the white shirt with his brothers Pat and Johnnie.

Tommy on the left with his sister Sadie, brother Colum and a neighbour, around 1940.

Tommy and Colum around 1942.

My grandmother's maiden name was Glenning, and she kept in touch with one of her cousins in Galveston, Texas. Margaret Glenning's parents were both Glennings. They had gone to Galveston and were married there. They were first cousins. Margaret's father (I don't know his name) grew roses for a living. One of Granny's cousins in Galveston became a millionaire and was murdered by his valet. None of his money came back, apparently. He left it all to the Marsh Rice College, Galveston.

My Granny had a sister who died young as a result of a vaccination. My mother refused to allow any of us to be vaccinated against anything! I didn't know why until recently. Granny visited Wexford regularly, presumably to visit relatives, but sadly, I don't know who they were.

My mother, as with other mothers in the area, was known to us as 'Mam'. I didn't hear the words 'Mum' or 'Mummy' in my childhood. She was one of three children, the other two being boys, Tommy and George. Uncle Tommy lived in Blundell Street, halfway between our house and my grandmother's, while Uncle George lived in Dovecot, a new suburb. My Uncle Tommy was the leader of St. Vincent's Parish Brass Band. He, like my mother, was a good singer, but, while she sang around the house, he sang in concerts in St. Vincent's Parish Hall. His repertoire included arias and songs from the music halls, as well as such Irish songs as *The West's Awake*. He was a carpenter by trade, and made billiard tables for an old established Liverpool company named Ashcroft's. We didn't see much of Uncle George when we were small, but I got to know him well later. He wasn't a singer but was very funny and could get a joke out of any situation. He was a French Polisher by trade and, apart from working on banks and chemists' shops, would often finish the billiard tables made by his brother.

My mother was not at all like her mother. Granny was

12

always cool and calm. She sat and read no matter what was going on around her. Like the other women of her time, her clothes all reached the floor. Although the other women of her age in Blundell Street wore shawls, she always wore a coat going to church, or to the cinema, or indeed anywhere.

She had a wonderful gramophone with a big brass horn, which was always shining. The records I can remember are John McCormack singing *She is far from the Land* and other such songs. Her favourite writer was Thomas Moore and she loved any of his songs. She wasn't a great singer and recited the lyrics of songs such as *The Meeting of the Waters*. Jimmy O'Dea's records were all there! *Biddy Mulligan on the Tram* was one: Biddy took her tripe onto the tram, causing a gentleman to complain of 'the abominable odour'. *Casey at the Dentist* was another favourite.

Granny had chickens in a coop in the backyard and we had a regular supply of eggs. She built the coops herself and maintained them. Whenever she returned from one of her visits to Wexford, she brought a box, with air holes, full of day old chicks. Occasionally, we would go to St. John's Market in the city centre to buy hens, which we would carry home by the feet, with the body hanging down. She knew all the breeds and would discuss whether Rhode Island Reds were better layers than Leghorns or Plymouth Rocks.

Granny and my mother would take us to St. James's Cinema to what was known only as 'the pictures'. On the way, we would go into St. Vincent's Church to light candles. Granny's favourite statue was St. Anthony, halfway down on the left. He is still there in the same position. Because of that, I was eventually to take Anthony as my confirmation name. I remember when I was about eight years old; I had a bad abscess on my leg which wasn't getting better. I was taken to the Franciscan Church of St. Mary of the Angels where one of the Franciscan priests placed a relic of St. Anthony on the abscess. He was the first Franciscan I had ever seen, and when I saw him approach, I thought it was Saint Anthony! The abscess was better in no time!

My Granny was a tailoress, 'not a dressmaker', she would say. Every little tin box or glass jar in the house, for pins, buttons … anything! had a little, beautifully made, cloth lining cut perfectly to size and with perfect stitching.

My mother was known as May to all the neighbours and customers and, indeed, as 'Auntie May' to many of them. She was not a bit cool and calm like her mother. She was perpetual motion and was continually on the go. She didn't have the patience to sit and read. I don't think I ever saw her sitting down for the sake of sitting. She frequently ran rather than walk. It didn't occur to me as a child that she was doing two full time jobs, running the shop as well as the home.

At that time, only the women did any housework, and she did all the cooking, cleaning and washing-up, and laundry … and no machines for any of those tasks.

My mother always sang as she worked. *The West's Awake* and *Skibbereen* were her favourites. *Skibbereen*, also known as *Dear Old Skibbereen*, is an Irish folk song, in the dialogue of a father telling his son about the Irish famine and the impact of the British Government in Ireland. The son in the song proceeds to ask his father why he left the village of Skibbereen, in County Cork, Ireland, to which the father tells him of the hardship he faced in his homeland. It ends on a vengeful note expressed by the son.

Dear Old Skibbereen

Oh father dear, I often hear you speak of Erin's isle
Her lofty hills, her valleys green, her mountains rude and wild
You say she is a lovely land wherein a prince might dwell
So why did you abandon her, the reason to me tell.
Oh son, I loved my native land with energy and pride
Until a blight came over all my hopes; my sheep, my cattle died
My rent and taxes went unpaid, I could not them redeem
And that's the cruel reason why I left old Skibbereen.

Oh well do I remember that bleak December day
The landlord and the sheriff came to take us all away
They set my roof on fire with their cursed foreign spleen
I heaved a sigh and bade goodbye to dear old Skibbereen.

Your mother too, God rest her soul, fell on the snowy ground
She fainted in her anguish seeing desolation 'round
She never rose but passed away from life to immortal dream
She found a quiet grave, me boy, in dear old Skibbereen.

And you were only two years old and feeble was your frame
I could not leave you with my friends for you bore your father's name
I wrapped you in my cota mor in the dead of night unseen
I heaved a sigh and bade goodbye to dear old Skibbereen.

Oh father dear, the day will come when in answer to the call
All Irish men, brave Irishmen, will rally one and all
I'll be the man to lead the van beneath the flag of green
And loud and high we'll raise the cry, Revenge for Skibbereen.

The West's Awake
by Thomas Davis

When all beside a vigil keep
The West's asleep, the West's asleep
Alas! and well may Erin weep
That Connacht lies in slumber deep
There lake and plain smile fair and free
'Mid rocks their guardian chivalry
Sing, Oh! let man learn liberty
From crashing winds and lashing sea

For often, in O'Connor's van
To triumph dashed each Connacht clan
And fleet as deer the Normans ran
Thro' Corrsliabh's Pass and Ardrahan
And later times saw deeds as brave
For glory guards Clanricard's grave
Sing, Oh! they died their land to save
At Aughrim's slopes and Shannon's wave

And if, when all a vigil keep
The West's asleep! the West's asleep!
Alas! and well may Erin weep
That Connacht lies in slumber deep
But, hark! a voice like thunder spake
The West's awake! the West's awake!
Sing, Oh! Hurrah! let England quake
We'll watch till death for Erin's sake

I think I knew every word of both as a tiny child ... and they never left me!

As with all the other local families, a regular meal was scouse. This is a stew dish in which everything, including the potatoes, went in together. A variation was 'blind scouse' in which there was no meat. Sunday dinner was always a roast meal. Chicken, or other meat, and always roast potatoes.

Pudding was usually rice pudding, made in a huge brown dish with plenty of grated nutmeg on the top. The skin of the rice pudding was either loved or loathed. I never remember hearing that anyone 'liked' or 'disliked' any particular food. Everyone ate everything that was put on the table. Chicken usually started out live with 'wringing its neck' being the first task. Even if it was bought dead, it was certainly complete with feathers, head, feet and innards.

The giblets, all of the innards, were precious for soup. Children would play with the feet and pull the sinews to make them open and close. Rabbits were a regular meal, particularly a little later during the war, when they weren't included in the rationed foods. Again, the rabbit came complete with fur coat, though there would usually be a slit down the stomach and the guts were removed. My mother was an expert at preparing chickens and rabbits for the table. Chickens had to be plucked and I often gave a hand with that job. Rabbits fascinated me as they were prepared for the pot. My mother would make a few, quick cuts with the knife, then the entire skin would be pulled off ... back legs, front legs, body, then a final chop removed the head and the entire skin, leaving the skinned rabbit ready to be cut up for the stew.

Friday was fish day. Again, the fish would be bought whole, and had to be gutted and prepared for table. On top of all this, my mother would wash all the clothes with a dolly tub and rubbing board, boiling the whites on the cooker. The fireplace was blackleaded with Zebra polish, steps were scrubbed and finally donkey stoned to give them a nice, coloured edge. We always had a cooker in what was known as the back kitchen. A lot of houses didn't have a cooker, doing all the cooking on the fire in the kitchen. There was usually an oven heated by the fire. A big kettle on the fire provided all the hot water and the oven at the fire was used for making bread. The other room on the ground floor was the parlour. In some houses in Blundell Street, the parlour was let off to another family. There were no living rooms, sitting rooms, dining rooms or lounges in those days.

While my mother was doing all this housework when the shop was shut, she was continually interrupted by the people in the street coming to the back door for something they had forgotten while the shop was open. I remember that one boy always seemed to come on Sunday at tea time for something from the shop. He never went away without some cake from our table. On Saturday nights, my mother would get the tin bath from the yard and have the kettle full and we'd have a bath in front of the fire. In very cold weather, when we were going up to bed in the unheated rooms, she would take the shelf out of the oven and wrap it in an old sheet and put it in the bed. The first hot water bottle?

Apart from the cinema, my mother loved the theatre and went to The Pavilion, The Rotunda and The Shakespeare to see stars like Cavan O'Connor (The Strolling Vagabond), Evelyn Laye, and, on one occasion, she often recalled, Charlie Chaplin.

Like so many others born in Liverpool, her Irish blood was very close to the surface and she wouldn't have a word said against Ireland or Irish people. In my experience, Irish people born in Liverpool are either 'more Irish than the Irish' or they simply aren't interested. There's also a smaller group who appear to resent having an Irish name and who are extremely anti-Irish.

My father was known as Colum, although his birth certificate said Colman. When I asked the reason for this, his family in Carraroe said that the authorities at the time, before Independence remember, always recorded details in English, even though Irish was the spoken language. Brigid became Bridget, They would have regarded Colman as an English language version of Colum, incorrectly, of course. He was about 5ft 10in in height, of strong build, and as a young man, was very dark and handsome. He was a pipe smoker who regularly bit though the stem of his pipe. Although he never dispensed with the bowl of his pipe, new stems were needed regularly. When he was younger, he gave up the pipe for Lent, but as he got older, he managed to go without it on Good Friday only. In Blundell Street, he didn't go to the local public houses, though he was not a non-drinker. In later years, he went to the local pub with the man next door, for a few drinks, but I never saw him under the influence of drink, nor did I ever hear him swear. In hot weather, he would go into a pub at the dock gate, depending which dock he was working in, and have a glass of beer on his way home.

He smoked plug tobacco, cutting it up into the palm of his hand with a pen-knife. A top seller in the corner shop was a long stick of black tobacco which the men would buy by the ounce, a few inches of the stick which was weighed on a little brass scale. However, my father smoked *Battleaxe Plug* which was in a little red box. A special treat was when one of the family was in Ireland and brought back *Clarke's Perfect*, or *Mick McQuaid*.

In later years, he used *Battleaxe Sliced* to save him cutting it, and later again, at 90 years of age or so, he used 'ready rubbed'.

Filling the pipe was a ritual which only those familiar with pipe smoking will appreciate: the bowl was emptied and ash and unburned tobacco turned out and kept separately while the bowl was cleaned thoroughly and blown through. The new tobacco was then packed very carefully; next came the unburned tobacco from the previous smoke, and finally, the ash. The lighting, by match or strip of newspaper, was often interrupted by conversation, and fingertips were invariably burned but it never seemed to be a problem.

He had no interest whatever in fiction of any kind, in book, film, or radio. He listened to every news bulletin on Radio Athlone, and read the papers from cover to cover. The same thing applied when T.V. came along in his later life. His main sporting love in his earlier life was boxing. He knew about every world championship fight of any weight. He knew every weight and category: Bantam, Fly, Cruiser, and so on. Benny Lynch and Peter Kane were as familiar names in our house as Jack Dempsey and Gene Tunney. He always listened to the world heavyweight championship fights which were invariably on at 3a.m. our time. My brother, Colum, and I would be whispered awake and creep downstairs. Madison Square Garden was a magic venue and I tingled all over when I saw it on my first visit to New York almost 50 years later. The Joe Louis v Tommy Farr fight and Louis v Schmelling still ring bells for me, while my father would talk about the Dempsey v Tunney fight of 'the long count' which I was too young to remember.

The big treat was yet to come. Always, after a world title fight, the Tatler News Theatre in Church Street, Liverpool, would show the film of the fight. My father would take my brother and myself to see that. Only short news films were shown, apart from the fight, and Pathé News, The Tatler was the only cinema he ever went to, and when the advent of T.V.

20

caused it to close, he never went to a cinema again.

The only interest he ever had in T.V. was racing and boxing. His heroes were Pat Taaffe and Martin Moloney and other Irish jockeys.

One of his annual treats was to walk the Grand National course at Aintree on Jump Sunday, which was an open day on the Sunday before the big race. Irish wins at Aintree or Cheltenham brought him enormous pleasure as did any Irish win in sport, such as Rinty Monaghan or Ron Delaney. Even wins for Ireland at soccer or rugby, in which he had no interest, brought him great pleasure.

In 1934, he had walked through the Mersey Tunnel after it was completed and before it was opened to traffic. He had a huge awareness of what was historic while it was happening.

We had a wireless in the house which was unusual in the street and, because we had no electricity, it was powered by a battery. I thought the wireless WAS Athlone because it was the only programme I remember hearing. Mind you, I do remember hearing Lord Haw Haw, and I don't suppose that was Athlone. One of us went to O'Neill's shop in St. James Street every day for the Irish Press. It was on sale on the day of issue. It came by boat, of course.

If, for any reason, the Irish Press was not available, he would do without an Irish paper. He simply would not allow the Irish Independent into the house. The simple and obvious reason was that it had called for the execution of the leaders of the Easter Rising in 1916. Many years later, I was to realise that the whole business of the Transport and General Workers Union and its sister organisation, the Irish Transport and General Workers Union, its role in the Dublin Strike in 1913, and the role of William Martin Murphy, had much to do with his attitude. William Martin Murphy had organised the Dublin Employers, and they were refusing to employ members of the Union, whose families suffered

21

dreadfully. The same William Martin Murphy was the owner of the Irish Independent.

By coincidence, James Larkin, who was prominent in both Trade Unions, was born in Combermere Street, a few minutes walk from Blundell Street.

When my father started work on the Liverpool docks, he joined the Transport and General Workers Union and remained a member until the day he died about sixty years later. Regular invitations to 'days out' and parties for the 'pensioners' amused him. He never availed of those opportunities but I think he was pleased to get them.

The work on the docks was, of course, casual. The men stood in a pen each morning and hoped to be called for a job. If they weren't, it was back to the pen at dinner time. Lunch wasn't a word used in Liverpool for another generation. If they didn't work, there was no pay. Even if they were taken on, it would be to discharge the ship only. Loading was a different job, and required another visit to the pen. They worked in the open, either on the quayside or in the hold of the ship. No protective clothing, no shelter from the weather, no toilets, nowhere to eat. If the load was not properly distributed, the ship was in danger of sinking, but the men who accepted this grave responsibility were deemed to be unskilled.

My father was almost invariably working in the hold of the ship, storing the load from the shed to the ship.

These new skills were added to the skills he had acquired while still at home. He was as good as the best at swinging a scythe to cut a field of oats, or hay, at footing turf at the bog and was particularly good at, and had a love of, rowing a currach. He was never happier than when out on the Atlantic between the Aran Islands and his home Tishmane. Like others, the real love was being out in the currach, but it was a huge bonus to catch fish. These would be brought home and immediately gutted and salted to see the family through the winter.

Concessions were to be gained very slowly and the Liverpool dockers were to become known as a very militant group.

Advert: 1944
1,000 Dockers wanted.
Minimum wage £4.2.6d.
The first guaranteed wage!

As in so many cases, the men who worked and died in those conditions didn't enjoy the improved conditions, which came later. I remember dockers who, if they were working on animal hides found nobody would stand beside them because of the smell. Others worked on lampblack and were literally jet black, with only the whites of their eyes showing. These men were going to homes with no hot water, no bathrooms. Some lived in 'courts' with one cold water tap serving several houses. Apart from dockers, there were other trades. Very recognisable were scalers. These were men who went inside ships' boilers and de-scaled them by chipping the scaling off by hand.

My father was a native Irish speaker, who would have spoken little or no English until he came to England. He thought in Irish and prayed in Irish until he died at almost 99 years of age. Yet as a child, I remember, him reciting, in English, *The Wreck of the Hesperus* and *Morrissey and the Russian Giant*. Both were very many verses long. It WAS in the forty-seventh round, that Morrissey floored the Russian!

Our house was about 200 yards from the gate into the docks. Kings Dock on the right, and Queens Dock on the left. The Limerick boats tied up in Queens Dock just at that corner. The Limerick Steamship Company sailed between Liverpool and the west coast of Ireland. My father usually worked on the Limerick boats, and the crews often came into the shop. The two boats which served the route for many years were the S/S Moyalla and the S/S Kyleclare. Many years later, one of them, the Moyalla, sank in Galway Bay off Salthill and the mast was clearly visible from the road out to Carraroe. Over several years I saw the mast clear above the waves until after some years, it was no longer visible. Limerick was obviously one of the ports of call, then any of Galway, Westport, Ballina, Kilalla, and Belmullet.

The main ports of call of ships using the south end docks were Africa and the Isle of Man as well as Ireland. Ships from the Far East and America used the docks at the north side of the city.

The tools of my father's trade were his docker's hooks which were always shining and were stored very safely. We were allowed to see but not touch, it was not necessary to put them out of reach. 'Don't touch' ... we didn't!

Opposite the Limerick Boat berth was a huge red brick warehouse. Children would throw stones at the rats running in and out. That warehouse is now a block of luxury flats known as Wapping Quay. When built, they sold at about £150,000 each. If a docker working there worked for 50 years, he earned about £10,725.

St. Vincent's was our local church and we were all baptised there and went to St. Vincent's school. My brother, also Colum, and I were altar boys there from the time we were old enough to learn and answer in Latin. The sheer beauty of the church which was designed by Pugin escaped me at the time. Many years later, when the church was closed due to reduced population, I was horrified. After some years, it was reopened by Fr. Patsy Foley, a former Kilkenny hurler, who ran two other parishes too. It was a very mixed neighbourhood as you would expect so near the docks. Chinatown was a few minutes away, the oldest Chinatown in Europe, I understand. Chinatown, at that time, started at Cleveland Square and extended up to Pitt Street. In those days, only the Chinese community and perhaps a few seamen ate in Chinese restaurants. The main Chinese businesses used by others were the small laundries.

Many of our neighbours were Spanish and Norwegian who had their own church nearby in Park Lane. It is still there, and is a beautiful building. Nearby were people from African countries. One of these families was the Contehs, one of whom became a world champion boxer. He was John Conteh. Most of the African people were from Lagos, Freetown, Takoradi and other places in West Africa. One of my St. Vincent's memories is of Asians who were known as coolies and who were always addressed as John. They would leave the church walking backwards, never turning their back towards the altar.

I had long left the area before I learned that Crosbie Street, which was the street next to Blundell Street, was full of Irish people many years before I was born. John Denvir said Crosbie Street was totally Irish speaking in the years after the Potato Famine during which thousands of Irish people had poured into Liverpool. In 1881, the census says there were 1,544 people living in Crosbie Street. They were the recorded residents. At that time, there was one water pump in Crosbie Street and one in Blundell Street.

While many dockers were Catholics, none of the shipbuilding firms would employ a Catholic. All ships' carpenters were members of the Orange Order. John Denvir says the 12th July was known as 'Carpenters' Day'.

Three Irish people living nearby, and working on the docks with my father, were Tim Foley from Mayo, Ned Healy from Kildare, and Paddy Conneelly from The Claddagh in

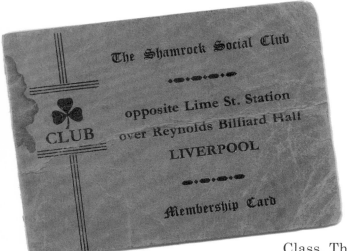

Galway. Two generations later, my daughter, Kathleen, and Paddy Conneelly's granddaughter, Mary Tuite, were to become close friends through their Irish Dancing Class. Their families have remained in touch with me. I remember pointing out Kevin Conneelly to my father when Kevin was appearing as a wrestler on T.V. and telling him he was Paddy's son. My father's great-granddaughter and Paddy Conneelly's great-granddaughter, Sinead and Olivia, are now best friends and do their Irish dancing together.

Other Irish people living nearby who were also shopkeepers, were the Osbyrnes and the Murphys. Osbyrnes was a chandler's shop and was known as 'the paraffin oil shop', while Murphys was a newspaper shop and was opposite St. Vincent's Church. Kathleen Murphy later married Eddie O'Reilly from Kerry, and they eventually opened and ran The Shamrock Club in Lime Street, a focal point for the Irish Community in the 1950s. The Murphys and Osbyrnes were cousins. Kathleen and Peggy Osbyrne became involved in Irish music, Kathleen as Kit Hodge, was a member of the famous Liverpool Ceili Band which won two All-Ireland Championships.

Kit was a founder member of both the Liverpool Branch of Comhaltas Ceoltoiri Eireann, and of the Irish Centre, Liverpool. She then returned to Ireland and became full-time Administrator of Comhaltas Ceoltoiri Eireann in their Monkstown headquarters. Meanwhile, Peggy (Peakin) formed the Brian Boru Ceili Band, which was hugely popular around Merseyside. I was often M.C. at Ceilithe she played at, and we got used to being introduced by a local person as 'Brian Boru and his Ceili Band'! Although she didn't live in the area, a close friend of the Murphys and Osbyrnes was Maírin Bolger who followed her family tradition of teaching Irish Dancing, and was to run the

Irish Centre Dancing Class from its opening until it closed its doors in the 1990s.

Also living in the area were Hylands, Barretts, Loftus's, McGraths, and O'Haras, while local publicans were Dick Whitty and Martin Naughton. Most of the people with Irish names would not be aware of their Irishness, and I now realise that they were almost certainly 'famine Irish' whose forebears would have come into Liverpool with hundreds of thousands of others back in 'black 47' and other years about then. Having an Irish name in Liverpool doesn't mean you know anything about your Irish origins.

The next parish to St. Vincent's, a few hundred yards south, is St. Patrick's. A beautiful stone Celtic Cross was erected in the grounds of St. Patrick's in memory of the ten priests who died tending to the victims of typhoid which struck those Irish people who had fled the potato famine shortly after they arrived in Liverpool. I was not aware of the cross when I was a child growing up in the area. Just

The Shamrock Club in Lime Street, opposite the station, played a huge role in the life of the Irish community in Liverpool. It was the most popular meeting place for young Irish people in the city and was run by Eddie O'Reilly and Mick Gill. It is generally agreed that the Shamrock Club was in the building on the right of this picture. There was a billiard hall on the first floor and the dance hall on the second, which would place it behind the Schweppes sign. It closed in 1964.

The membership card belonged to Tommy's dear friend Vin Boyle.

St. Patrick's.

another hundred yards or so on the other side of St. Patrick's, is Combermere Street, where James Larkin, the Trade Union leader, was born.

Illnesses such as diphtheria and scarlet fever were quite common among children at the time, as were rickets. Children I went to school with died of diphtheria, while others were missing for months in the 'fever hospital'. The fever hospital was in Mill Lane about four miles from the city centre, but nobody around there knew where it was. They knew there was such a place, but that was all.

In the area between Park Lane and the docks, there were as many warehouses as dwelling houses. Huge brick buildings, seven or eight storeys high, with access to all floors by hoist and sling to load and unload wagons on the street below. These were almost all horse-drawn wagons with just a few steam-driven wagons. A man used to come into the yard early on, to light fires under the wagons to build up steam for the drivers coming in later. One of our neighbours, Mr White of Simpson Street, did this job for many years.

The main products handled were brown sugar from the West Indies, coming into Tate and Lyles refinery, and bales of cotton from America. It was impossible to stand in any of those streets without having wagons in your vision. If brown sugar was the load, there was, almost certainly, at least one young boy hanging on the back, cutting the sacks and filling pockets and making a large pocket by holding the hem of the jersey in one hand to hold more sugar. Brown sugar at this stage was known as *togo*.

Most of the wagons had one Shire horse, but there were bigger wagons for bigger loads with teams of two horses. These were usually bigger than average horses, and were magnificent beasts.

Where there was a slight incline in the street, an extra horse would be brought and hooked up until level ground was reached. The extra horse would be taken back to assist another wagon up the slope. Carters, as the men were called, were extremely skilful. In heavy rain, they wore empty sacks around their shoulders.

Accidents were different too, in those days. Men working many floors up taking in sacks or bales, would occasionally fall. Sometimes a sack of sugar or other heavy item would land on a carter below. Such accidents were usually fatal.

There was great excitement when a horse collapsed in the shafts in the street. The bystanders would remain until the knacker's wagon arrived and pulled the poor horse onto the wagon by the neck.

Because we had the corner shop surrounded by docks and warehouses with the goods station built on the site of Crosbie Street beside us, we knew these men well and regarded them as friends. Their own big day was May Day when they spent all night preparing their horse for the parade. When decorated, these horses were a magnificent sight.

The surrounding workshops included rope and fender makers and other trades serving the shipping industry. Workers were always to be seen with wooden spikes for splicing ropes, and very sharp knives in their belts.

I often walk along the Riverside Walk now. The old docks are decorative. One of them is a feature of the new Customs and Excise building. Another, nearby, is a marina with numerous small leisure boats. Hundreds of new homes, apartments and houses are built around the docks … all for sale, not rent! All up-market. As I watched the development proceed, I thought with sadness of all those men who sweated and slaved and didn't enjoy the comforts of this place. Then I thought … the boatowners and homeowners are probably the grandchildren of those dockers, scalers, and seamen.

The magnificent Celtic Cross outside St. Patrick's Church in memory of the 10 priests who died while administering to the poor people who had left Ireland during the Great Hunger.

The dockers in the 1930s assembled in 'cocoa rooms' at midday or to wait for the pen to open again, particularly if they lived a long way from the dock. Occasionally, there would be great excitement as fleets of black Marias (police wagons) would drive up and there would be a raid. All the men would be taken off to the police station. They had been found betting on horse racing, and street betting was illegal. Bets would have been 3d or 6d, (1p or 2p in present money). The people running horse racing, making laws and presiding over the courts were, literally, a different class. If you could afford to go racing, or have an account, you had no problem. Other main pastimes of the men were toss schools and olleys. Toss schools were also occasions of illegal betting. On almost every corner there were groups of men or boys. An essential part of the scene was the lookout who kept an eye out for the police. Two coins were tossed. Bets were placed on two heads, two tails, or one of each. Olleys were played on any fairly large piece of waste ground. There were three holes scraped into the ground, about 30-40 yards apart forming a triangle. Olleys were a large version of children's glass marbles, but were made of stone. Looking back, it occurs to me that the game was a crude form of golf, which was a game I hadn't heard of. The objective was to get the olley into the holes with the smallest number of attempts.

Because I lived over a shop in 1930s Liverpool, I had the opportunity to experience at first hand the way of life, hear the language, know the people, more than otherwise would have been the case, and certainly, to know what people were buying. Most of our customers lived in sight of the shop. Because we were so near the docks and the warehouses, I had the added experience of meeting people who worked in the area, as well as those who lived there. Most exciting of all, was meeting people from all over the world, namely the seamen.

30

They were mainly from African countries, usually East African, Indians (from the whole of India before Pakistan) and Chinese. There were also a lot of Scandinavians, but many of them were sailing out of Liverpool on British and every other country's ships. I don't think there were Liverpool/Scandinavian routes. Many Scandinavians lived locally, and there were Norwegian lodging houses. Belgians came in regularly but they were mainly officers on ships sailing into what was then Belgian Congo. It was the Norwegians who gave Liverpool its traditional dish...scouse. I think they call it lobskous. Other nationalities sailed into the north end docks, particularly from the middle and far East. Europeans sailed into the east coast ports.

There was a word which was common to every nationality ... savvy. No savvy was a variation. Understand? Don't understand!

All seamen bought block salt. We bought it in blocks about 2ft. long and 1ft. by 1ft. We cut it up with a joiner's saw into blocks about the size of a brick (or a sod of turf) and wrapped them in newspaper. I remember packet salt being introduced, but I don't think anyone thought it would catch on. An item we stocked mainly for Africans was blue-mottle soap. It was about two feet long and about three inches by three inches. The soap was white with a blue vein, a bit like Danish Blue cheese. Apart from obvious things like bread and tinned foods, groceries like tea and sugar, we sold potatoes by the peck.

Potatoes were delivered in large jute sacks, and were sold by the peck, which were 20lbs. Half pecks and quarter pecks too. The only cigarettes we sold were *Woodbines*. I suppose that means our customers were 'Woodbine Willies'. There was no mention of cigarettes being harmful to health and young people or anyone else short of money, would buy 'a loosie', a single cigarette. Detergents were not invented and soap powders like *Glee* and *Rinso*, were big sellers. The only soap powder which became a detergent and kept its name was *Persil*.

Because we were near the local wash-house, the women on their way to the wash-house would call in for soap, usually *Sunlight*, soap powder, and dolly blue 'for the whites'. Many of them had an old pram chassis without the top part, especially for the wash-house. More of them, especially the older ones, carried the washing wrapped in a blanket in a huge bundle on their head. I don't know how they lifted it up, let alone walk across the road. I didn't know then, and I don't suppose the women did, that this wash-house was historic. It was the first public wash-house in Britain and was started by Kitty Wilkinson, an Irish woman.

If a woman reached nine months of her pregnancy and the baby hadn't arrived, the advice of the older women would be to 'take a load of washing to the wash-house' ... and they did! Some women took other people's washing as a source of income, and they might go every day. In any weather, the temperature in there was probably 100 degrees or more, and it was difficult to see because of the steam.

Sticky fly-catchers were a must, especially in summer. Zebra black lead for grates, Brasso for the brasses which were in every house, often as fire irons. Donkey stones were big sellers, to keep the front steps nice. There were four or five stone steps (no concrete) up to all the front doors and these were scrubbed regularly. The donkey stone was used to put a nice edge on the steps.

We sold a lot of mothballs. Many men's' suits and other clothing were taken to the pawn shop every Monday morning, so had to be kept in good condition. Back studs and front studs were always available. One shirt and half a dozen collars would be standard for most men. Unfortunately, most of the customers used the 'tick' system, and I'm sure my mother lost a huge amount in unpaid bills.

Some of the items we didn't stock and which are now standards, would be electric light bulbs. We did sell gas mantles. Crisps were not yet invented, and toilet rolls were not on the shopping lists in that area anyway. Yet another use for the *Echo*! Coffee had still not appeared on the scene, and when it did arrive, it was Camp liquid chicory and coffee extract. In Ireland, it was known as Irel. Teabags were still unheard of but tea played a huge part in people's lives. Bottled milk was sterilised only, but the most popular milk was tinned condensed milk. Calf was the big seller, but a smaller seller, the Nestle brand, was the top quality brand.

Dockers, carters and other manual workers, made their tea in a can and drank it from the lid. A 'brew' was a little parcel of tea and condensed milk, which was a mixture of sugar and milk. It was wrapped in greaseproof paper. The brew was hung over the edge of the can and boiling water poured over it. Tea, sugar and milk, all in one. The can was swung by the wire handle to brew the tea. Can lads could be seen making their way to boiling water with up to a dozen cans suspended on a brush pole. A can, with lid, was the size of a pint milk bottle.

In 1941, Count John McCormack gave a concert for Liverpool dockers. I have been unable to establish how it went down. Despite the abject poverty of the time, and I suppose because everything is relative, and life was as we saw it around us, I was never aware of poverty or hunger. I don't think this was because we had a shop, although food would have been more readily available to us. Ours was a very, very happy home, and as far as I was aware, so were most of the other homes around us. As children, we were taken to Carraroe every summer, though I never heard the word 'holiday'. I was never aware of any of our neighbours going away anywhere, even to visit relatives, except our own family.

It took about twenty-four hours to get to Carraroe. We went down to Princes Dock at night, boarded the old *B and I* boat to Dublin. We got the bus to Galway the following morning, then another bus to Carraroe. The final leg of the journey out to Tishmane was the best. Cousin Johnnie would meet us with the pony and trap. He always had Connemara ponies.

My father's eldest sister, Mary, went to Boston in 1912. She was followed by her sister, Sarah (Sala) in 1916. I grew up remembering that my father said his sister Sala worked in the post office in Carraroe. He remembered her coming home from work one day after Easter, saying she had received a telegram from Padraic Pearse telling the people to lay down their arms, the Rising was over. More than 50 years after hearing that story, I visited my aunt in Boston. I sat on the side of her bed and asked her did she remember taking a telegram. 'From Padraic Pearse', she said. Like my father, seventy years after leaving home, she still prayed in Irish. I was so glad I had enough Irish for us to pray together. We said the rosary in her native tongue.

In 1939, in September, World War II broke out. I was serving at 11a.m. Mass in St. Vincent's and heard the Parish Priest, Fr. Hodson, announce that Britain had declared war on Germany. Immediately, (after Mass!) there was a scramble to get the children to safety. All our school friends from St. Vincent's were evacuated, mainly to North Wales or Yorkshire. No one had ever heard the word evacuee before. The idea that we might go to Wales was never considered. We were sent off to Carraroe, that is the three youngest who were still at school. The idea was, of course, to miss the bombing that was expected. This war was going to be different and each country was expected to bomb the other's civilian territory. It transpired that there was a 'phoney war' when no bombing took place, and we eventually returned to

The interior of Kitty Wilkinson's wash-house, built in 1842. Kitty was born in Derry and is buried in the Anglican Cathedral graveyard. The wash-house was in Upper Frederick Street, near St. Michael's Church, and was the first public wash-house in England.

Blundell Street around Christmas 1939.

The months in Carraroe were very happy. Irish was, and still is, the spoken language there. We were very lucky that most of our cousins spoke excellent English, and all of them were very kind to us. We lived in the old house that my father had lived in before he left home in 1922, with his brother, Padraic, his wife, Mary, and their family. My grandmother (Mamo) was there too, and cousins Colum, Johnnie, Sala, Nan and Brigid. Two of our cousins, Mary and Maggie, were married and they lived in sight of the old house. Looking back, it must have been incredibly inconvenient for them to have us three children added to the household but, of course, I didn't appreciate that at the time.

We went off to the local National School, Naoimh Mhic Dara, and that presented its difficulties. Many of our school friends spoke little or no English and we spoke even less Irish. Regardless of our problems, we were very happy there, as we were made so welcome by the pupils and teachers.

The house was full of music, singing, storytelling, and especially dancing. Johnnie's favourite dance was the Stack of Barley and it was a regular feature.

We helped (or maybe hindered!) with the work in the fields, and with the turf from the bog, bringing in the hay and the oats all of which were cut by hand with the scythe. It seemed that cousin Colum could swing a scythe all day. Hour after hour with perfect rhythm. The donkeys were great. They were very popular with us, and they were great help with the work. We were picking up Irish, of course, and had we stayed, we would have become Irish speakers. It is my greatest regret that I never became fluent in Irish.

My eldest sister, Mary, was staying in Ballina, County Mayo, visiting friends my mother had made through the boats coming into Queens Dock at the bottom of Blundell Street. They were the Killeens of The Quay in Ballina. *The*

Moyalla was built especially for the depth of water in Ballina. So it was named ... Moy for the River Moy in Ballina, and Alla for Killala.

Sadie, Colum and I went to Ballina and all travelled back to Liverpool together. We were still living in Blundell Street when the bombing started. It was August 17th, 1940 when the first bombs landed in Caryl Street, just a few minutes from our house. We remained in Liverpool for the rest of the war. I suppose by that time, travel was almost impossible.

Truth and news being the first victims of war, we were not allowed at the time to know the full details of the blitz, but we heard, and saw, and smelled the results. Recently demolished property, involving explosives, fire and dust have a very distinctive smell. After the blitz, it was many years later that I was in Talbot Street in Dublin the morning after the bombing there, and I recognised the smell immediately.

The dock area was the main target for the bombers, and we now know that the nerve centre for the 'Battle of the Atlantic' was less than a mile from our home. We didn't know it then, of course, but the other side probably did. Lord Haw Haw seemed to know, judging by some of his references to Liverpool.

It was a horrendous time. I can still hear the whistle of the high explosive bombs. We knew the sound of all the different bombs. There were high explosives, land mines, and incendiary bombs. Breadbaskets were the bombs which showered incendiary bombs over a large area on impact with the ground. Most of the property damage was by fire.

My mother, sisters and brother and I spent the nights in the cellar of our home in Blundell Street. My father would spend the night keeping the area from around the house free of incendiary bombs. A supply of sand bags was always kept, and one would be placed on any incendiary bomb that came near.

For those of us underneath, the high explosives were the most frightening, because we heard them coming. They whistled for what seemed like ages before the explosion and the shaking of the house and the sound of breaking glass. The explosion of land mines came without warning because of the parachute. Fires from the incendiary bombs caused loss of life and huge property damage. On the night of November 28th, 1940, over 200 people were killed, which almost doubled the total killed since the blitz began. The worst single loss of life that night involved the basement air raid shelter in Durning Road School. Almost three hundred men, women and children were in the shelter when it was hit by a land mine. It was a busy shelter anyway, and two trams were passing at the time of the siren and the passengers went in too. The entire building was demolished, three floors had collapsed onto the basement shelter. One hundred and sixty-four people were killed with a further ninety-six injured. Winston Churchill later described it as 'the worst single incident of the war'.

Around Christmas time in 1940, a land mine landed in Blundell Street and every house in the street with the single exception of ours was destroyed. We knew before we came out of the cellar that something dramatic had happened, and the devastation was total. Fortunately, we were the only family in our own house, everyone else being in air raid shelters. No one was killed or even seriously hurt. Our house, though it was still standing, was unfit to live in, and all the residents were dispersed. We went to live with an uncle and aunt in Dovecot, a suburb of Liverpool, but as the corner shop at number 13 was just about able to stay in business, we came back and somehow managed to live there until a house in Edge Lane Drive was allocated to us. That became the family home for all of us. My sisters, Mary and Sadie, and myself were married from there, my mother and father died there, and my brother Colum lived there with his wife, Mary, a native of Bundoran, and his four children, for many years.

It was in the month of May 1941 that Liverpool took its worst pounding. Presumably Hitler decided that Liverpool docks had to be put out of action at all costs. About one thousand tons of high explosives were dropped on poor Liverpool in those raids. Every morning the streets were littered with pieces of shrapnel, and boys collected them as they now collect pictures of footballers.

On May 13th, 1941, five hundred and fifty people were buried in a common grave in Anfield Cemetery. Near the gates of Ford (Catholic) Cemetery, as you walk towards the Fenian Memorial and the graves of leaders of the Irish Community in Liverpool, you pass two graves, on the left, beside the footpath. One says: *Annie Neary. Age 38, and her children James 18, Joseph 15, Charles 11, Gerard 9, Teresa 7, Mary 5, Andrew 3, and Kathleen 1. Killed by enemy action 13th March 1941.*

The next grave reads: *Mary Jane Neary 34, and her children Mary 13 and Luke. Killed by enemy action 13th March 1941.*

Doesn't that say it all about the futility of war and man's inhumanity to man?

The last air raid on Liverpool was on January 10th 1942 when four high explosive bombs fell on Upper Stanhope Street, and killed fifteen people. Oddly enough, the last bombs, as with the first, fell only a few minutes walk from where we were living in Blundell Street. Out of a total of 282,000 houses, 11,000 were destroyed and 185,000 were damaged.

Talking about Upper Stanhope Street, the Liverpool Echo occasionally refers to the fact that Adolf Hitler's uncle, Alois, was married to an Irish woman, Brigid Dowling, and they lived in Upper Stanhope Street. In her memoirs,

Brigid, says that their nephew, Adolf, stayed there with them from November 1912 to April 1913. She said she didn't like him! She also said he was there to dodge being drafted for the Austrian Army. That could be the reason Adolf did not mention Liverpool in his own writings. I have a mental picture of Adolf Hitler being told about those bombs falling on Upper Stanhope Street. 'Oh no! Not Upper Stanhope Street … no more bombs on Liverpool.'

And there weren't! Or was it, 'At last! You got Upper Stanhope Street … now you can leave Liverpool alone!'

All over the city throughout the war, there were barrage balloons. These were huge grey balloons similar to airships except that they didn't carry passengers. They were parked near the ground all day, and every evening, they would be released to the end of their cable length to climb into the sky as part of the defence of the city. The nearest to Blundell Street was on the corner of Norfolk Street and Jamaica Street, about 100 yards from Saint Vincent's church door. There was great excitement when one occasionally 'escaped' and sailed away with a snapped cable dangling. On May 1st, 1941, one of these barrage balloons, which were of course for defence, caught fire. It fell on the ship *Malakand* which was berthed in Huskisson Dock. *Malakand* was carrying one thousand tons of high explosives. The firemen put the fire on the ship out but the dock shed was ablaze, and the ship caught fire again and went up in one of the most spectacular explosions of the war.

Another memory I have of that period was that every evening, as daylight was fading, a military type formation of men, not marching, but walking in formation, dressed in scruffy ill-fitting uniforms with large coloured patches all over, would walk down our street to the warehouses and dock sheds, These were prisoners of war and conscientious objectors who were placed in the warehouses as firewatchers.

I don't suppose I realised, until many years later, when I had children of my own, how difficult it was for my parents, and the other parents. Just making the decision whether to go into a shelter, as many did, or stay in the cellar, as we did, was a matter of life and death. I simply can't imagine how I would cope with being in a situation in which I could do nothing to protect my children from likely death.

~

A language has been lost in my lifetime. I think it was T.V. that did it. Most of the words which were particular to Liverpool have gone, to be replaced by a national language, if not an international (from films) language. Only the accent remains.

When people were desperately short of money, they went to the Parish Office which dispensed charity. This gave rise to the expression 'Your face would get you the parish'. Mugging was treating people – not the opposite as it is now. If someone came up on the horses, they mugged their family and friends ... bought them a drink or whatever.

A jigger was a back entry, a scuffer ... a policeman. A cat was a moggie, a halfpenny was a meg. Hence the meg specs were cheap seats in the cinema. People called males, friends, workmates ... wacker. If you hear a mother in Connemara call her son 'a mhac', you'll know where it comes from – Crosbie Street?

When children were not turning the mangle for 'me mam' or 'me nan' (and we all knew someone who got their fingers caught in the mangle), they were playing in the street, while the women sat on the steps talking. The girls played skipping rope, sometimes singly, sometimes with anything up to 10 kids in a long rope. 'I call in my very best friend' brought in the next girl. Sometimes a mam would be walking down the street and would run in to skip ... to squeals of delight from the kids. 'All in together, to see Cinderella' brought a rush of all the girls to the rope.

I call in my very best friend ...
On the mountain stands a lady,
Who she is I do not know.
All she wants is gold and silver,
All she wants is a nice young man,
So call in my very best friend,
very best friend, very best friend,
Call in my very best friend,
While I go out to play.

Girls again, and only girls, played 'two balls' or even 'three balls' against a wall, with their skirts tucked into their knickers. Playing marbles in the gutter was usually left to the boys. Swinging on a rope hung over a lamp-post was popular. They had to make way for the lamp-lighter when he came around to light the gas mantle with his long rod with the hook on the end. 'Relievo', 'Hide and Seek', and 'Kick the Can' (boys only). Were regular street games. Top and whip, and yo-yos were regular games but they needed a purchase where most street games did not. Hop scotch was a game which left evidence on the street. An old bike wheel with no tyre or spokes was a great hoop and with a stick to drive it, boys could run around the block all day. An old orange box on a set of old pram wheels was priceless and was a great help to go to the wash-house as well as a toy.

Before the war, funeral parlours were unknown in our area. Bodies were laid out in the person's own home, by an old lady who did it because she always did it. In our street, it was Mary Foster who lived in nearby Simpson Street.

42

Then, on funeral day, the beautiful horse-drawn hearse would arrive. The horses were always black, and they would go to Ford Cemetery which was on the north side of Liverpool, about ten miles away.

I remember when funeral parlours came into existence, it was regarded as scandalous by the neighbours if a family used one and didn't wake the corpse in their own home. I remember a lady who was a very nice and charitable person. Her brother, who was married, died. His widow put him into a funeral parlour, and her sister-in-law never spoke to her again. It took a generation for the habit to change.

Because, during the war, regular visits to Ireland were impossible, our knowledge of Ireland was fed by Radio Athlone. I was aware of the verbal exchanges between Winston Churchill and Eamon de Valera without fully understanding, and exulting in what we considered to be the victory of Dev over Churchill.

Our local parish was now the suburban parish of Christ the King. A totally different environment to the inner city dockside. Because the family shop was still in Blundell Street, we maintained a presence in the old neighbourhood, especially my mother who ran the shop. My father still worked on the docks, in the same area and he continued to go into the shop every day at midday. I appeared to be destined to be the shopkeeper of the future, mainly because all my older siblings were doing something else. My brother, Colum, and I travelled by tram every Sunday morning to retain our altar boy status by serving the 11a.m. Mass in St. Vincent's. Meanwhile, we were altar servers in Christ the King for the rest of the week.

At 11 years of age, I started attending the local school attached to St. Edward's Orphanage and stayed there until I reached the normal school leaving age of 14 years. This was the first time I attended any regular school since

St. Vincent's closed down in 1939, when I was nine years old. In the meantime, most of the children were still in North Wales together with most of the teachers. Some retired teachers opened their parlours for a couple of hours a day on some days and took classes. I remember walking to a house in the shadow of the Anglican Cathedral to Miss Cole's house for lessons.

September 1941. New school. A big boys' school. Full time education. Scary! St. Edward's Orphanage and School was run by the Brothers of Charity. Side by side, on the same site they ran the orphanage for boys who lived in and were called interns, and the school for boys of the surrounding parishes, who were called externs.

The congregation of the Brothers of Charity established a base in 1903 at Thingwall Hall Merseyside. Initially the Brothers of Charity were invited to establish an orphanage for boys from Liverpool and surrounding areas.

We all attended classes together. My three years there were very happy. At home, we no longer spent nights in the cellar (we had no cellar) and I really enjoyed going to school. The teachers were mainly Brothers, with a few lay teachers. Other Brothers were there who were not teachers.
St. Edward's was famous for its brass band, which apart from many other engagements, played at Everton's Goodison Park at all home games.

There were regular film shows, where silent, black and white films were shown. Non-residents could attend for a penny or so. My first teacher was Brother Abbott who, coincidentally was a parishioner of St. Vincent's. All my other teachers were Irish. My second year teacher was Brother Mayne, and Brother Phelim was my third year teacher. The headmaster was Brother Fergus. Brothers Timothy and Botulph were the woodwork teachers. I remember them all with affection and, years later, I called to Lota in Cork where I met Brother Timothy and others.

They all carried a leather strap which was the traditional means of applying corporal punishment. The cane was gaining in popularity and was used by the lay teachers there and in other schools. Corporal punishment was standard procedure in the society of the time, as well as in schools. While no one enjoyed it, I was never aware of any resentment about it. I was never aware of any parents suggesting it should not be used. It simply was not a topic of conversation, which seems strange in the present climate of examining the past and being critical of those times. Perhaps the reason there was no demand for an end to corporal punishment in schools was that it was tame compared to much of the thrashing at home.

During those three years at St. Edwards, I became friendly with Vin Boyle who had lived in there for much of his life and who was in my year. We were to meet again two or three years after leaving school when we both became involved in the Gaelic League and in the Gaelic Athletic Association. We remained very close friends until his death many years later. I was indeed privileged to be named by him to the hospital authorities as his next of kin, and with other friends of his, including the late Bishop Kevin O'Connor, arranged his funeral.

More than fifty years on, I live in the same area as what was St. Edward's Orphanage, now Thingwall Hall, and frequently walk through the grounds. The Orphanage, of course, is long gone, including all the old buildings, except what was the chapel and the old Brothers residence. Modern villas are now in the grounds and adults with learning difficulties are cared for.

After three years at St. Edward's. I passed what was grandly called an entrance examination for Old Swan Technical School. It was the only examination I ever remember taking or passing.

I subsequently left school at 16 years of age without any qualifications of any kind, and, of course, though it was never decided, but was never in doubt, went straight into the little corner shop in Blundell Street, over which I had been born.

After School

DECIDING HOW to spread my wings socially after leaving school was also easy. The only places I was allowed to go to, by my parents, were the Seán O'Donovan branch of the Gaelic League and to the various parish Ceilis in Liverpool.

The Gaelic League was by far, my most regular haunt. My sister Sadie was on the committee at the time, and was usually going on the night I wanted to go, so I was allowed to go without difficulty.

At that time, the Gaelic League was situated upstairs in rented premises at 18 Wood Street in the City Centre. It had previously been located at 22 Wood Street. Apart from the Sunday Ceili, I usually attended an Irish language class on a mid-weekly evening. My teacher was Michael Walsh who was a motor mechanic by trade. He was fond of songs in Irish and always included one in the lesson.

Committee members included Mick Flood who was Chairman. There were several families who were prominent. Peadar, Michael and Maírín McCarthy who lived in a pub opposite St. Anthony's, Scotland Road. The McDonnells – Peggy, Pat, Tess and Patricia – lived in the same area. The Luddens – Denis, Frank and Seán from Wirral, or 'over the water' as we call it in Liverpool. The McNamaras, the boys were fiddlers of renown, and the girls were dancers. Seán was the youngest of the family and was nearest to me in age. We became very good friends, and have remained so throughout our lives. Seán became a founder member of the famous Liverpool Ceili Band and of the Liverpool branch of Comhaltas Ceoltoiri Eireann. They were quite separate, but started about the same time in the late 1950s.

The regular Sunday Ceili was always excellent. Strictly ceili dances only, no Old Time waltzes allowed. *Sixteen Hand Reel, Eight Hand Reel, Siege of Ennis, Haymakers Jig, Harvest Jig, Fairy Reel, Stack of Barley, Humours of Bandon*

Tommy aged 18 in Spiddal, Co Galway, 1948

Tommy's wedding photograph is the only picture he has with his parents and his wife all together. From the left: Colum and Mary Walsh, Tommy and his wife, Kathleen, and her parents Elizabeth and Michael Redmond.

47

and *High Caul Cap* were some of the dances.

All the dances were announced in Irish only, and there was always a rush onto the floor. There were those who were going for years but never learned the names in Irish, as well as newcomers, who said 'what is it?' when Cor Seise Deag was announced (it was a Sixteen Hand Reel).

Another regular activity was rambles in the countryside around Liverpool at weekends. They were usually on the Wirral across the Mersey, and were usually referred to as 'hikes'. We would get to a given spot by tram and ferry and walk from there. Having some music which enabled us to dance a Stack of Barley or whatever, at a crossroads, or in a café was a bonus. Seamus O'Connor would sometimes take his bagpipes and play while we walked. Little did we think that those ferries across the Mersey would one day become famous in song, and that people would come from all over the world to take a ride.

It was there, in Wood Street, that I met up with Vin Boyle again. We had been at school together for three years taught by Brothers of Charity in the school attached to St. Edward's Orphanage. From then on, we became inseparable. We both became 'committee types' who enjoyed a meeting as much as a social occasion, and we were to be on committees together until Vin died. On Sundays at Wood Street, the music was played by Addie Brophy on the piano. In the last hour, he would be joined by musicians who, like the rest of us, had paid the shilling admission. Addie played Mozart's Rondo Alla Turca for the High Caul Cap in perfect reel time. I think Addie got ten shillings for his night's work.

Some of the 'Gaelic Leaguers' but not all, would also go to parish ceilis. Old Time waltzes would be allowed at those dances, and they were advertised as 'Ceili and Old Time Dance'.

The more complicated ceili dances would not be danced

at those dances. The bands playing for those nights would be Peggy Osbyrne (who became Peakin) and her Brian Boru Ceili Band and the Shannon Star Ceili Band run by Teresa and Sue McQuaid.

I was frequently M.C. at those dances. I had to be aware of which dances would be suitable for the particular hall. If I didn't think there were enough ceili dancers present, to make a 16 hand reel feasible, I wouldn't call it.

St. Alphonsus' Parish Ceili, on a Saturday night was big! Fr. Michael Colman from County Cork ran a tight ship. St. Monica's, Bootle was run by Fr. Oliver Brady of County Cavan. Another Cavan priest running a weekly ceili was Fr. Cornelius McEnroe of St. John's. He was a cousin of John McEnroe of tennis fame. Other regular venues were St. Aloysius in Huyton, and St. Vincent's, my old school.

There were two other branches of the Gaelic League, running full programmes of Ceili and language classes at the time. They were Craobh Sean Mhisteil (John Mitchels) and Craobh Ceithre Mhaistir (Four Masters) in Eldon Street and Crosby, respectively. One of the prominent members in Crosby was Peggy Atkins, who was later to become the pianist in the Liverpool Ceili Band, and was with Seán McNamara when they were All-Ireland Champions in 1963 and 1964. In all the Gaelic League Branches, the Ceilis were fior-ceili (no waltzes allowed).

So at that time, in the late 1940s and throughout the 1950s, there were three Gaelic League branches and numerous parish ceilis running weekly in Liverpool as well as St. Anne's, Rock Ferry and other venues across the Mersey.

The venues I remember being used by the Irish Community include:

PARISH HALLS
Christ the King
Holy Cross
Holy Trinity
Our Lady of Mount Carmel
Our Lady of Sorrows
St. Aloysius
St. Alphonsus
St. Anne's (Marmaduke Hall)
St. Anthony of Padua
St. James
St. John
St. Joseph
St. Mary, Highfield Street
St. Mary of the Angels (The Friary)
St. Matthew
St. Monica
St. Oswald
St. Patrick
St. Peter, Seel Street
St. Peter and Paul, Crosby
St. Philip Neri
St. Sebastian
St. Teresa
St. Vincent
Sacred Heart (St. Helens)
St. Marie (Southport)
St. Anne (Rock Ferry)
St. Werbergh (Birkenhead)
Our Lady Queen of Martyrs
St. Clare
St. Alexander

IRISH DANCING CLASS VENUES
Gallaghers
S and M Kelly, St. Teresa's
St. Anne's, Rock Ferry, M. Bolger
Irish Centre, M. Bolger
Holy Cross, M. Bolger
St. Michael's, K. Cunningham
George Ferguson
King Academy

HIRED HALLS
Bootle Town Hall
Broughton Hall (Feis)
Bootle Stadium (Feis)
Litherland Town Hall
Mecca (Dale Street)
Reeces, Parker Street, City Centre
St. John's Hall, Oriel Road
State Ballroom, Dale Street
St. George's Hall
St. George's Concert Hall
Stork Hotel
Philharmonic Hall
Picton Hall, William Brown Street
Crane Theatre
Neptune Theatre (same as Crane Theatre)
David Lewis Theatre
Green Lane GAA (E. O'Reilly)
Sun Hall, Kensington
Gay Street (Pre-1930s Scotland Road. Area)
St. Helen's Town Hall
Birkenhead Town Hall
Wallasey Town Hall
Wirral College
Fearnley Hall, Birkenhead
Kingsland Hall
Grosvenor Hall, Liscard

GAA FIELDS
Greenwich Park, Aintree
Dingle Brook Farm, West Derby
Thingwall Hall (St. Edward's Orphanage)
Sefton Rugby Ground
Yew Tree Field
Hanson Road, Aintree
Buckley Hill
Whetstone Lane (Ellesmere Port)
St. Patrick's, Widnes
Bootle Stadium
Waterloo Rugby Ground
Newsham Park
Greenbank Road

GAELIC LEAGUE

Bold Street (Sean O'Donovan)
Wood Street (Sean O'Donovan)
St. Cuthbert (Sean O'Donovan)
Eldon Street (John Mitchels)
Crosby (Four Masters)

FEISEANNA

St. Anne's, Rock Ferry
St. Teresa's, Norris Green
Broughton Hall
Bootle Stadium

OTHER VENUES

Islington } Lawlor
St. Anne Street } Lawlor
Shamrock Club, Lime Street, E. O'Reilly, M. Gill
Rialto
Blair Hall
Gay Street
KSC Iona House
Sampson & Barlow, London Road
Dermot Gallagher & 98 Shop
Burton's (Over shop)
Royal Iris Ferry
Geraldo (St. Helens)

Looking back at the Liverpool ceili scene, people divided into several groups. Those who attended Gaelic League fior-ceili only, and wouldn't dream of dancing a waltz, those who attended their own parish ceili and no other, and those who went to many parish ceilis only and didn't go to the Gaelic League, and thought 'they' were a bit odd.

Of course there were many who went to all, maybe with a first loyalty to their branch of the Gaelic League, and to other venues as an acceptable second best. There was a strong point of view in the Irish Community that Gaelic Leaguers were living in a 'Celtic Twilight'. It was a view I argued against at the time, but, looking back, they were probably right. Many Gaelic Leaguers, almost all born in Liverpool, could, and did, quote chunks of Padraig Pearse's oration at the grave of O'Donovan Rossa, the Proclamation and Robert Emmet's speech from the dock.

About this time, I became a member of the committee of the Seán O'Donovan branch and became involved in the local GAA club too, attending meetings regularly from about 1947. At that time, my club was the St. Patrick's Hurling and Football Club. The Club had previously been named the Eire Og Club, and had almost gone out of existence during the war. About that time, Fr. Paddy Spain of Kilruane, Nenagh, Co. Tipperary came on the scene.

He was a young curate and was based in St. Patrick's, Widnes. He got the Club going again and the newly revived club was re-named St. Patrick's after Fr. Spain's parish. A

In England, it could only happen in Liverpool – a greetings card featuring one of Ireland's great heroes, Robert Emmet. Austin Harford was to become Liverpool's first Catholic Lord Mayor.

This was a meeting of three branches of the Gaelic League in Liverpool. The Joint Committee came together to run major events such as the Liverpool Feis and St. Patrick's Day Mass and Concert. **Back row**: Eileen Goodwin, Tess McDonnell, Sheila Goodwin, Steve McKeon, Joe Graney, Bernard Bradley, Monica Smith, Tommy Walsh, Michael Walsh, Vin Boyle and Bob Gormley. **Front row**: Kath Gordon, Rita (Fry) Gormley, Maureen McNally, Sadie (Walsh) Redmond, Aileen McNally. Probably about 1948.

few years later Peter Delaney and a few other young men, the Marrays and Lynskeys among them, all members of the Sean Mhisteil branch of the Gaelic League, formed a Gaelic football team which they called John Mitchels Gaelic Football Club. As with other branches of the Gaelic League, they were not attracting Irish born players and didn't last long.

They amalgamated with the existing GAA club, St. Patrick's, and as a gesture to them, the club was renamed the St. Patrick's Hurling and John Mitchels Gaelic Football Club.

While GAA meetings were attended by both Irish born and Liverpool born people, meetings of the Gaelic League were attended mainly by Liverpool born people only. This suggests that 'the Famine Irish' became involved in Irish affairs with the single exception of Gaelic games. In Liverpool, Sinn Fein, Ancient Order of Hibernians, Irish Self-Determination League and the Anti-Partition of Ireland League were all active and they, like the Gaelic League, had primarily Liverpool born people as their members.

Sadly, during that period there was no Irish Centre in Liverpool, nor in any other English city. Nowhere to provide advice or information. They were to come too many years later. The absence of such structures didn't mean that there was no help for newcomers: GAA clubs, Irish priests and dance hall proprietors found digs and jobs for new arrivals. Above all they helped one another. A newly arrived person had only to meet other Irish people in social surroundings or at Mass, to hear of digs and where 'the start' was available. Certainly the dressing room at GAA games was a hive of information about jobs and digs.

Within a year or two of becoming involved in the Gaelic League, I had found the Gaelic Athletic Association – or it had found me! Young people who would attend meetings were unusual enough, and were often flattered by being nominated for positions on the committee. Many refused and escaped! At about the same time, I became involved in the committees of both the St. Patrick's GAA Club, and the Seán O'Donovan Branch of the Gaelic League. Vin Boyle was also involved in both. He had left St. Edward's Orphanage at age 14 having been trained as a tailor. He had found lodgings with an old lady in St. John's Parish in Kirkdale and a job with a Jewish tailor in Chicago Buildings, Whitechapel in the city centre. St. Edward's had assisted him as was their usual practice.

Vin quickly became friends with a number of Irish families in the city. One of the first would have been the O'Connors who, like Vin, were parishioners of St. John's. They were to become life long friends. Seamus was a Gaelic League activist and Vin became equally involved. Other O'Connor family members – all Gaelic League members were Arthur, Marie and Sheila. Younger brother, Kevin, was away to be a priest. He was to become a Bishop of Liverpool and was destined to say Vin's funeral Mass.

Vin and myself became equally involved in the GAA and came under the influence of two truly remarkable men. Fr. Paddy Spain, to whom I have referred and Sean McInerney. Sean McInerney, born in Liverpool of a Clare family, was the most dominant person in committee affairs, as distinct from the playing field. Sean was an accountant by profession and looked after the finances. He stood at the gate on a Sunday and took the collection.

He was the accepted authority on procedure at meetings and on County Board and Provincial Council affairs. He knew the GAA Official Guide inside out. Because of him, Vin and I became involved in the Lancashire County Board at a very young age.

Despite changes of name, and some hard times, the GAA has been active in Liverpool for a century or so.

In 1928, the GAA was strong enough to stage an exhibition match between Dublin and Cork, who had been All-Ireland Champions in 1927-1926 respectively. This game and one in London, were arranged by Central Council in Dublin to start the Provincial Council of Britain.

It was because of my involvement in the committee side of the Club that I met my wife, Kathleen. In those days, GAA meetings were held in the homes of committee members, and most were held in the Redmonds' house at 65 Derby Lane in the Old Swan district. 65 Derby Lane was the unofficial HQ of the Club. Hurleys were repaired and hooped in the cellar by members. Sliothairs (sliothairs are hurling balls) were stitched again, usually by Flann McCarthy of Clare, who lived across the road. His expertise saved the club valuable shillings.

One of the perks of having meetings in houses was that refreshments were served during the evening and Kathleen Redmond, the youngest in the family, invariably brought in the tea and biscuits. In a mirror image of my own situation a few years earlier, she was allowed to attend ceilis only, and on condition that her older brothers were going. As her brother Tom and my sister Sadie were courting and went on to be married, it follows that the younger brother and sister were attending the same functions. Our courting days were at the Yew Tree GAA field every Sunday and at various ceilis around Liverpool.

They were good days for the GAA in Liverpool, Lancashire and Britain generally, How could it be otherwise when the cream of Ireland's young men and women were pouring into Britain? Hospitals in Merseyside were full of Irish nurses and young Irish men were building up British cities after the war – and soon the motorways would be built. Irish dance halls all over Britain were booming.

St. Patrick's Hurling Club had a group of doctors, mainly from Cork, based in the Providence Hospital, St. Helens. In one team alone, I remember we had Doctors Bernard Murphy, Jimmy O'Reilly, Tim Broderick, Mick Herlihy and Mick Desmond. It was said that applicants for positions in the hospital were asked 'do you play hurling?' before qualifications were discussed! Jim Butler was one of the members of that team who stayed on after his playing days to become a club officer, County Board Chairman and later, Chairman of the Irish Centre in Liverpool.

After many years, when emigration had dried up, St. Patrick's was unable to field a hurling team and so the Club became the John Mitchels Gaelic Football Club which it is today. It is a Club which claims great loyalty and many families have remained involved for many years and for several generations.

The stalwarts of St. Patrick's in the great days included Michael Redmond from Wexford and his sons, Tom, Nick and Eddie, all of whom played hurling and football for the club and Lancashire County. All were also involved in the administrative side of affairs. Michael Redmond and his wife, Elizabeth, were neighbours' children from The Ballagh in County Wexford and they and their family became the base of the 'Wexford Connection' for which the Club became famous. Their daughters played camogie, and as I have said, their house became the venue for club meetings, equipment repairs, and every other Club activity. The Wexford connection continued with Sim Donoghue from Castlebridge and his son Michael who played in goal for both Club and County at both hurling and football. Also from Wexford was Jim Cosgrave. Then the Kirwans arrived from Kilmuckridge, Pat, Aidan and John, Tom and Hubert Sheils from Gorey. Others from Wexford were Pat Fortune from Gorey and Chris Morrissey from Kilmuckridge. No wonder the atmosphere was great when Wexford were playing!

Before my time, but I just remember them, were the Brennans, who were more famous for their greyhounds. That was in the days of the Liverpool Stanley track and the other dog track in Lower Breck Road.

An Irish organisation attempting to appeal to a wide spectrum of the Irish community is the Irish Fellowship in 1939. There were many people involved and they were, as far as I am aware, the first group of people to make a serious attempt to open a premises for the use of the Irish community in Liverpool. Whether the 'Irish Ireland' organisations stayed away or whether they weren't invited, I don't know.

Why the Irish Fellowship failed in their bid to secure the Wellington Rooms (which was destined to become the Irish Centre 25 years later) we'll never know. Was the £500 too much? Was the outbreak of war on September 3rd in that year the reason? It's worth pointing out they were trying to rent, not buy.

The absence of a bar may have been OK in 1939 but it

wouldn't have suited later. The signatories of the letter indicate the movement was distinctly 'up-market'. Would they have attracted the majority of the Irish community? Did they want them? We'll never know!

I believe 'The Irish Fellowship Letter' is a most remarkable document. It is the only original copy I have seen. It asks more questions than it answers. Why did this huge project sink without trace? How was it possible to get so many signatures on one document?

The building had opened as The Embassy Rooms in 1923, having been the Wellington Club from 1816 to 1923. The Embassy Rooms were put up for auction on 26th March 1930. The collection of names, all of whom were Hon. Vice Presidents apparently, was very interesting.

The President, Willie Loughrey, who was a barrister, was associated primarily with the St. Patrick's Day Banquet Society. They held their Annual Banquet in the Adelphi Hotel and were usually known among the Irish community as the 'one day a year Irish people'. The other three names were very different: Pat Taggart was an Irish language teacher at the Seán O'Donovan Gaelic League. Seán Bolger was an Irish dancing teacher and was also a member of the Gaelic League. The remaining one was Dwyer Doyle who owned the famous '98 shop in Liverpool. Irish newspapers and other items were available there. The other 45 Vice Presidents were prominent Irish names in the city, such as Dr. Bligh, Peter Murphy and Fr. M. O'Ryan OMI. In most cases, they were prominent Catholics. It appeared to be almost obligatory to have a degree.

What is certain is that 25 years later when the Irish community bought the premises to house an Irish Centre, none of the gentlemen of 1939, and they were almost entirely men, came forward to claim their connection with the premises.

President :	*Vice-President* :	*Secretary* :	*Treasurer* :
W. J. LOUGHREY, Barrister-at-Law	P. TAGGART, F.S.A.A.	SEAN BOLGER, B.A.	DWYER DOYLE, M.Sc.

An Ʒaeƌeal Caṗaƌaṙ

THE IRISH FELLOWSHIP

— Established June 1, 1938 —

ON. VICE-PRESIDENTS

W. BAKER, L.D.S.
J. BARRY, M.D.
P. BLIGH, M.D.
RANK CLANCY.
CLARKE, M.D.
HE VERY REV. M.
    COADY, P.P., V.F.
V. COGHLAN, M.D.
HILIP COYNE.
. J. CROGHAN, M.D.
HN CURTIN, M.A.
. P. DAVIS, K.H.S., J.P.
HE MISSES DEERY.
. DEVLIN, M.D.
J. DOYLE, J.P.
DUFFY, M.D.
FOLEY, B.L.
EV. W. GREENE, P.P.
. HARDING, M.D.
HAWE, Ch.M., F.R.C.S.
EV. J. HOWARD, M.A.
ISS M. JOHNSTON,
    M.R.S.T.
. P. KELLY, M.R.S.T.
. KEARNEY, B.D.S.
SEPH KENNAN.
D. L. KING, J.P.
. LYNSKEY, LL.B.
HE VERY REV. A. W.
    CANON MADDEN,
        V.F., P.P.
SEPH MAGUIRE.
RS. B. J. MARMION,
    M.A.
HE RIGHT REV. MGR.
  J. P. MOLONEY,
  O.B.E., D.S.O., M.C.
ENIS MOONEY, J.P.
MORRISSEY, M.D.
MURRAY-BLIGH.
    F.R.C S.
ETER MURPHY.

Dear *Madam*,

January, 1939.

For many years past there has been an urgent need for the establishment of an Irish centre in Liverpool where the Irish community could assemble in a place worthy of our people.

The Irish Fellowship was formed in June last and in the course of a few months without any great effort by the Committee a membership of 300 was secured.

This almost spontaneous response is clear proof of the need in Liverpool for such a society and for the objects for which it stands.

A responsible Committee has been appointed to take steps for the acquisition of premises suitable to our purpose and to the needs of the Irish community.

An opportunity has now been presented to us to acquire a tenancy of The Embassy Rooms in Mount Pleasant, which would provide an ideal solution to our problem.

These premises contain a Theatre or Ballroom suitable for the production of Irish dramas, the holding of Irish concerts, dances, meetings, and other popular functions.

There are also several other rooms in the building which would be suitable for games, reading rooms, library and other purposes of a social and educational character. It is further proposed that light refreshments be provided, but the Committee are unanimously opposed to anything in the nature of a club for the sale of alcoholic liquor.

Such an institute as it is proposed to establish would prevent a large proportion of our youth from being swallowed up in surroundings which are hostile to both their religious and national convictions.

The Embassy Rooms are excellent premises for our purpose. They are premises of which any Irish person can be justly proud. The initial cost, however, will be somewhat high. The Committee must raise at least £500 before they can equip them and give the project a proper start.

Already as evidence of our sincerity a substantial sum has been raised by the members present at a General Meeting of the Irish Fellowship on Wednesday, November 2nd, and the Committee now appeal to you to assist them in furthering their praiseworthy object.

Once equipped and started the Committee are confident that the proposition will be a paying concern. Several Societies have promised assistance by offering to hold their dances and other social functions to be held there, this being possible without in any way interfering with the normal activities of the organisation.

From this source alone, a very substantial revenue can be obtained quite apart from membership subscriptions and other functions to be organised by The Irish Fellowship itself.

The Committee having gone carefully into the figures feel they will have no difficulty in defraying expenses in the years to come. The initial expense, however, is the great difficulty.

May we count on your generosity to enable us to provide what has been a long felt want in Liverpool ?

Yours faithfully,

W. J. Loughrey President.

P. Taggart Vice-President.

Sean Bolger Secretary.

T. D. Doyle Treasurer.

The next grouping of Irish Societies was the 'Irish Association of Liverpool and District'.

AN GAEDHEAL – CHONNRADH, LIVERPOOL

Again, as was so often the case in the past, the primary objectives were to invite 'persons of Irish birth or descent' and to 'assist other Irish Societies in furthering any part of their objects' and to 'promote unity, goodwill and co-operation among all sections of the Irish race'.

Nowhere was there an aspiration to obtain premises for use by the Irish community. I, personally, find that remarkable.

In the 1940s, apart from the Gaelic League and the Gaelic Athletic Association, another Irish organisation active in Liverpool was the Anti-Partition of Ireland League. Like the other two organisations, this was part of a nationwide organisation with branches all over Britain. Local people involved were Harry McHugh, Peter O'Hanlon, Sean (Jack) McCann and Paddy Garrigan. Gerry McCormack from St. Helens was also active and was a member of the National Council.

Other people who were active nationally were Frank Short of Birmingham and Bill Halley, Jack Griffin and Jim Kirby of Portsmouth. All of these gentlemen were to become friends of mine many years later. Frank Short was an officer of the Provincial Council of Britain GAA. His daughter, Clare Short, became a prominent politician.

Bill, John and Jack were founders of the Federation of Irish Societies, Southern Region. In 1974/5 and 6, Bill and I were to serve together as the first officers of the Federation of Irish Societies after it became an all-Britain organisation. I was Chairman while Bill was Secretary. My sister Sadie, who was on the committee of Seán O'Donovan branch of the Gaelic League way back in the 1940s, was the first Treasurer

(f) The Trustees shall have power to enforce from any Officer or Sectional Committee the production of accounts, submission of accounts to audit and payment or transfer to the Trustees or under their directions of all balances of moneys or other properties.

5.—Bye-Laws. Until the first Annual General Meeting, the Executive Council shall make all rules, bye-laws and regulations for the conduct of the Association, which shall remain in force until the first Annual General Meeting in 1931. At the Annual General Meeting in 1931 the Executive Committee shall submit for adoption, amendment, and final determination, a copy of the principal rules for the regulation of the Association, including within such Rules power for the Executive Committee to make bye-laws. As from the date of such Annual General Meeting, the principal rules so defined shall be amended only by General Meeting of the Association.

6.—Annual General Meeting. The Annual General Meeting shall be called in February in each year, by advertisement, and there shall be laid before such Meeting an account made up to the preceding 31st December, together with Auditor's report thereon.

7.—Audit. The accounts of the Association shall be audited annually by a person carrying on the work of a professional accountant, and his fees shall be paid by the Executive Council. The Executive Council shall make the first appointment, and thereafter the Annual General Meeting shall make the appointment annually.

8.—Winding Up and Vesting of Property. The whole of the property of the Association shall belong to the whole of its continuing members in an undivisible whole, and if the Association determine by resolution of an Extraordinary General Meeting to wind up, the whole of its assets shall vest in the Trustees for division among existing organisations in Ireland having objects partly or wholly similar to the objects of the Association. The Trustees' power of application of the assets shall not be limited in any way, and the Trustees shall be deemed discharged from all Trusts so soon as the Auditor of the Association certifies his satisfaction that the balance of any property has been paid over as aforesaid.

9.—Alteration of Rules. These rules shall be altered only by the Annual General Meeting of the Association and shall be printed in both the English and Irish languages. The Executive Committee shall not in any way be limited in supplementing these Rules until the first Annual General Meeting of the Association.

The
IRISH ASSOCIATION
OF
LIVERPOOL & DISTRICT.

Constitution

AN

GAEDHEAL - CHONNRADH
I
LIVERPOOL.

CONSTITUTION.

1.—Name. The name of the Association shall be the "IRISH ASSOCIATION OF LIVERPOOL AND DISTRICT."

2.—Objects.
(a) To unite persons of Irish birth or descent in a non-political and non-sectarian society for social, cultural, educational, recreative, thrift and benevolent purposes, according with Irish traditions.
(b) To assist other Irish Societies in furthering any part of their objects which are similar to any objects of the Association.
(c) To promote unity, goodwill and co-operation among all sections of the Irish race.
(d) To promote schemes (including the appointment of Trustees or nominees to act on bodies corporate), for the provision of social and cultural intercourse, education, recreation, thrift and benevolence, insurance, etc., for the benefit of members, and to co-operate with any other body offering such provision to its members.
(e) To celebrate Irish festivals in a fitting manner.

3.—Membership and Subscription.
(a) Membership is open to all persons upwards of fourteen years of age.
(b) The annual subscription shall be due on the 1st January in each year after the year 1930. In the year 1930 the subscription shall be due on the date of adopting this Constitution. The annual subscription shall be 2/6 except as shall hereinafter appear.
(c) The annual subscription shall be reduced to 1/- per annum in the case of persons being members of other Societies which enter into co-operation agreements with the Association.
(d) Membership shall lapse when a subscription is three months due and unpaid.
(e) Members shall be entitled to privileges in relation to admission to all public proceedings promoted by the Association. Such privilege shall consist of a cheaper charge for admission, or admission to reserved seat or portion.

4.—Officers, Etc.
(a) The business of the Association shall be entirely controlled by an Executive Committee to be appointed as hereinafter appears.
(b) The Executive Committee shall appoint for such period not exceeding three years as their resolution shall determine :—
    (i) One or more Honorary Presidents.
    (ii) Three Trustees.

(c) The Executive Committee shall appoint annually from its number :—
    (i) A President.
    (ii) Two Vice-Presidents of whom one shall be senior.
    (iii) A Secretary or Secretaries (who may be paid a stipend or other remuneration).
    (iv) A Treasurer to act under the direction of the Executive Committee, subject to the control of the Trustees.
    (v) Departmental Chairmen to preside over and be responsible for work of sectional committees.
(d) The Executive Committee shall consist of twenty members of the Association elected as follows :—
    (i) For the year 1930, 12 persons shall be appointed by the meeting adopting this Constitution and these twelve shall have power to co-operate eight other persons.
    (ii) One half of the twenty persons so appointed (who shall be selected by lot) shall retire at the first Annual General Meeting, but shall be eligible for re-election.
    (iii) In 1931 and subsequent years, one half of the members of the Executive Committee shall be appointed to hold office for two years, and in each year after 1931 those members of the Executive Committee who have been continuously in office for two years without reappointment shall retire, but shall be eligible for re-election.
    (iv) Casual vacancies shall be filled by resolution of the Executive Committee, and each person appointed to fill a vacancy shall be subject to the same rules of retirement as would have affected the person who created the vacancy.
    (v) No act of the Executive Committee shall be invalidated merely for the reason that any member of the Executive Committee has ceased to be a member of the Association ; and in any such case the Executive Committee may declare that a casual vacancy exists.
(e) SECTIONAL COMMITTEES. The Executive Committee shall from time to time determine how the work of the Association shall be divided into sections, and shall establish, amend or maintain regulations for the work of the Association to be carried out by the Sectional Committees. The convener of each Sectional Committee shall be appointed by the Executive Committee, and one-half of each such Committee, in addition to the Chairman, shall consist of members of the Executive Committee. Sectional Committees shall not have power to pledge the credit of the Association, and shall in all matters be subject to the Executive Committee.

61

of the All Britain Federation of Irish Societies.

Maurice Roche in Huddersfield and Sean Hogan in Manchester were also involved nationally in the Anti-Partition of Ireland League. I became friendly with both of these great Irishmen in later years.

During my youth as I have described it, I was leading a very 'Liverpool Irish' life. Only much later in my life did I realise what a strange life it was. As I became older, I slowly, over a very long period, became aware of what a truly remarkable city I live in. There is more Irish history in Liverpool than in many Irish towns.

Superficially, the history is simple. Because of the boat link between Liverpool and Ireland, there has always been an Irish community in Liverpool. The two Diaspora: At the time of the failure of the potato crop in the 1840s, and about 100 years later after World War II, brought huge numbers of Irish people to Liverpool.

The people were very different. In the 1840s, the people were mostly families who walked away from their homes, often after eviction by a landlord. There was usually no one left behind so there was no family to keep in touch with. They had often walked from the west coast of Ireland, possibly 150 miles to the boat in Dublin. There, near where the beautiful but haunting famine memorial is now, they boarded the Liverpool boat. It is estimated that 1,300,000 people landed in Liverpool between 1845 and the early 1850s. 1847 (Black '47) was probably the worst year.

Many stayed in Liverpool, many walked out of Liverpool towards St. Helens, Manchester and Yorkshire. Liverpool was the gateway to the 'new world' and those with some money bought tickets for America and Australia.

The worst of the ships were called coffin ships. Sadly, many, many of these poor Irish people died. They died in Liverpool of hunger or typhus, or 'famine fever' as it was known. Thousands were buried in mass paupers' graves and many more were buried in the Atlantic Ocean.

Of course there was no famine in the true meaning of the word as we know the word 'famine' today. All crops other than the potato were growing as normal but potatoes were the staple food and the animals were used to pay the rent. However, a tradition has evolved and the people who came in the 1840s and 1850s have become known as 'the Famine Irish'. The descendants of the Famine Irish often don't know where their families came from in Ireland because there was no tradition, for them, of going home to grandparents. Very often, they simply know they have an Irish name.

There is little evidence of Irish community activity in the 19th century. Simply living was the ultimate objective. Having a social life was impossible for those poor people.

The second Diaspora was very different. Nearly all the exiles from the mid 1940s and 1950s were single. They left their parents behind and headed for Liverpool to look for work. As was the case 100 years earlier, many stayed, and many moved on to other parts of England. Those who chose to go to America or Australia usually travelled directly from Ireland.

So what was Liverpool like for those Irish people who came here in the 1840s and '50s?

LIVERPOOL AS THE 'FAMINE IRISH' FOUND IT

They arrived into Clarence Dock perhaps a mile from what is now the Pier Head. Cotton Street was opposite and would lead the people to Scotland Road. I have read that immediately opposite the Clarence Dock there was a public house with a statue of St. Patrick on the wall above the door.

I have also read that this statue was transferred to St. Patrick's Church, Park Place and is the famous statue still in a place of prominence on the church. As the information on the leaflet shows (see p74), the church was opened on

"I feel this sculpture is not complete until the figures are crossing an ocean of names, names cast in bronze and set into the cobble surround, thousands of names, names of those who have pledged to care"
Rowan Gillespie

THROUGH THIS INITIATIVE, THE IRISH FAMINE COMMEMORATION FUND AIM TO RAISE £10 MILLION TO ASSIST THE HOMELESS, UNEMPLOYED AND DISADVANTAGED YOUTH OF IRELAND.

Rowan Gillespie six bronze figures on the North Wall in Dublin portrayed just a few yards from the boat to Liverpool. At the other end of the voyage, they would pass through the gates of the Clarence Dock into Liverpool.

23rd August, 1827 so the story is simply not true.

There had been a lot of Irish people in Liverpool long before the 1840s. The geographical location meant it was inevitable. It could be argued that without Ireland, Liverpool wouldn't exist. In 1207, King John, who was establishing his hold on Ireland needed a port on the west coast of England to move soldiers in and out of Ireland to service the garrison. He granted Liverpool its Charter that year – 1207.

Regular contact has been maintained. Inevitably, there were Irish people at the Liverpool end of the route ever since, and much movement back and forth. Many Irish people arrived immediately after the 1798 Rebellion, which affected many parts of Ireland, particularly Wexford, Antrim, Mayo and Down.

There was also a considerable influx around 1801 as a result of the Act of Union. The Census of 1841, before the failure of the potato crop, showed that there were 49,639 Irish born people in Liverpool.

The next Census in 1851 showed a total of Irish born people of 83, 813 or 22.3% of a total population of 375,955. We clearly shouldn't think the first Irish people to come to Liverpool came to escape the 'potato famine'.

Such a huge increase in population generally, apart from the fact that they were mainly Irish, must have placed huge demands on the city at the time. Thomas Burke in his 'Catholic History of Liverpool' says 'In 1809 there was another influx of Irish immigrants, due to the severity of Irish landowners.'

What must be borne in mind is that quite apart from the problems in Ireland which resulted in all those hungry and sick people coming in a short period of time, the situation in Liverpool was already extremely distressing with people living in appalling conditions.

In a survey of the Vauxhall district in 1842, John Finch obtained information from 4,814 families (a total of 23,892 people). Only 1,490 heads of family were in full employment. 1,342 families were without *any* visible income, while a further 3,045 families had an income of less than 40 shillings a week.

As far as living accommodation is concerned, 982 families were living in cellars, and a further 1,236 families were lodgers, namely 'not owning furniture'. These consisted mainly of persons who had pawned or sold all that they possessed for food, and had therefore taken lodgings.

As this was the Liverpool that the 'famine Irish' came in to; it was sad that they were to be blamed for the conditions in subsequent years.

A typhus epidemic struck early in 1847. The names of the dead indicates that a large percentage of Irish were among the victims. By the end of June 1847, 3,753 paupers, including 1,584 infants had been buried in the St. Mary's burial ground, Mulberry Street. While many of these were from the Vauxhall area, 224 of them came from the workhouse in Mount Pleasant. The Catholic Cathedral is now on this site.

Edwin Chadwick in a report to the Government in 1842 suggested 'that for the general promotion of the means necessary to prevent disease it would be good economy to appoint a district medical officer independent of private practice, and with special qualifications and responsibilities to initiate sanitary measures ...' Doctor William Henry Duncan (1805-1863) was appointed to be the Medical Officer of Health in 1847. The first in Britain. Duncan was surprised by the extreme poverty of so many people in Liverpool and in particular, by the poor housing conditions, associated with poverty. He put a series of statements to the Town Council and to the Literary and Philosophical

Society of Liverpool from 1842/43 onwards. In one he said 'the vicious construction of the dwellings, insufficient supply of out-offices and of receptacles for refuse and excrement, the absence of drains, deficient sewerage and overcrowding is ... increasing the mortality in Liverpool.'

Describing the notorious cellars, in 1844 he reported: "the cellars are ten to twelve feet square, generally flagged, but frequently having only the bare earth for a floor and sometimes less than six feet in height. There is frequently no window, so light and air can gain access only by the door, the top of which is often not higher than the level of the street. In such cellars ventilation is out of the question ... as a result of defective drainage, they are generally damp ... a back cellar used as a sleeping apartment has no direct communication with the external atmosphere. ... There are, in the twelve wards forming the Parish of Liverpool, 6,294 inhabited cellars, containing 20,168 inhabitants."

Doctor Wm. Farr, Superintendent of the Statistical Dept. of the Registrar General's Office, said in 1885: "Of 100,000 children born in the healthy districts of England 96,339 are alive at the end of the first month of life. In Liverpool, only 94,551 would be alive. At the end of the second month, the figures are 95,178 and 92,088. At the age of seven months 91,932 children are alive in healthy districts while in Liverpool only 84,373 survive. So unfavourable are the unsanitary conditions in Liverpool, the mortality rate of children under one year of age is 229 out of every 1,000."

Apart from the cellars, many other poor people in Liverpool were housed in 'courts'. In evidence before a House of Commons Committee on the Health of Towns, Dr. Duncan said, "As some of the Members may not be acquainted with the construction of courts in which many townspeople reside ... they consist of two rows of houses

66

placed opposite each other ... usually nine to 15 feet apart ... six or eight houses in each row. The court is linked to the street by a passage or archway about three feet wide ... the farther end being closed by a high wall ... forming a cul-de-sac with a narrow entrance ... it bids defiance to the entrance of air and renders its circulation a matter of impossibility. I do not know of a single court which communicates with the sewer by a covered drain."

Few of the streets in working-class Liverpool were sewered anyway. Farr's report says 243,000 persons were living in a square mile in London ... while the ratio in Liverpool was 460,000 per square mile. In a small specific area, the ratio rose to 657,973 persons in a square mile. This was based on an area of 49,000 square yards with a population of 8,000.

It was into this situation that in 1846 and the next few years, scores of thousands of 'famine Irish' arrived. It was estimated that about 20% of the working class population lived in cellars, many others lived in courts. In larger courts there were usually two privies with an ash pit between them. These privies were often situated within 3-4 feet of the doors and windows of the houses. The ash pits became full to overflowing long before the nightmen came to empty them.

Many of the cellars had been closed as a result of the Health Act of 1842, but in his report for 1847, Dr. Duncan has this to say: "The pauper immigration is steadily increasing. By the end of June not less than 300,000 have landed in Liverpool. Of these, 60,000 to 80,000 have located themselves amongst us, occupying every nook and cranny, filling lodging houses and forcing their way into about 3,000 closed cellars. In parts of Liverpool, 50 or 60 people had been found in houses of three or four small rooms, with upwards of 40 sleeping in a cellar."

The overcrowding in insanitary conditions was resulting in epidemics of various diseases affecting towns and cities. Typhoid became known as the 'Irish disease' because an outbreak occurred at the time of the huge influx of Irish immigrants in 1847. In that outbreak 5,845 people died, and, of course, they were mainly from the poorer people living in poor conditions. Then, in 1848, there was an outbreak of Asian cholera. It came via Glasgow and Dumfries. On 10th December 1848, an Irish family arrived by steamer from Dumfries where an epidemic was at its height. One child and both parents went down within 24 hours of their arrival. All three died, and on 15th December, a woman who had washed the bodies, and the bedclothes, also died. By the summer of 1849, hundreds were dying every week. The epidemic burned itself out and when cholera returned in 1854, its impact was much less.

One of the first people to recognise the part that dirty, overcrowded conditions played in disease epidemics was not a medical person, but a poor, hard-working woman named Catherine (Kitty) Wilkinson. She had come from her home in Derry in 1912. In the cholera epidemic of 1832 she allowed and encouraged her neighbours to wash their clothes in her back kitchen. Her husband happened to work as a porter for William Rathbone. When the first public wash-house was opened in Frederick Street, Thomas and Kitty were the first superintendents.

Because of the success of this Liverpool venture, the Bath and Wash House Acts of 1846 and 1847 came into existence. Doctor Duncan was concerned that lodging houses were centres of infection in various epidemics, and introduced inspection and control. Bye-laws for the regulation of lodging houses were introduced in August 1848.

Nightly visitations were introduced in February 1849. Duncan said: "Up to the end of 1850, I inspected nearly

68

1,100 houses for which registration was required, in order to ascertain the number of lodgers each was capable of accommodating, with due regard to health. Nine tenths of the keepers are Irish … few can be relied on for carrying out Bye-laws unless closely watched. The Bye-law for requiring windows to be opened daily is habitually neglected … although their condition since registration is materially improved in respect to overcrowding, cleanliness and ventilation. There is still room for improvement."

The *Morning Chronicle* of 15th July 1850, in a long article on the dreadful reception awaiting the thousands of people fleeing from the potato famine, had this to say: "It is in the neighbourhood of the Waterloo Dock and northwards to the Clarence Dock that the principal lodging houses for poor immigrants are to be found, more especially around Denison, Regent, Carlton, Porter, Stewart and Great Howard Streets, most of them the filthiest kind, externally and internally. The wretched accommodation provided for the multitudes of emigrants that daily pass through Liverpool, to await the departure of the vessels by which they have secured their passage, and the robberies of all kinds to which they are subjected during their stay, are evils that the philanthropic citizens of Liverpool, who feel for the misery of their fellow creatures, might well hasten to remedy."

John Denvir, in his book, *The Life Story of an Old Rebel*, described how an attack on Crosbie Street by Orangemen was thwarted by a force of police headed by Michael Whitty who was Chief Constable of Liverpool at the time. He was a Wexfordman and was a very interesting character.

He was educated at St. Peter's College, Wexford, before going to Maynooth to study for the priesthood. He left Maynooth and headed for Liverpool where he became editor of *The Journal*. Then he became a policeman and was the first man to fill the post of Head Constable. He remained in the post from 1836 to 1844. He claimed to know every policeman by name and rank. When he came to office, it was estimated that 20,000 people were living in cellars, while 40,000 were living in courts. Conditions were already appalling before the arrivals from the potato famine in Ireland. Orange and Catholic divisions were apparent in the police force and it was Whitty who established the force as a disciplined body. John Denvir describes an attack on a Hibernian Club in Crosbie Street. The attack was made from Blundell Street side where the houses were back to back with the courts in Crosbie Street. Denvir's uncle, Hugh Roney, lived in Blundell Street and Denvir was visiting with his mother. He was in a first floor room with his mother and Uncle Hugh. He says every room from cellar to garret was crowded with dock labourers, all Irish. The Orangemen were armed, he says - with guns, swords, and ships carpenters' hatchets. They were thirty yards from Hugh Roney's when Michael Whitty marched out of Simpson Street with a force of policemen. There was a 'desperate engagement', and the police, freely using their batons, routed the Orangemen.

Whitty resigned from the police in 1844 and went back to journalism. He founded the *Liverpool Daily Post* which, together with its evening version, the *Liverpool Echo*, is still Liverpool's main paper. His sub-editor was Stephen Joseph Meany, a prominent figure in the Young Ireland and Fenian movements.

Whitty wrote a book, *Life of Robert Emmet*, which John Denvir reviewed for the *Catholic Times*. Michael Whitty died in 1873, and is buried in Anfield Cemetery.

Many years later, in my own lifetime, and before, my Grandmother ran a lodging house in Blundell Street, beside Crosbie Street. Her lodgers were invariably Irish. My Mother told me she remembered that men used to come in at night with lamps and count the men in every room. This was presumably to comply with Dr. Duncan's Bye-Laws.

Although the vast majority of the 'Famine Irish' crowded into the Vauxhall area, there were one or two pockets in the south end where concentration occurred. One of these was in and around Crosbie and Blundell Streets. John Denvir, in his book *The Life Story of an Old Rebel* says: "I had an aunt … married to Hugh Roney who kept a public house in Crosbie Street. Nearly all in Crosbie Street were from the West of Ireland, and amongst them there was scarcely anything but Irish spoken."

Crosbie Street consisted mainly of courts. The courts usually contained seven or eight houses. In one, there were 118 inhabitants. In that court, the local Dispensary attended to fifty cases of fever. In number 12 Court there were, in the 1851 Census, 85 persons in the seven units.

No.1	No.2	No.3	No.4	No.5	No.6	No.7
10	16	9	14	12	18	6

Sixty-seven of the eighty-five gave their place of birth as Ireland. All of the others were children of Irish-born parents. The men's occupations were given as carter, dock labourer, dock lumper, agricultural labourer, sailor or pauper. The women were mostly oakum pickers but there were also washerwomen, basket girls, servants (some unemployed servants) and seamstresses. Most of the children were recorded as scholars. In the same Census (1851) in the Dryden Street area of Scotland Road, there were 583 people in six courts, 202 of whom were born in Ireland. In the fourteen political wards in central Liverpool, there were 47,472 Irish-born people in 1841, and 72,978 in 1851.

It is ironic that Liverpool had many of the finest buildings in England reflecting the prosperity of the people

Victorian courts.

The image shows a Victorian court with the following labels:

NARROW COURT – allowing little sunlight to penetrate

ENCLOSED ON ALL FOUR SIDES APART FROM THE ALLEYWAY AT THE ENTRANCE

BACK-TO-BACK HOUSES (i.e. another court on the other side)

HOUSES TEEMING WITH PEOPLE

NO KITCHENS – if a family could afford a joint of meat it was roasted in the nearest baker's oven or in an oven serving all the people in the block

BADLY FITTING WINDOWS AND DOORS

ENTRANCE THROUGH TUNNEL

SOLITARY STANDPIPE – supplying water to all the houses

COMMUNAL PRIVY (LAVATORY) The cesspit was emptied into large buckets and taken away at night – but the job was often neglected and sewage overflowed into the court

NO DAMP COURSE = DAMP HOUSES

SOME PEOPLE LIVED IN CELLARS

OPEN SEWER OR GUTTER FOR SLOPS – many houses lacked even this

WATER SUPPLY – often contaminated by cesspit if it came from a well

involved in shipping, commerce and the slave trade, and at the same time the worst housing in England.

Ten years after the huge influx of starving poor people, the situation was little better. William Rathbone still seeking to help those most in need, was introduced, by Florence Nightingale, to Agnes Jones. He persuaded her to become Lady Superintendent of the Brownlow Hill Workhouse, in 1865

Margaret Simey in her book *Charitable Effort in Liverpool in the 19th Century*, quotes Agnes Jones: "There was on the ground floor a Bridewell for women, consisting of huge cellars, bare and unfurnished – damp stone floors called oakum sheds. Voluntary creatures, driven by hunger, destitution or vice-begging a few nights shelter and a piece of bread, in return for which they picked their allotted portion of oakum. I went to the oakum sheds ... filled with women and girls – more than 200. I sat on the floor and picked oakum. They laughed at me and told me my fingers were no good for that work." Oakum was fibre from old ropes which when 'picked' and waxed was used to caulk deck planks on ships.

Agnes Jones was a remarkable woman whose likeness is included in the stained glass window of great Liverpool women in the Anglican Cathedral.

CENSUS RETURNS 1851

Below are details from Census returns for Crosbie Street
(situated between Park Lane and Queens Dock). From these
you can get an idea of numbers of people/families living in
each household, where they were born and the jobs they did.

Crosbie Street 12

Court No. 1

Name	Relation	Status	Age	Occupation	Birthplace
Charles O'Donnell	Head	Married	45	Carter	Ireland
Margaret O'Donnell	Wife	Married	50		Ireland
Henry O'Donnell	Son		15	Works in Smithy	Ireland
John O'Donnell	Son		12	Scholar	Lancashire, Liverpool
Charles O'Donnell	Son		6	Scholar	Lancashire, Liverpool
Margaret O'Donnell	Daughter		10		Lancashire, Liverpool
Ann O'Donnell	Daughter		3 months		Lancashire, Liverpool
James Thompson	Head	Married	27	Dock Labourer	Ireland
Bridget Thompson	Wife	Married	27	Washerwoman	Ireland
Margaret King	Lodger		18	Basket Girl. Fish	Ireland

Court No. 2

Name	Relation	Status	Age	Occupation	Birthplace
Catherine Connor	Head	Married	40	Oakum Picker	Ireland
Michael Connor	Son		16	Clay Pipe Maker	Lancashire, Liverpool
Bridget Connor	Daughter		19	Oakum Picker	Ireland
Mary O'Connor	Daughter		10	Oakum Picker	Lancashire, Liverpool
Mary Moghen	Lodger		28	Oakum Picker	Ireland
Anthony O'Connell	Head	Married	48	Dock Labourer	Ireland
Cicely O'Connell	Wife	Married	46	Oakum Picker	Ireland
Ann O'Connell	Daughter		18	Oakum Picker	Lancashire, Liverpool
Bridget O'Connell	Daughter		14	Oakum Picker	Lancashire, Liverpool
Catherine O'Connell	Daughter		10	Oakum Picker	Lancashire, Liverpool
Margaret O'Connell	Daughter		8	Oakum Picker	Lancashire, Liverpool
Anthony O'Connell	Son		12	Scholar	Lancashire, Liverpool
John O'Connell	Son		5	Scholar	Lancashire, Liverpool
Mary O'Connell	Niece		13	Oakum Picker	Lancashire, Liverpool
Denis Cain	Lodger		28	Dock Lumper	Ireland
James Cain	Lodger		35	Dock Lumper	Ireland

74

Court No. 3						
Honor Connor	Head	Widow	68		Ireland
Patrick Connor	Son		19	Sugar Baker	Ireland
Jane Cain	Head	Married	36	Oakum Picker	Ireland
Mary Cain	Daughter		18	Oakum Picker	Ireland
Richard Cain	Son		16	Labourer	Ireland
Mary Dean	Visitor		21	Oakum Picker	Ireland
Barbara Dean	Visitor	Married	40	Oakum Picker	Ireland
Court No. 6						
Bridget Neelty	Head	Widow	36	Oakum Picker	Ireland
Margaret Neelty	Daughter		14	Oakum Picker	Ireland
Bridget Neelty	Daughter		11	Oakum Picker	Ireland
Catherine Coyne	Lodger	Widow	50	Oakum Picker	Ireland
Winifred Coyne	Lodger		18	Oakum Picker	Ireland
Ellen Coyne	Lodger		9	Oakum Picker	Ireland
Catherine Clerk	Lodger	Widow	26	Oakum Picker	Ireland
Catherine Clerk	Lodger	Widow	27	Oakum Picker	Lancashire, Liverpool
Mary McDonnell	Head	Married	32	Oakum Picker	Ireland
John McDonnell	Son		10	Scholar	Ireland
Mary McDonnell	Daughter		2		Ireland
Bridget Cain	Sister		26	Oakum Picker	Ireland
John McGowen	Lodger		45	Dock Labourer	Ireland
Michael Hogan	Lodger		36	Sailor	Ireland
Mary Dunworth	Lodger		58	Seamster Sewer for Slop Shop	Ireland
Catharine Dunworth	Lodger		22	Seamster Sewer for Slop Shop	Ireland
Matthew Dunworth	Lodger		17	Journeyman Shoemaker	Ireland
William Dunworth	Lodger		11	Journeyman Shoemaker	Ireland

Court No. 7

Francis Donnelly	Head	Widower	36	Dock Labourer	Ireland
Francis Donnelly	Son		8	Scholar	Lancashire, Liverpool
James Donnelly	Son		6	Scholar	Lancashire, Liverpool
Bridget Farens	Sister		46		Ireland
John Farens	Nephew		17	Scholar	Ireland
John Buckingham	Lodger		50	Dock Labourer	Ireland
Thomas Preston	Son-in-law	Married	27	Labourer	Ireland
Ann Preston	Daughter	Married	25		Ireland
Mary Preston	Grand-daughter		4		Ireland
Bernard Quinn	Visitor	Widower	63	Agricultural Labourer	Ireland
Bridget Quinn	Visitor		22	Unemployed Servant	Ireland
Mary Morison	Room-keeper		25	Basket Girl, Greens	Ireland
Mary Johnston	Lodger		22	Unemployed Servant	Ireland

Court No. 4

Nancy Geraghty	Head	Widow	68	Oakum Picker	Ireland
Bridget Dean	Daughter	Widow	42	Oakum Picker	Ireland
Michael Bourke	Son		20	Dock Labourer	Ireland
Thomas Bourke	Son		18	Dock Labourer	Ireland
Matthew Naughton	Lodger	Widower	69	Dock Labourer	Ireland
John Dougher	Lodger		26	Dock Labourer	Ireland
Henry Wallace	Lodger	Married	28	Dock Labourer	Ireland
Nancy Wallace	Lodger	Married	24	Oakum Picker	Ireland
James McHale	Head	Married	60	Pauper	Ireland
Bridget McHale	Wife	Married	60	Oakum Picker	Ireland
Thomas McHale	Son		27	Journeyman Joiner	Ireland
John McHale	Son		22	Dock Labourer	Ireland
Catherine McHale	Daughter		20	Oakum Picker	Ireland
Mary McHale	Daughter		18	Oakum Picker	Ireland

Court No. 5

John Bourke	Head	Married	34	Dock Labourer	Ireland
Mary Bourke	Wife	Married	35		Ireland
Patrick Bourke	Son		4	Scholar	Lancashire, Liverpool
Mary Bourke	Daughter		3		Lancashire, Liverpool
Catherine Bourke	Daughter		7 months		Lancashire, Liverpool
Judith Lavell	Lodger	Widow	48	Oakum Picker	Ireland
Anthony Lavell	Lodger		7	Oakum Picker	Ireland

The house in which I was born, 15 Blundell Street, was just
a few yards from the Crosbie Street courts.

St. Anthony's Scotland Road, was at the heart of the 'famine Irish' community. A booklet produced by St. Anthony's contains the names of 7,219 paupers who died in Liverpool in the bleak year of 1847. 2,303 of these poor souls were buried in St. Anthony's crypt. In later years, T.P. O'Connor, who was the only Irish National Party M.P. to be elected outside Ireland, attended Sunday Mass there. Afterwards he met his constituents at Dandy Pat's pub, The Morning Star, at nearby Scotland Place.

In 1997, 150 years after Black '47, a Great Hunger Commemoration Service was held in St. Anthony's. The Archbishop of Liverpool, Patrick Kelly, was principal concelebrant. Listed too are the 10 priests who 'died of typhus' in 1847 as a result of carrying out their Sacramental responsibilities to the Irish in Liverpool.

The beautiful Celtic Cross in St. Patrick's Church, Park Place, is a tribute to these 10 brave men who made the supreme sacrifice. Among the details of many people who

Scotland Place, the heart of Irish Liverpool. The bar is the Morning Star of which Patrick Byrne, or Dandy Pat as he was known, was the owner. In the centre is the famous 98 shop, where Irish newspapers and other items were available. The Dandy Pat Memorial beside the telephone kiosks has since been re-located to St. Anthony's Church grounds.

St. Patrick's Parish

THE PRESBYTERY,
22 PARK PLACE,
LIVERPOOL L8 5RA
Tel: 051-709 1136

Foundation and Building of the Church

The history of St. Patrick's goes back as far as 1816, at that time there were no Catholic Dioceses in England, the Church was divided into four districts, the London, the Western, the Midland and the North, Liverpool belonging to the North District, each of these Districts being presided over by a Vicar Apostolic. Priests were few and scattered over a wide area, and it was frequently left to laymen to provide Churches and living accommodation for the priests.

In 1816, a group of laymen saw a growing need for a church in the south of Liverpool, and formed the Society of St. Patrick for this purpose. The first meeting of the society which is recorded took place in Mrs Glover's in Whitechapel on Sunday, 16th November, 1816, a committee of fifteen was formed under the chairmanship of Matthew O'Connor and 105 members were entered on the roll. The first report of the Committee was submitted to members some weeks later, authorising the committee to negotiate the purchase of a suitable site. The report also states that several plans for the proposed new church had been submitted and that they had selected one—'combining elegance of appearance, economy of expense, convenience of structure with dimensions of a very large extent.'

The Society of St. Patrick meanwhile seems to have met with considerable opposition to their proposals from the Catholic community. It was thought by many that the number of Catholics did not warrant the erection of a new church. The Society of St. Patrick therefore decided to hold a census themselves to prove the need, adding that 'frequently you will behold numbers of churchmen in the open air and in the most inclement weather complying with the obligation of attending divine worship, a sight which fills one with pity and admiration.'

The society then purchased, after long negotiations, the site in Park Place, they engaged architects and builders and the foundation stone was laid on the 17th March, 1821, by the Reverend Father Thomas Penswick of St. Nicholas Church, and a sermon in support of this charitable work was given by Reverend Father T. M. Kirwan of St. Michans, Dublin. The ceremony commenced with a procession from St. Anthony's Church, Scotland Road, with six bands supported by officers and men of the 88th Regiment of Foot, the Royal Connaught Rangers. The number of people present at the ceremony was estimated to be over 15,000.

The following is a contemporary account of this great event:—

The non-commissioned Officers and Privates of the 88th Regiment of Foot, or Royal Connaught Rangers, were marshalled in the Procession by their own desire, and contributed one day's full pay in aid of the undertaking. It had been intended to place the procession regularly upon the ground: but upon its arrival, a scene took place, which baffles description. The anxiety to obtain favourable situations, acting simultaneously upon thousands, the whole of the large area with the surrounding grounds, were in a few minutes completely covered; towards the spot where the foundation-stone was to be laid, the crowd was so dense, that it was with extreme difficulty a passage could be obtained for the Clergy. In the centre of the upper surface of the Stone a cavity had been prepared in the form of a cross for the reception of the articles to be deposited therein, consisting of a printed statement of the Catholic Chapels and Chaplains, with the number of their respective Congregations in the County of Lancaster; and some recent local specimens of printing, closely soldered up in a case of lead, over which were placed five deeply-engraven metal plates, each measuring 13 by 8 inches. These filled up the shaft or upright part of the cross, in the arms of which were then placed a considerable number of silver and copper coins, enclosed in lead, comprising those of England and Ireland, of the Papal States and of several foreign countries, given by friends anxious to contribute a memorial of the event. A portion of Shamrock, the national emblem of Ireland, which had been blessed for the occasion, was next enclosed. The whole was then covered with a strong plate of lead and soldered down, in all probability, not to be again viewed by the eye of man for centuries to come. The procession was then again formed and marched away in the same order, in which it had come. After its departure, a scene occurred, which no pen can describe, which none but the truly pious mind can appreciate, and which was most affecting, as it was totally unexpected; great numbers of persons who had remained until the departure of the bands of music had restored comparative silence, now begged that they and their children might be allowed to touch the Sacred Stone. The request was readily complied with by those to whose care it had been consigned; and so great was the concourse of persons, who desired this favour that it was necessary to appoint officials for the express purpose of marshalling their regular advance and departure from the interesting spot. Many approached with great reverence, imploring the divine blessing upon the undertaking. The manifestation of religious feeling continued until the approach of evening rendered it necessary to adopt measures for its safety.

The solemn opening of St. Patrick's took place on Wednesday, 22nd August, 1827, some six years after the laying of the foundation stone and in 1828 the Vicar Apostolic took over the remaining debt on the church and the deeds of the property were passed over to the church authorities, and so began the long history of the parish church, starting in 1827 and continuing through 150 years of history right down to the present day.

There are two points here of immediate interest, the founding of St. Patrick's was a strictly lay initiative, laymen as members of the church saw a need and took active steps to fulfil this need, even to the extent of providing a future annual stipend of £370 for the maintenance of the clergy, and this was in the year 1816.

The second point which in these ecumenical days is even more illuminating is the financial assistance provided by the Anglican and non-Conformist churches in the building of the church, and we quote here in full from the minutes of Society of St. Patrick, again in the year 1816:—

'It is by no means the intention of the society to confine this appeal to Catholics only, they appeal to the benevolence of all (they contemplate with delight the gradual extinction of those prejudices founded in unmerited suspicion and wicked misrepresentation which have so long operated to their serious injury and degradation, they appeal with confidence to their extended liberality which has never been applied . . . in vain, and which has marked the British public with that superiority of character so justly admitted by the whole world—In the words of their first address they appeal 'To the charity of Christians of every religious persuasion on behalf of an object so closely connected with the cause of Religion, Benevolence and Social Order;' they invoke the liberality of an enlightened public to furnish their poorer brethren with the means of worshipping God, of acquiring religious instruction, and thus of becoming (what they cannot otherwise become), virtuous and useful members of society.'

The charitable terms of this statement could not be improved upon today, what went wrong in relations with our fellow christians in later years?

The Picture of the Crucifixion

The large picture of the Crucifixion seen above the High Altar was painted by the well-known artist, Nicaise de Keyser of Antwerp. It had been exhibited in the city in the early 1830s and we are told that 'a general desire was expressed to retain it within the town.'

The 'Manchester Guardian' at that time reported 'We have seen this truly splendid picture and we cannot sufficiently express our admiration of the talents of the artist. In conception and in execution it bears the impress of the genius which immortalised the works of Rubens and Titian.'

The picture itself measures 30ft x 22ft, the figures in the foreground being over 8ft. high, and has been described as a production of fine dramatic power, as grand in its effect as in its dimensions. It is interesting to note that another of this famous artist's work, depicting William II of Holland, at the Battle of Waterloo, is at Windsor Castle.

The Great Plague of 1847

During the 1830s and 1840s and particularly following the Irish Famine immigration from Ireland increased tenfold and from the Mother Church, St. Patrick's, Missions were founded in other parts of the south end of the city, e.g. St. Vincents in 1843, Mount Carmel in 1865, St. Bernards in 1876 and so on continuing throughout the century.

St. Patrick's faced its greatest crisis in 1847 when in the words of the famous Monsignor Nugent 'a terrible plague struck the city.' In 1847 a fever epidemic broke out in the city, 800 cases were reported in February and this was followed by an outbreak of typhus. The authorities set up 4 sheds in Mount Pleasant and a hospital ship was anchored in the Mersey to cope with the terror. The position was not helped by the living conditions of the people of the parish. Thousands lived in rat infested cellars, covered by stagnant pools of water. During all this period the priests of the parish went among the sick and dying giving comfort to the people. A witness at the time described the situation 'I can remember a messenger coming to the Pro-Cathedral and saying hurriedly, for God's sake will some of you come to St. Patrick's and bury the dead, the church is full of corpses, and all the priests are now down. The dead and the dying are lying together and the little children, soon to wither in the black death, played with the shavings on which they lay. St. Patrick's church was closed, the presbytery door stood open but there was no priest within, and when Sunday came silence reigned around the altar.'

The white memorial in front of the Church facing Park Place commemorating 10 Priests of the City who died in the typhoid epidemic of 1847, this was erected in 1898 and solemnly blessed by Bishop Whiteside on Sunday, October 2nd 1898, the sermon being preached by Monsignor Nugent.

There is a further poignant reminder of these terrible times, look at the Memorial to the Burns Family in the corner of ground to the left of the Church, to the memory of their five young children who died during this period, with ages ranging from 7 years to 2 months.

St. Patrick's Parish Newsletter.

died is the inquest report on John Waters. His wife gave evidence. John and herself and their seven children, had walked from their home in Mayo to Dublin. John was a labourer aged 'upwards of 50 years'. Their walk to Dublin had taken nine days. On arriving in Liverpool, they set out to walk to Sheffield, as John had a brother there. They passed through Prescot and Warrington. They reached Stockport where John died.

Another inquest was for Nancy Doherty. Nancy, 50 years old, was found lying in a passage at the night asylum. Nancy and her daughter could not get in to the night asylum as it was full. They lay down and went to sleep. When the daughter woke, her mother was dead.

The Times on 5 April 1847 said: "50,100 Irish people had arrived in March. 3,500 last Sunday. Large sheds have been hired in Great Howard Street to hold between 400/500 fever patients at a rent of £900 per week".

The vast majority of the newly arrived Irish people stayed on the north side of the city, in the Scotland Road and Vauxhall area. In other words, they hardly moved out of the area in which they had walked out of the gates of Clarence Dock.

St. Anthony's Church was at the heart of the Irish community and yet had very different origins. The parish was founded by Father Jean-Baptiste Antoine Gerardot in 1804. He was a refugee French priest who fled from France at the time of the French Revolution and settled in Liverpool in 1800. Fr. Gerardot's successor, Father Peter Wilcock, realised a much bigger church was needed on the north side of Liverpool. Funds were raised and a site beside the Throstle's Nest Tavern was purchased. The foundation stone of the present church was laid on 17th March 1832. Only St. Mary's in the city centre was on the north side of town, while St. Peter's was also city centre but on the south side. St. Patrick's was built in 1827, again on the south side. These churches were to provide Mass facilities for the newly arrived Irish people.

Another aspect of old Irish life in Liverpool was the belief that St. Patrick himself may have visited Liverpool. In his article in the Irish Centre Silver Jubilee brochure Harry McHugh said: "a small group of monks may have arrived here before they set sail to convert the Irish".

What is certainly true is that the earliest map of Liverpool shows a Celtic Cross named Patrick's Cross and a road named St. Patrick's Hill running down to the pool which gave Liverpool its name.

The site of the cross was where today Tithebarn Street, Vauxhall Road and Marybone meet. The cross disappeared from Liverpool maps about 200 years ago, during road-widening. Harry McHugh and Bob Parry, the Labour MP for the area worked extremely hard to bring back a long lost Irish landmark.

In 1985, the illustrated plaque was erected on Holy Cross

Holy Cross plaque.

The beautiful memorial to those who died in the Great Hunger. It is located in St. Luke's Churchyard in Leece Street, Liverpool. It was unveiled by President McAleese.

Church about 100 yards from the original site. Unfortunately, Holy Cross Church has since been demolished. It is a sad fact that thousands of Irish people – children and adults of all ages – died in Liverpool in the 1840s and 1850s. Normal, single graves could not possibly cope, and there were numerous graves which contained many, many bodies. They were known as mass famine graves.

Ian McKeane of the Institute of Irish Studies in Liverpool University has talked and written on the subject and he and Greg Quiery of the Great Famine Commemoration Committee have caused a number of plaques to be erected in the city marking the sites of relevance during the Great Hunger. They have called the collection of sites the Irish Heritage Trail.

The front of the leaflet is a beautiful reproduction of the Famine Memorial, which was unveiled by President Mary McAleese in the St. Luke's Churchyard at the top of Bold Street.

As recently as 2006, the subject of mass famine graves was in the news again. Tom Slemen, who is a local writer and radio contributor, wrote about a situation in St. Oswald's grounds in Old Swan, about four miles from the City Centre. St. Oswald's Church was built in 1842, so was there when the 'famine Irish' came to Liverpool. In 1973, a site was being cleared to build a primary school for St. Oswald's. They found a mass grave in which there were 3,561 coffins. As Tom said: "The mystery deepened because there were no records in the register of St. Oswald's Church and stranger still, because the Home Office ordered the cremation of the remains of the unknown dead".

No cemetery existed on the site of the grave. A local criminologist, Keith Andrews, believes he can solve the mystery of the mass graves. He says his suspicions were raised because there were no children's remains. The bodies were all in boxes made from the same type of wood in an efficient and well-organised manner.

Keith Andrews believes the bodies were the victims of a mass murder committed by soldiers in the summer of 1848. Keith said: "It's an historical fact that in the summer of 1848, over 2,000 armed soldiers from London, encamped in Everton with orders to deal with the 'Irish insurgents'. As well as these soldiers, 20,000 special constables were sworn in and the police were augmented with 500 extra officers, and 800 members of Cheshire Yeomanry joined their forces."

Keith says that the children of the dead were either sent to orphanages, the workhouse, or transported to Canada and Australia.

K.A. Williams (former Principal Environmental Health Officer for Liverpool) said Keith Andrews was incorrect in his allegations. However, no acceptable explanation has been given concerning the remains.

Many Irish people made their marks in Liverpool in the distant past. More knowledgeable people than I have written about them. My book is not intended to be about a few people who became famous, so much as about the huge, nameless Irish community of Liverpool. In particular, I am interested in people who dedicated themselves to their own Irish community, and I hope my book will do justice to them. Some of the better known Irish people with a Liverpool connection are:

Michael James Whitty (1795-1873) He was born in Enniscorthy, County Wexford. Enrolled at Maynooth with a view to becoming a priest. Came to Liverpool in 1829. In 1836, he became Head Constable - Liverpool's first! He founded *The Liverpool Daily Post* in 1855 as the first penny daily newspaper. He died in 1873 and was buried in Anfield Cemetery.

Kitty Wilkinson Arrived from Derry in the 1830s. Some 10 years later, the typhus epidemic struck the city which was full of 'famine Irish'. She realised that hygiene was crucial. She started the first public wash-house. She is buried in the Anglican Cathedral graveyard.

John Denvir Born in Bushmills, County Antrim in 1834. Moved to Liverpool as a child. Wrote two great books *The Irish in Britain* and his autobiography *Life Story of an Old Rebel*. Posthumously awarded an Irish Post Community Award. He was a journalist and set up *Denvir's Irish Library*. His aunt married Hugh Roney who kept a public house in Crosbie Street. The same Crosbie Street of courts which were full of Irish-speaking people.

James Larkin Born in Combermere Street near St. Patrick's Church in 1876. Became an organiser for the National Union of Dockers. When he was 31, he went to Belfast and later to Dublin where he founded the Irish Transport and General Workers Union. His story is well told.

Robert Tressell Author of *The Ragged Trousered Philanthropist*. Born in Dublin as Robert Noonan. His life here was brief but his Liverpool connection became permanent because he died here in 1911 in the Liverpool Royal Infirmary. He is buried in a pauper's grave in plot T11 in Walton Park Cemetery.

Douglas Hyde Didn't live in Liverpool but was married here in St. Nicholas's Church, Blundellsands in October 1893. Became the first President of Ireland.

Percy French Perhaps the most prolific of writers of Irish songs. His local connection is that he died while visiting his cousin at St. Luke's, Formby and is buried there. At the request of the Irish Centre in Liverpool, Brendan O'Dowda, the best interpreter of Percy French's songs, unveiled a plinth on his grave on January 25th, 1970 (50 years after his death). *Come Back Paddy Reilly* and *The Mountains of Mourne* are just two of his songs.

Patrick Byrne Known as Dandy Pat. A native of Ferns, County Wexford which is where he is buried. A drinking water fountain was erected by public subscription outside his old pub 'The Morning Star' in Scotland Place. Unfortunately, the fountain was demolished during the redevelopment of Scotland Road. However, a small committee led by Michael Kelly and Bernard Morgan located most of the remains of the memorial and re-erected it in the grounds of St. Anthony's, Scotland Road.

T.P. O'Connor was the only Irish Nationalist M.P. to be voted for a constituency outside Ireland. He was elected for Liverpool Scotland constituency. Another indication of the depth of Irish people in that area.

Father James Nugent As far as I'm aware, Fr. Nugent is the only Catholic priest to whom there is a statue erected in England. It is in St. John's Gardens in the city centre. There is a little boy in the statue to remind us that Fr. Nugent founded premises to provide shelter for homeless children. He was born in Hunter Street near Scotland Road in 1822 so was a young man when the worst of the conditions of the 'famine Irish' was evident. His father was from County Meath.

Desmond Greaves dedicated his life to improving the lot of working class people. He was an acknowledged authority on the lives of James Larkin and James Connolly. He was a frequent visitor to the Irish Centre, Mount Pleasant.

After the 'famine Irish' people of the 1840s and 50s had found their feet and by hard work had improved their lot, they turned their attention to the spiritual and temporal needs of themselves and their families.

They moved slowly, usually in a northerly direction, into better housing conditions and turned their attention to schools and churches. While there may have been some council and government help, the emphasis was very much on self-help.

Churches went up at an extraordinary rate in Liverpool. Parishes were established as follows:

1804	St. Anthony's (had been established by the French priest I've already referred to)
1826	St. Peter and Paul's, Crosby
1842	St. Oswald's, Old Swan
1843	St. Anne's, Overbury Street
1845	St. James, Bootle
1845	St. Francis Xavier's, Shaw Street
1845	St. Joseph's, City Centre North
1849	St. Augustine's, Vauxhall
1849	St. Alban's ('Over the Bridge')
1850	Holy Cross, City Centre North
1852	St. Vincent's, City Centre South
1854	Our Lady's, Eldon Street (Scotland Road)
1856	Our Lady's, Everton
1861	St. Michael's, West Derby Road
1862	St. Alexander's, Bootle
1864	St. Philip Neri, City Centre South
1865	Our Lady of Mount Carmel, South End
1870	St. Brigid, Scotland Road Area
1871	St. John's, Fountains Road, Kirkdale
1871	Our Lady's, Wavertree
1872	All Souls, North
1872	Blessed Sacrament, North
1875	St. Sylvester, Scotland Road
1878	St. Alphonsus, Scotland Road
1879	St. Paul's, West Derby
1883	St. Francis of Assisi, Garston
1883	St. Francis De Sales, Walton
1884	Star of the Sea, Seaforth
1886	St. Joseph's, Blundellsands

1886	Sacred Heart, Hall Lane, Liverpool
1890	St. Clare, Liverpool South
1890	All Saints, Anfield
1892	St. Charles, Aigburth Road, Liverpool
1895	St. Winifred's, Bootle

There were a total of 80 parishes established between 1840 and 1900. Has there ever been such a programme of church building anywhere in the world? Schools were established and built in all these locations. Places like St. Helens and Wigan, where the Irish had gone in large numbers, are also a vital part of the Liverpool Archdiocese.

The first signs of political activity happened after the potato famine, around 1867, when the Irish in Liverpool and around the world showed an active interest in the Fenian movement in Ireland. There were probably more Fenians in Liverpool and America than there were in Ireland. The old Irish song *Come to the Bower* summons the Irish people abroad to 'Come to the Land of O'Neill and O'Donnell'.

So it took just about 20 years from 1847, for people in the depths of despair, living in the total degradation of life in the cellars, to want to make a contribution to 'the most distressful country'. What remarkable people.

The beautiful monument in Ford Cemetery is worthy of them – and is well worth a visit. For many years, on Easter Sunday, a group of Irish patriots walked from the gates to the monument and, after a decade of the rosary in Irish, the Proclamation was read. I took part in the ceremony a number of times. The priest I best remember leading the rosary was that wonderful Kerryman, Fr. Donie Coffey. He was sometimes late with the huge workload he would have had at the time but the bike would eventually appear through the rear gate and across the graves. The simple ceremony linked two of the many bids for freedom – the Fenians of 1867 and Easter 1916 in both of which Liverpool was deeply involved.

Sadly the monument has been the target of vandals in recent years. The restoration work was carried out quickly due to the generosity of Patrick Doran and his wife Eileen who not only provided the labour and transport, but who covered the cost themselves. Liverpool has remained a city with a vibrant Irish community ever since the dreadful days of the 1840s.

The beautiful Fenian Memorial in Ford Cemetery erected in memory of Liverpool men who took part.

The memorial has often been defaced. The picture in the centre shows Patrick Doran who was responsible for restoring the monument at no cost to the Irish Community.

Apart from the GAA and Gaelic League, there have been several occasions when a number of different organisations have come together, usually to run major functions. Not until 1960 when the Irish Centre Building Fund was born was a serious attempt made to establish an Irish Centre, although the Irish Fellowship in 1939 and Irish Association of Merseyside in the late 1940s did state an Irish Centre as an objective.

The Sean O'Donovan Branch of the Gaelic League lost its Wood Street premises and moved to St. Cuthbert's, Fairfield. The branch never thrived the way it had in Wood Street.

The GAA thrived as a result of many young men coming in from Ireland. The Shamrocks formed in Birkenhead in the early 50s. The Shamrocks and St. Werbergh's amalgamated in 1957 and were re-named Clan-na-Gael. Another new club, Sean McDermotts was formed in 1959. The Club was based at the Fearnley Dance Hall in Birkenhead and had strong connections with the Shamrock Club in Liverpool.

Unfortunately, the Gaelic League didn't benefit from the incoming Irish tide in the way that the GAA did and the three established branches faded out over a period of several years. There was a new branch formed in Great Mersey Street near St. Alphonsus dance hall, but it didn't last very long either.

A treasured memorial is transformed

CLEAN-UP: The Fenian monument in Liverpool's Ford Cemetery, after the removal of the racist graffiti. Local Irish people want support in completing the transformation.

Liverpool's Irish community has removed racist graffiti taunts of "IRA scum" and "No surrender" from an Irish monument in the city's main Catholic cemetery.

The damaged parts of the memorial, erected by Liverpool's Council of Irish Societies in 1931 in memory of 16 Fenians buried in Ford Cemetery, have been transformed and locals aim to complete the renovation as soon as is practical.

Vandals struck last February in the same week that racist rioting forced the abandonment of the Republic's soccer game with England at Dublin's Lansdowne Road. Attackers daubed "IRA scum" over the names of the memorial's dead and "No surrender" was added in red paint. Vandals then climbed part of the way up the monument to throw paint over a statue of St. Patrick and crowbars were apparently used to lever off two large, carved stones on either side of it.

The new-look monument was unveiled in a moving ceremony organised earlier this month at the cemetery by the John Mitchel's GAA Club. Amongst those attending were: Liverpool-based Downman Pat Doran and his wife, Eileen, who arranged the graffiti's removal; Harry McHugh, author and activist in the now-disbanded Anti-Partition of Ireland League; and Tommy Walsh and Chris Johnston, treasurer and chairman respectively of the John Mitchel's Club.

Tommy Walsh told the unveiling ceremony: "What happened here was an act of desecration and is difficult for us to understand. For generations, the communities of the two traditions in the city of Liverpool lived uneasily side by side and there were occasional black eyes and bloody noses, but we believed in the same God, though we both thought he kicked with a dif-

ferent foot. Above all, we respected each others' graves and places of worship.

"We believe that whoever was responsible for the desecration was not anyone of any Irish tradition. We don't want any groups of any philosophy to use this place as a stick with which to beat each other. We hope that in future this place will be left to the Irish community on Merseyside and that no other group should congregate here.

"When we heard about the damage here, Chris (Johnston) and I were as sad as anyone else. We were particularly upset because Sean McInerney (former John Mitchels' chairman and a former president of the GAA in Britain), who was dear to us, and to others here, was central to the whole idea of erecting this monument in 1931. He himself lies only a short distance away, in this same graveyard.

"When discussing what we could do we realised that, as is always the case in the Irish community, there was one of our own who had the expertise and the experience and, above all, we knew we would only have to ask and it would be done.

"So we spoke to Pat Doran, who immediately suggested picking us up and coming out to have a look. He took samples of the red paint and black bitumen with which the entire memorial was defaced. The samples were sent to a laboratory and within days the necessary work was done and here we are.

"It isn't the first time that Pat Doran has placed his resources at the disposal of the Irish community in Liverpool. On this occasion, he has refused to take a penny towards the expense incurred. We must be honest and say that a man who works here had already started to do something about it, and we thank him on behalf of all of us.

"Perhaps before we go we

should all make a promise that we will now and again keep an eye on this place. There are three statues or figures missing and two pieces of stone are also missing from the sides. If anyone has any suggestions about how we might complete the transformation, we'd like to hear your ideas. Surely we would all want the memorial in its original state."

Chris Johnston added that the restoration was an example of Liverpool's Irish community in action and that no group had the right to put it at risk.

Those gathered in Ford Cemetery said a decade of the Rosary and paid their respects at the nearby grave of Sean McInerney, who died in 1962.
■ The now defunct Liverpool Council of Irish Societies was an umbrella grouping for all the city's various Irish groups during the inter-war years.

For many years, Harry McHugh organised an annual ceremony at the Ford Cemetery monument on behalf of the Anti-Partition of Ireland League.

Attempts to bring the community together included:

1929 COUNCIL OF IRISH NATIONAL SOCIETIES
Affiliated were:
Irish National Foresters
Gaelic League
Sinn Féin
Irish Self-Determination League
Irish Musical Society
There was a meeting on July 4, 1929 of the Council of Irish National Societies and the purpose of the meeting was to disband and to disperse the funds.

On February 9th, 1930, a new Irish umbrella group was formed. It was called 'The Irish Association of Liverpool and District / An Gaedhal Chonnradh'.
The affiliated societies were:
GAA
Gaelic League
Padraic Pearse Pipe Band
Irish National Foresters
Sinn Féin
Fianna Fail
Musical Society and Drama
University Irish Society
Kirkdale United Irish League
Bootle Dramatic Society

Individuals included Austin Harford – who became first Catholic Lord Mayor of Liverpool.

It is reasonable to assume that this amalgam of Irish Societies came about as a result of the Council of Irish National Societies folding up only seven months earlier. Many of the affiliated societies were the same.

1947 Comhdhail na nGaedhal Cois Mersi
The Irish Association of Merseyside 'Cois Mersi' attracted individuals rather than societies but had the support of the Gaelic League and GAA whose members were active. Kathleen Carroll, who was Secretary, was highly regarded throughout the community.

1949 Liverpool Feis Committee
3 Branches Gaelic League
GAA
Anti-partition of Ireland League
Padraic Pearse Pipe Band
Camogie Club

Late 1950s The Gaelic Council
GAA
Gaelic League
Comhaltas Ceoltoiri Eireann
(Forerunner of Irish Centre Building Fund)

The period between the end of World War II and the 'Second Diaspora' saw the established Irish community organising themselves.

There were several big concerts.
The GAA was re-establishing.

In 1948, the Anti-Partition of Ireland League, brought Eamon de Valera over to Liverpool and to other venues in Britain. It was a huge occasion for the Irish Community here. It was probably the first post-war event which appealed equally to the older Irish people and to the newly arrived.

The Stadium in Bixteth Street was the venue. The Stadium was the home of boxing and wrestling then, but is no longer there. Harry McHugh was one of the main local organisers of the event.

Although there was no Irish Centre as such, the young Irish people newly arrived from Ireland were catered for by Mr. & Mrs. Pat Lawlor in their halls in Islington and St. Anne Street, and by Eddie O'Reilly and Mick Gill in the Shamrock Club in Lime Street. Eddie O'Reilly of Kerry was a noted Gaelic footballer while Mick Gill of Galway played hurling for St. Patrick's Club and for Lancashire. The Shamrock Club closed as a result of compulsory purchase in 1964. The St. George Hotel was built near the site. There had been a hotel on the site earlier in which Michael Davitt had founded the Liverpool branch of the Land League.

Although diminishing, there were still some halls running ceilis, many of the people involved in the old Irish community lost touch as times changed. Equally, very few newcomers joined the Gaelic League. Some of them saw ceili dancing in Liverpool for the first time in their lives. Meanwhile the Gaelic Leaguers could not understand why the 'new Irish' weren't interested in ceili dancing. The 'commercial halls' had mainly old time waltzes and quicksteps with a Siege of Ennis and Haymaker's Jig thrown in. These ceili dances were danced with more abandon than in the Gaelic League, where 'buzzing' was not allowed. Buzzing was four dancers in the centre of a Siege of Ennis forming a wheel and spinning together. Up to this, and certainly in the Gaelic League, the four dancers in the centre formed a star while the outside couples swung together.

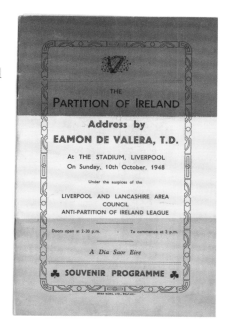

One of the biggest events ever organized by the Irish Community in Liverpool was the visit of Eamon De Valera in 1948. Harry McHugh, Sean McCann, Charles McMullan and Barney Earley were among the local organizers. Others were Alderman J.P. Mannion (Wigan), Gerry McCormack (St. Helens) and Frank Short (Birmingham) whose daughter, Clare, was to become a Government Minister.

The Irish Centre - Mount Pleasant

WAR-TIME RESTRICTIONS made travel impossible during World War II between 1939 and 1945. Liverpool was so badly damaged by bombing it wouldn't have been a nice place to come to. About 3,840 people were killed in the city and a further 2,424 seriously injured, by bombing. Many of the houses and business premises were damaged or destroyed.

The combination of travel restrictions and damage to property during the war led to a huge number of Irish people coming into the city after the war. The young men were attracted first by the work in the construction industry. Then, in 1948, the National Health Service came into existence and thousands of young women were attracted to the hospitals where they became nurses. Training in those days was 'on the job'. Walton, Broadgreen, Smithdown Road (later Sefton), Mill Road, Whiston, Providence (St.Helens) and St. Catherine's (Birkenhead) were among the hospitals which attracted Irish girls.

Long gone hospitals like the Southern, the Northern and Bootle Hospital also had many Irish women. There were also Irish doctors, who, in those days, were mainly men. Many of the young Irish people who sailed into Liverpool Princes Dock went to Manchester, Leeds, Birmingham and many other towns. Most of the Irish people bound for London came over via Holyhead.

Many of the shops in Lord Street, Church Street and Whitechapel had been destroyed. South Castle Street and Red Cross Street, had been completely removed from the map, as well as the beautiful Custom House in Canning Place at the bottom of South Castle Street. Chinatown was also almost wiped out in Cleveland Square and transferred to Nelson Street and surrounding streets.

The area around my home was destroyed too. The docks were very busy. This was the time before containerisation

This is the photograph which proves the only way into the Cathedral was through the Irish Centre!

91

and every bag, bale and box was handled by the dockers.

I was living among dockers and serving them in my little corner shop in Blundell Street near the gate of Queens Dock. It is now the way in to the new Liverpool Echo Arena car park. I saw the dockers close up and resented very strongly the bad publicity they got. They, the dockers, became public whipping boys by the media, and they were blamed for every problem in the country.

Brown cane sugar was giving way to beet sugar and cotton was being replaced by nylon. These two products had been major goods shipped into Liverpool. It wasn't the fault of the dockers that this business was lost to the city.

The best indication of young Irish males leaving home has always been the GAA. When emigration is high and GAA clubs in Ireland are losing players, the GAA abroad thrives and new clubs spring up. Equally, when times are good at home, and the young people stay at home, the GAA clubs in Britain and elsewhere in the world have difficulty fielding teams.

In the late 1950s, the GAA, Gaelic League and Comhaltas Ceoltoiri Eireann came together as the Gaelic Council to run occasional major functions such as Annual Concerts and St. Patrick's Day Ceilis. The GAA and Gaelic League were unable to arrange functions which included 'foreign dancing'. GAA Rule No. 29 said 'a club shall not organize any entertainment at which foreign dances are permitted'.

In 1961, a group of Gaelic footballers travelled up to Manchester for a game which I refereed and which included an all-priests team. The teams afterwards went to the newly opened St. Brendan's Irish Centre for refreshments. That did it! Father Michael O'Connor, a young Kerry priest, based at Christ the King parish in Childwall said, 'If Manchester can do it, why can't Liverpool?'

Shortly afterwards, the next meeting of the Gaelic

92

Irish Centre — nuacht
127 Mount Pleasant
Liverpool 3

NEWSLETTER SIX TIMES A YEAR

FOR some time the Executive Committee, in conjunction with the Manager, have been examining more effective ways of communicating with the members and others who regularly attend the Irish Centre. We have discussed and rejected a number of schemes but now at last we have agreed on a publication, which we believe is worthy of the Irish Centre.

It is planned to publish the new newsletters on six occasions during the year and it will include pictures and articles on all the major events taking place at the Centre. As far as possible future events, with the names of artists and bands will be included but where this is not possible, members can obtain the necessary information by phoning the Centre.

One of the major items discussed, when considering a venture of this nature is the cost. The Irish Centre has now been opened over thirteen years and as you are aware the membership fee has not been increased during that time. We all know how the cost of paper, printing and postage have increased but due to a combination of good management and our consciousness of the service we provide for the Irish Community on Merseyside, we have so far managed to absorb this increased cost.

YOUR SUPPORT, PLEASE

In order to help offset the cost of this new newsletter we have decided to include advertisements. These will help financially and also provide a service for the members of the Centre. We will be delighted to accept advertisements from Irish organisations in this area and also from our own members who are shop-keepers, traders, or those involved in professions which can help fellow members. Anyone wishing to avail of the service should contact the Manager, Mr T. Walsh, at the Irish Centre.

Finally, I hope you find the new newsletter informative and enjoyable. If it is to be a permanent feature of the Irish Centre, we must have advertisers and I would appeal to each of you to give your full support to those who advertise and thus enable us to bring you a publication of which we can all be proud.
J. F. ENGLAND
Chairman

CONCELEBRATED MASS IN HONOUR OF ST PATRICK

Thursday, March 16,
at 8.00pm
in the Metropolitan
Cathedral of
Christ the King

Principal Concelebrant:
Archbishop
Derek Worlock

Special Preacher:
Rev. Michael Cleary
cc Ballyfermot,
Dublin

The Centre will be open afterwards for refreshments—all welcome

St Patrick's Day

ST PATRICK'S WEEK

| Saturday 11 March | Sunday 12 March |
| THE ANTELOPES FROM CO. CORK | LEO McCAFFREY and the GLENSMEN |

Monday 13th
COMHALTAS CEOLTOIRI EIREANN
An informal music session

Tuesday 14th March
CEILI 50p INCLUDES SUPPER

Wednesday 15 March
CONCERT
starring
DERMOT HEGARTY
LEO McCAFFREY
TONY GARRIGAN   THE SKIBBEREENS
8.00pm   IRISH CENTRE DANCERS   Tickets £1 and 80p

| Saturday 18 March | Sunday 19 March |
| DENIS & THE CLUBMEN | DERMOT O'BRIEN & The Men of the West |

There is, of course, a function on St. Patrick's night but tickets are distributed to members on a first come first served basis. Tickets are not available to non-members.

DERMOT HEGARTY

Irish Centre — nuacht
127 Mount Pleasant
Liverpool L3 5TG
051-709 4120

Community Award 1978

'There is a style—even an elegance—about how things are done at the Liverpool Centre.'

WE are delighted and proud to announce to you that we, the Irish Centre, Liverpool, have been nominated to receive one of this year's Allied Irish/Irish Post awards. The citation refers to us as follows:—

An award goes to the Irish Centre, Liverpool, for the excellence of virtually everything it has done over the past thirteen years. Every year has been one of achievement for the centre and 1977 saw its excellence maintained and further enlarged.

It is no reflection on any other Irish club or centre in Britain to say that Liverpool has down the years been a model and an inspiration. Many of the more recently founded Irish community venues started by going to Liverpool to see how it should be done.

From the outset Liverpool managed brilliantly to combine social, cultural and welfare activities—each complementing the other. The Irish language, music, dancing and Gaelic games have since it opened been an integral part of activities in Liverpool.

It is also the only lay community headquarters in Britain to have a full-time wel-

fare department.

There is a style—even an elegance—about how things are done at the Liverpool Centre. It has always been a credit to itself and to our community at large.

In latter years too, some of its officers have made a tremendous contribution to the Federation of Irish Societies.

The award will be presented at a function in the Tara Hotel, London, on Friday, 5th May, and some of the officers and the manager will accept the award on behalf of the Centre.

Mary from Dungloe

ONCE again, this year, we intend to send a girl to represent us at the Mary from Dungloe International Festival, Co. Donegal. The Festival will be held from 31st July to 6th August. Our Selection Dance will be held on Friday, 26th May.

The sponsors of our dance will be Aer Lingus and Guinness. Both companies will provide a judge on the evening. Aer Lingus will provide the ticket for the winning girl to travel to the Festival, while the Guinness Company will provide Draught Guinness at only 20p. per pint to all the customers on the evening of the dance.

MATT TALBOT'S GFC VISIT

EASTER weekend saw the visit to Liverpool of Matt Talbot's G.F.C. Two games were played against John Mitchell's at two different age levels. White the Liverpool young lads won, the older Dublin boys were victorious so honours were even. Matt Talbot's also played games against St. Patrick's, Ellesmere Port, and all three clubs got together in the Centre for a rousing send off before catching the boat home on Easter Monday evening.

Playgoers

THE next production of the Irish Playgoers is the ever popular 'June and the Paycock' by Sean O'Casey. We find we are always being asked for Sean O'Casey plays in book form, in the shop, by senior students. Please be sure your teenage family know about this particularly if they're studying English literature. As for yourself just sit back and enjoy it.

MARY FROM DUNGLOE SELECTION DANCE
A NIGHT OUT AT HALF PRICE
FRIDAY 26th MAY
Dancing to
FINIANS RAINBOW
and DISCO

8.30 to 12   Bar extension applied for   Tickets 25p

DRAUGHT GUINNESS
ON SALE AT 20p per PINT. YES — 20p! — ALL EVENING

Irish Centre — nuacht
127 Mount Pleasant
Liverpool L3 5TG
051-709 4120

THURSDAY 15th MARCH
Annual
St. Patricks Concert
STARRING
JACK CRUISE AND SEAN O'SE

THE SKIBBEREENS
IRISH CENTRE DANCERS
TONY GARRIGAN

TICKETS £1 and 80p ON SALE NOW.

PLEASE NOTE:
The Centre will be closed for normal business on the night. Concert ticket holders only admitted.
The bar will be closed while the concert is in progress. It will be open before the Concert and during the interval.

SEAN O'SE. The highlight of his performance will be a tribute to P.H. Pearse in his Centenary Year.

SPECIAL ATTRACTIONS	
TUESDAY 20TH FEBRUARY	**MONDAY 19TH FEBRUARY**
DERMOT O'BRIEN	**Comhaltas Annual Concert** 'A Glimpse of the Real Ireland'
8.30 TO 12 £1	TICKETS £1 ON SALE IN THE CENTRE
TUESDAY 27TH FEBRUARY	**THURSDAY 8TH MARCH** John Mitchells Juvnile GFC
SUPPER CEILI LIVERPOOL CEILI BAND 50p (INCLUDES REFRESHMENTS)	**DERMOT HEGARTY** 8.30 TO 12 TICKETS £1 Proceeds to Dublin Trip Fund

TICKETS for St Patricks Night will, as usual, be made available to members only on a one member, one ticket basis. Any tickets unsold in this way will be made available to regular users of the Centre from March 3rd by personal request. No orders by phone please. Admission to the Centre will be strictly by ticket only.

Irish Centre — nuacht
127 Mount Pleasant
Liverpool L3 5TG
051-709 4120

AN TOSTAL
IRISH FESTIVAL
MONDAY MAY 7th IN THE IRISH CENTRE

TUGO O' WAR Ladies & Gents	FANCY DRESS Children & 'OPEN'	IRISH CENTRE PIPE BAND	TEDDY BEAR STALL
IRISH CENTRE DANCERS	TOMBOLA	WHITE ELEPHANT STALL	GOLF & POOL
MUSIC SESSION	'SCORE A GOAL'	CHILDRENS CORNER	SIDE SHOWS & STALLS

ADMISSION BY PROGRAMME ADULTS 10p CHILDREN 5p. B & I £60 VOUCHER TO HOLDER OF LUCKY ADULT PROGRAMME, PRIZE TO HOLDER OF LUCKY CHILDRENS MINI-PROGRAMME.
ONLY FIRST CHILD IN FAMILY TO BE PAID FOR!
(NO UNACCOMPANIED CHILDREN)
12 NOON TO 5 PM. BAR OPEN 12-3 P.M. CATERING & SHOP 12-4 P.M.

Gifts for Tombola and White Elephant Stall will be gratefully accepted. Groceries, Toiletries, Bottles, Clean Records and Books, Toys etc., etc. (No clothing please).
THE TOSTAL COMMITTEE THANK BANK OF IRELAND FOR SPONSORING THIS PAGE

IRISH CENTRE BUILDING FUND

This handbill was released by the Irish Centre Building Fund Committee in May 1964. It speaks for itself. It is probably the biggest ever announcement by a unit of the Irish Community in Liverpool.

A Chara,

We promised that when we had found a premises suitable to become the Liverpool Irish Centre, we would call a public meeting.

We have found the premises and we most cordially invite you to the Public Meeting :-

Sunday, 31st May, 1964

at 8.0 p.m.

The Wellington Assembly Rooms,

Mount Pleasant, Liverpool.

(Opposite the Convent)

Please come and see these magnificent premises and bring any friends who are interested.

Yours sincerely,

The Irish Centre Building Fund Committee.

Council was held in Hugh Cullen's house in Cornice Road, Old Swan. Hugh was a Gaelic League member and was the Treasurer of the Gaelic Council. It was 24th March 1961 and Father O'Connor said: "we should try to buy an old cinema or house which would be suitable as an Irish Centre such as recently opened in Manchester."

It was realised that an Irish Centre could only be viable if it catered for the whole of the Irish community, providing not only Irish music and ceili dancing, but 'modern music and dancing'. The simple fact was that the majority of Irish people in Liverpool would not attend dances at which there was only ceili dancing.

After a lengthy discussion in which the Gaelic League

94

and GAA delegates said the proposals may contravene their rules, it was agreed that individuals, and not delegates, would attend a meeting on April 6th, at the same venue. At that meeting, it was decided that the Irish Centre Building Fund should come into existence.

I was elected Chairman, while Tomas O'Canainn, a native of Dungiven, County Derry, now living in Cork, who was lecturing in Liverpool University was Vice-Chairman. The Secretary was to be Kit Hodge and the Treasurer, Hugh Cullen. The Assistant Secretary was Peggy Atkins.

Would we succeed where so many others had failed?

The general opinion in the Irish Community was NO!!!

Pessimism was widespread. So much so, that no donations were asked for. The money that was raised by the Irish Centre Building Fund consisted of the profits from various functions held mainly in Christ the King Hall, Queens Drive and a major Annual Concert held in the Philharmonic Hall. There were donations too from bishops and priests in Ireland to whom we appealed for help.

The committee would do two things only. It would raise money and look for a suitable premises. Some committee members soon dropped out while others were invited to join and accepted. It was the most ruthless Irish committee ever in Liverpool. Members were simply dropped if they didn't attend meetings or if they didn't attend and help to run all our money-raising events.

Although there was pessimism about the outcome, there was also much encouragement. Many of the Irish people in Liverpool said, 'what makes you think you can succeed where so many have failed in the past?' Some said, 'we have contributed in the past and have never seen a brick'.

However, the outstanding feeling was of hope that, after 100 years of striving, we would find 'a home of our own'. Not in a back street, not in a cellar or upstairs, but at

Fr. Michael O'Connor was the inspiration of the Irish Centre "in the beginning". Here the Chairman, Joe England, presents Fr. Michael with a Waterford Crystal gift on the occasion of the Silver Jubilee of his ordination.

ground level in one of Liverpool's main thoroughfares.

In Liverpool, promises of money, 'if we are successful and open a centre', were sought. Forms were distributed and many were signed and returned. At this stage, the meetings were held in St. Cuthbert's, Stanley, in the home of Fr. Bill O'Connell, the Parish Priest.

In September 1962, we rented a small room upstairs at 19 Tithebarn Street in the city centre. This was suitable for committee meetings which were now being held weekly.

Early in 1964, Fr. Michael O'Connor heard at a clergy meeting that the Notre Dame Sisters in Mount Pleasant were selling a Grade II listed building called the Wellington Rooms opposite the convent.

I remember distinctly his 'phone call telling me the news. I, like many other people in Liverpool, was aware of the gloomy building without windows at the top of Mount Pleasant. Fr. Michael, Harry McHugh and myself went to have a look. An emergency meeting was called for Sunday 5th January 1964 to give them all the news.

A surveyor had looked at it on our behalf, and the Minutes read 'In their estimation it is worth £13,000, and suggested we make an initial offer of £12,000'. Those of us who saw it KNEW we had found a home for the wandering, renting, homeless, borrowing, hiring Irish people of Liverpool. We hardly noticed the lumps of plaster hanging from the walls, or the holes in the floor.

Then we discovered that the money we had scrimped and saved and begged for in the last three years wasn't enough for the building! It wasn't enough for the deposit! It wasn't enough for the solicitor's fees!

Our next news was that when we found the £12,500 to buy the building we'd have to spend (and find) another £20,000 to make it fit to open! Were we downhearted? Definitely ... YES!

That's where the larger than life Fr. Paddy Spain enters the story. Along with two other Tipperary men – Fathers Dinny Ryan and Jim Bergin – he was building new churches, schools, presbyteries and clubs in the new town of Kirkby. Wasn't it President Kennedy who said 'the impossible takes a little longer'? It was surely Fr. Spain he had in mind. He spoke to the Bank Manager and he told the Cornbrook Brewery to lend us £20,000 – or else! Most of all – he gave us the courage to take on the debt and the task. We also succeeded in getting a loan from Guinness of £4,000.

Before we bought the building, we 'borrowed' it for a public meeting. Hundreds turned up. We said 'There it is. If you want it – say so and we'll make an offer.' The response was tremendous. Promises were converted into cash, hundreds of membership fees were collected, but in financial terms the money still didn't pay the fees, let alone the deposit. What mattered was the outpouring of emotion. The feeling that as a community of over a hundred years we were taking our rightful place in the city of Liverpool. Older people wept openly and said they had believed it would never happen.

In August 1964, the builders moved in and I was invited by my colleagues on the Committee to accept the job of Manager – and I moved in with the builders.

Lá le Bhrigid, the Feast of St. Bridget, February 1st 1965, was the day of our formal opening. The St. Bridget's Cross became the symbol of the Centre.

For a week or so before the Centre opened, the place was a hive of activity. Opening of boxes of glasses, of crockery, furniture – and assembling it – and a thousand other jobs. Numerous people, many of whom didn't know one another, gave up night after night. One of those was the late Martin Foley, who had given his name at a concert in the Philharmonic Hall, and said he was willing to help in

The immortal winner of Olympic Gold in Melbourne in 1956 was Ronnie Delaney. As an executive of B+I Line, he was a regular visitor to the Irish Centre and always caused a stir. He is a gentleman who was always courteous and kind to his autograph hunters. Here, he signs the distinguished visitors book.

At the formal opening of the Irish Centre on 1st February, 1965. Archbishop Andrew Beck of Liverpool, Tommy Walsh and Frank Aiken, Tanaiste and Minister of Extenal Affairs in the Irish Government. They are viewing the parchment they both signed to declare the Centre open.

any capacity. From then, till the day he died suddenly in February 1989 – he never stopped!

Two bars and a beer cellar, as well as a kitchen had to be installed. The plaster work was restored and the best 'ecclesiastical decorators' in the country, Campbell Smith, were employed to decorate. Carpets with our logo, the St. Brigid's Cross woven into it, were made in Ireland for us. A different colour for each room. Some furniture was bought locally but a lot was made in Navan, County Meath ('only an hour from Dublin').

It was a deliberate decision to open informally five weeks or so before the formal opening. So many things can go wrong. New staff, not knowing where anything is, switches, etc. 'Teething problems' are very real.

The name Irish Centre Liverpool was very deliberate. Sadly, 'Liverpool Irish' had deservedly, or otherwise, become a description of the stage Irish character, often depicted as ignorant and over-indulgent. So, Harry McHugh and myself who did many interviews always corrected 'Liverpool Irish' to Irish Centre Liverpool.

We resolved that everything would start on time. Bands and artistes who did not comply would not be re-booked. The policy caused some internal strife at first, when people turned up late, but the majority liked the policy, and it stayed. On December 26th, we had our first function.

Around the Fire took its name from the popular Radio Eireann programme of the time.

The Irish Government had recognised the importance of what was happening in Liverpool, as had the City of Liverpool and the Catholic Archdiocese. The Tanaiste and Minister for External Affairs, Mr. Frank Aiken, the Irish Ambassador, Mr. Jack Molloy and Senator Tom Mullins were all present at the Formal Opening, as was the Lord Mayor of Liverpool, Alderman Louis Caplan and Archbishop G. Beck, Archbishop Conway of Armagh also accepted an invitation but just before the event he was informed he was to become a cardinal and his plans to travel to Rome for the ceremony prevented him coming. It was two years later when he came for the opening of the Cathedral that he paid his first visit to the Centre.

The opening was a glittering occasion, with massive media coverage. Irish and local newspapers were all there. We were learning all the time, of course, and like everyone else we learned from our mistakes. For the first and only time we employed a Toastmaster to call the guests to make their speeches. He had read on the menu card 'Frank Aiken T.D. – and called on 'Frank Aiken – holder of Her Majesty's Territorial Decoration!'

Michael O'Connell and Eithne Dunne sang.

The major test facing the Irish Centre was to become a Community Centre, serving the needs of the Irish people 52 weeks a year. Obviously this had to be on a trial and error basis, and some of the activities didn't last, while others flourished and required more and more space. Within weeks of the opening, Maírín Bolger had started an Irish Dancing Class.

As soon as the formal opening was over, I resigned as Chairman and continued with the post of Manager.

Harry McHugh took over as Chairman. Harry was well

GENERAL ELECTION
OCTOBER 25th, 1951

Bootle Parliamentary Constituency

VOTE FOR

HARRY McHUGH
The Irish Anti-Partition Candidate

Dear Elector,

Communism is threatening to destroy the Christian Way of Life in the world. There is not only the threat of armed force, but there is a more sinister spiritual threat; and I believe that the only way to meet both threats is by a rigid adherence to the principles of Christianity.

We must ensure that our children are armed against the spiritual threat by seeing that they receive a sound Christian Education.

We must ensure that the Government will always safeguard the rights of the family and of the individual before any other interests.

We must ensure that we gather about us as many friends as we can amongst the nations of the world ; and the only way we can do that is by helping those nations to enjoy the same benefits we wish for ourselves. Ireland must be granted the freedom and unity which the vast majority of her people desire, and the national dignity of the Persians, the Egyptians and all other peoples whose friendship means so much to our future must be similarly respected. If these peoples are convinced of our desire for equal friendship they will rally to our aid in time of need.

I believe in these principles, and I will work to my utmost endeavour for them. If you believe in the same principles, then you will give me your vote, and you can then rest easy in your conscience that you have done all in your power to preserve for yourselves and your children the Christian Way of Life which alone will enable us to face the future with confidence.

Yours sincerely,

Harry McHugh.

VOTE HARRY McHUGH   X

Harry McHugh was a member of the Anti-Partition of Ireland League. He was Chairman of the Irish Centre, Mount Pleasant from 1965-1968.

known in the Irish Community in that everyone knew *of* him. However, not too many knew him. He had been a very prominent member of the Anti-Partition of Ireland League. He had been one of the main organisers of Eamon de Valera's visit to Liverpool in 1948. He was unique in that he had stood as an Anti-Partition candidate in the General Election of 1951.

I knew him well because he was, like me, a member of the Sean O'Donovan Branch of the Gaelic League. He was not a member of the Gaelic Council but joined the Irish Centre Building Fund at my invitation shortly after we formed the committee.

He was almost immediately elected Vice-Chairman so he obviously impressed the members.

I remember one meeting when we were arranging a function in a parish hall. We discussed the band, the hall, the printing of tickets and handbills, the MC, the door staff and all the usual things. Harry had only ever been involved with major events in St. George's Hall or the Stadium. He was impatient and said to me (in the Chair), 'How much profit are we going to make on this?' I said, 'Perhaps £10'. He said, 'Let's all put £1 in and go home.'

Of course, he was missing the point that we were selling the whole 'Irish Centre for Liverpool' idea. No one else, in Irish circles in Liverpool, thought like Harry. I liked and admired him and it was an honour years later to be asked by his wife Frances to say a few words at his funeral. Harry had won an Irish Post Literary Award, had plays performed and had several books published.

Harry was a good Chairman, but he ruffled feathers. He was good for me as Manager. We agreed responsibilities, Manager and Committee. The Committee would decide policy. I would carry it out without interference. I had a free hand to run the Centre on a day-to-day basis. I had total

A 50th Wedding Anniversary family party in the Centre. A very well known Irish family, the Kilgallons. There were many such parties in the Irish Community. This was a very early party.

respect for Committee members and defended them when they were criticised.

I had my own slot at meetings and put forward any proposals I had before them. Frequently my ideas were strongly debated, but when a decision was made, like it or not, that was the end of it.

The Committee ran two events each year:

• The AGM for members when they reported the year's work to the members and put themselves up for re-election. Each member came up for re-election every third year.

• The Annual Dinner which was held on 1st February each year. The Committee invited the guests, and the speakers, usually an Irish Minister and an Irish Bishop. The dinner was followed by dancing. They were always great nights.

Before 1965, the community had gathered in small groups, such as the Gaelic League, the GAA, dancing classes, and

This was the first "Annual Concert" in 1965. Many of the Irish families in Liverpool are represented. Here among Mairin Bolger's Dancers: Maureen (Coyne) Morrison, the Administrator of St. Michael's Irish Centre is extreme right, front row. Tom O'Connor who went on to become a TV star is centre, back row. Val Fitzpatrick and Teresa Duffy were the stars from Ireland.

the Shamrock Club and Lawlor's in St. Anne Street and Islington. Suddenly there was a huge venue available 365 days a year, which could comfortably accommodate 3,500 people a week.

Despite all the longing for a 'place of our own' would the Irish people make their way to town and walk up the hill that was Mount Pleasant? There were very few cars, only limited street parking for the cars that were available, hardly any buses passing the door. On day one, there were no activity groups, no regular functions in the ballroom, no regulars in the All-Ireland Bar or Claddagh Room.

Those involved were torn between resting after the huge event of the formal opening and the essential 'bread and butter' arrangements for the present and the future.

There had been huge press publicity for the formal opening with full page coverage in the Irish papers and local press, and radio. Fairly quickly, the week-ends took shape. Fridays started as 'modern dance' and fairly quickly became Show Band nights.

Saturday nights at first were Ceili and Old Time while Sundays were Irish Folk nights. The resident duo were Tom and Brennie (Tom O'Connor and Brendan O'Sullivan). Brendan played guitar and Tom sang. While Tom O'Connor became famous on TV as a comedian and chat show host, he was a singer with us. He particularly liked Wexford songs, and Boolavogue was his favourite.

The weekend format settled down to Fridays: Show Bands, Saturdays: 'Take the Floor' with Ceili and Old Time Dancing. The Shannon Star Band were resident for many years. Teresa Ryan and her sister Sue Danham, John Danham on drums, Arthur James on accordion and Jim Terry on fiddle. For a number of years we had a guaranteed crowd. We also had a song contest every Saturday. About ten songs were put in a box and singers in the crowd drew them and sang them from their place in the hall. When it was over an envelope was opened with the name of one song, and the person who had sung that song, won a cash prize.

Friday nights drew by far the biggest crowds. There were no tables and chairs and 500 young people piled in. Every Irish nurse in Liverpool and Birkenhead was there, and every young single Irish man too. Numerous marriages resulted from Friday nights in the Irish Centre. These people became the pillars of both the Irish Community and the broader Liverpool community.

Their children and grandchildren became active in Irish affairs, particularly through Irish dancing and music classes. I regularly see grandchildren and great-grandchildren of my old friends of those days, in St. Michael's Irish Centre.

An early Chairman was Jim Butler, a former Irish Army Officer who had moved to Liverpool. He was a representative for a medicines' company and was a pillar of the GAA in Liverpool and was a friend of mine. Jim and I agreed that we should follow the GAA example and the Chair should remain in post for three years and resign. This became a tradition rather than a rule. It worked.

I recall a debate going on at Committee level for several meetings about the level of new lighting in the lounge. Once the Committee made a decision, I would deal with contractors. The problem was whether the lights should be

Seamus Wynne from County Louth was the first catering manager at the Irish Centre. He was particularly busy when the new Cathedral brought coachloads of visitors from all over the country.

good, bright ceiling lights as had always been the case, or the new-fangled wall lights which gave subdued lighting. I said I needed a decision that night if the work was not to be delayed. Jim made a ruling 'The light must be strong enough to read *The Tipperary Star* by'. Decision made.

The 'Diary', which was produced on a duplicator we had bought second-hand for Tithebarn Street, listed the following activities in July 1965. Children and Adults Dancing Classes, details of the next car rally/treasure hunt, Irish Language classes, a camera club. Welfare and maintenance committees were very active.

By the start of the 1970s, we were a well-established business. We were profitable; we had a small, full-time staff with a large pool of equally loyal and efficient part-time staff who were employed on a casual but regular basis.

I had three assistant managers, all full-time, with quite separate responsibilities, but who covered one another on days off and holidays. Whoever was on duty on a quiet night, or when someone was on holiday, was the 'duty manager'.

Nick Redmond was the Bar Steward, responsible for running the two bars, for staffing the bars and for maintaining stock levels.

Seán Murphy was, in many ways, the face of the Irish Centre. He was responsible for every aspect of reception, controlling admission at the door, ensuring that both the reception desk and the door were manned. Not simply manned, but presenting the right image to the clients, visitors, and the world. Of course, most of them were Irish people living in Liverpool and were regular visitors. I think Seán knew every one of them and they all knew him. He was very much the youngest of the staff, all the older women mothered him. He was a priceless asset to the Centre.

Phil Farrelly was the Entertainments Manager and booked the bands and entertainers. He was in charge of the

Three members of Management Staff in the Irish Centre. Sean Murphy, Bridie Ryan who ran the shop 'Croc An Oir' (Crock of Gold) and Phil Farrelly. Bridie was Sean's aunt.

ballroom on dance nights. Phil was to become manager when I eventually resigned in 1981.

We opened a small shop selling Irish goods called Croc An Oir (of which more later). We were very fortunate to have Bridie Ryan there. Bridie was Seán Murphy's aunt.

She was Tipperary and everyone knew it. Her running hurling rivalry with Fr. Seán O'Connor when Cork played Tipp in the Munster Final was a joy to behold. Bridie had no interest in the clock where her shop was concerned. Obviously, her busy spells were when there were functions on, but she was there whenever there was business! I think she knew every wife's birthday and would make helpful suggestions to husbands.

It was Fr. Seán who eventually conducted Bridie's funeral and it was a joyful occasion

Seamus Wynne was Manager of the Claddagh Room during 1967 when the Cathedral was opened and we had numerous coaches of visitors from all over England, coming to us for a meal. When Seamus went home to the Nuremore Hotel in Carrickmacross, Seán Dunne took over. Seán had a family connection too, as his mother, Pauleen, known to everyone as Pal, was one of Nick's senior bar staff.

Chrissie Murphy was Seán's deputy and eventually took over the catering department. Chrissie was loved by everyone, especially all the Show Bands. She met them with tea and food when they arrived and saw them off with tea

In 1978, the Irish Post gave a 'Community Award' to the Irish Centre, Liverpool.

'An award goes to the Irish Centre Liverpool, for the excellence of virtually everything it has done over the past thirteen years. Every year has been one of achievement for the centre and 1977 saw its excellence maintained and further enlarged. It is no reflection on any Irish Club in Britain to say that Liverpool has down the years been a model and an inspiration. Many of the more recently founded Irish community venues started by going to Liverpool to see how it should be done ... There is a style – even an elegance – about how things are done at the Liverpool Centre. It has always been a credit to itself and to our community at large.'

at 2am when they were hitting the road.

Chrissie's son, Vincent, and daughter, Mary were two more of Nick's senior bar staff. Vincent now lives in Roscommon with Mary and her husband Pat Mullen. Mary was the best maker of Irish Coffee I ever came across.

Having found and opened the premises, the challenge was to make it work. To be a focal point for all of the Irish Community in Liverpool.

Difficulties were created by the 'club structure'. To run a bar legally we had to run it as a club. Only registered members were allowed to purchase drinks, so everyone using the place had to join. The problem was that 'joining a club' was totally foreign to Irish people. A regular question/criticism was, 'Is this an Irish Centre or isn't it? I'm Irish. Why won't you let me in?'

The truth is that it was never our intention to open a club for members. The objective was to run a Centre to accommodate all Irish activities in Liverpool. The fact that we could only run it legally as a licensed club was always a difficulty. The man who represented me, as Licensee, in court was Bob Gaul. His son, Patrick, is now a committee member of St. Michael's Irish Centre.

It's worth thinking back to the Irish Fellowship in 1939. They intended to run a Centre, in the same premises, without a bar. Our Licence was a 'Justices On-Licence With Conditions'. The 'conditions' were basically that we were only allowed to serve members with alcohol, or those persons attending organised events.

There were frequent 'debates', 'arguments' about events which were not in someone's opinion 'culturally desirable'. Bearing in mind that I had been firmly in the Gaelic League and GAA camp, running events in premises without bars, I was virtually considered a traitor.

Fr. Paddy Spain said, "If you pay the rent you can

promote culture. If you don't pay the rent, you'll have no cultural activities."

In the early 70s we were still paying off the £20,000 brewery loan that Fr. Spain negotiated for us to enable us to buy the place, when Allied Irish Banks opened in Manchester and eventually opened the Liverpool Branch in Renshaw Street in 1972.

We negotiated an overdraft facility for up to £30,000 and immediately paid off the brewery. Naturally, we had been unable to negotiate prices and discounts while we were tied to the brewery. We now made very big savings on our bar purchases and our weekly cash income was immediately offset against the overdraft. A charter flight to Ireland was proposed. The Drama Group was planning a production. In addition to these 'activities' arranged by members, there was a full programme of entertainment arranged by the Centre management.

The Secretary's Report for 1965 shows that there were 1,635 members and separate committees for Reception and Membership, Entertainments, Public Relations, Culture, Welfare, Maintenance, Catering, and Outdoor Activities.

Early in 1965, it was decided that Sunday lunchtime opening would be a good idea. I remember opening the door on the first occasion at 12 o'clock and finding Phil McHale on the step. He got a free pint that day. I doubt if he missed a Sunday for many years. He was one of the Mayo McHale family, many of whom used the Centre.

One of the biggest events to happen in Liverpool in the 60s was the opening of the Cathedral in 1967. Our close proximity meant we had a major role to play, and we made the facilities available to the Archdiocese, and at the same time prepared to welcome the many Irish visitors to Liverpool.

Almost unbelievably, we soon found that this huge building wasn't big enough, and it was necessary to extend.

Options were limited as three sides of the Centre are in different streets and offered no scope. Attempts were made to purchase 125 Mount Pleasant in October 1969 but The Feathers Hotel were also expanding and they beat us to it. We were left with only a back yard 12 feet wide. Out of this, on four different levels, we built a beer cellar, dressing rooms, bar service area, a stage, an activity room, and an Executive Committee meeting room. Because of the building being of architectural importance, planning permission was extremely difficult to obtain. However, after much negotiation and inconvenience the extension was completed and opened by the then Ambassador Dr Donal O'Sullivan and blessed by Bishop Cathal Daly on February 1st 1973. A plaque on the edge of the stage commemorated the occasion.

After we had been open a couple of years, an Extraordinary General Meeting was called. This was done constitutionally by 30 members signing a request. There was one item on the Agenda. 'The dismissal of the Manager for insisting on punctuality, and not employing a particular band because he required them to start punctually, and remain on stage during the function.' A lot of people avoided eye contact with me about that time!

One or two told me they didn't know what they were signing. A very nice man who was a friend of mine who didn't like commerce raising its head said, "Michelangelo would never have completed the Sistine Chapel if the same attitude was taken".

In my response at the end of the motion, I said, "If Michelangelo was painting the Irish Centre ceiling, we may not be open yet!"

The then Editor of the Irish Post, Brendáin Mac Lua, speaking at one of the Anniversary Dinners said something like this, "Don't have your children grow up saying about you, their parents, they taught me Irish Dancing and Music, they

taught me Gaelic Games, but they didn't tell me about
Ireland". For me, that sums up the challenge of an Irish
Centre which should bring out the best in an Irish community.

In my office in the Centre in Mount Pleasant, I had a
card on the wall which someone had given me. It said
something like this, 'when a man does for a living what he
likes doing, he has found his job.'

I loved what I was doing. I was doing full-time what I
had been doing in all my spare time for years, organising
events for the Irish community. In relation to my job
content, and certainly with regard to the cash turnover, the
most important aspect was the bar. Buying, selling, stock
control and staffing were crucial. Run well, the bars made
the Centre profitable. Run badly, even taking your 'eye off
the ball' briefly, can be fatal, However, I was determined
that my objective would be fulfilled and maintained. 'There
is a bar in the Irish Centre, the Irish Centre is not a bar.'

Some of the outstanding
contributors to the Irish Centre
are here, on the occasion of the
visit of Cardinal Conway,
Archbishop of Armagh,. Left to
right: Fr. Oliver Brady, The
Cardinal. Fr. Michael O'Connor,
5th from left Vin Boyle – he and
Michael Murray (1st right) were
registrars of the Centre.
Between them is Fr. Patrick
Spain. These three men are
among the most remarkable
people in the history of the Irish
Community in Liverpool.

In 1973, the Irish Centre was extended and a new stage and a new 'All-Ireland Bar' were added. They are illustrated here as well as The Claddagh Room and the shop, Croc An Oir.

From day one, we had an extremely good bar steward in Nick Redmond. He too was from a GAA background and was, coincidentally, my brother-in-law.

From the day we opened, we had a fully fitted kitchen and a refreshment room known as 'The Claddagh Room'. From a cup of tea or coffee to a full meal.

Our flourishing branch of the Pioneer (Total Abstinence) Association kept a very close eye on me. Being a non-drinker, though not a Pioneer, I was well aware of the importance of the Claddagh Room to non-drinkers.

I think that the most personally satisfying facility in the Centre was the establishment of the CROC AN OIR (Crock of Gold). To this day, having done many things for a living, given one choice, I'd have to say 'I'm a Shopkeeper'. Perhaps as a result of having been born over the shop in Blundell Street. For some years, I had toyed with the idea of opening a shop in Liverpool City Centre for the sale of Irish made goods, but had never got round to it.

Here was my opportunity. For the Irish Centre rather than for myself. We started with Irish provincial papers and greetings cards. We were soon selling huge quantities and I decided that, to do the job properly, we needed a full-time member of staff. Bridie Ryan was from Kilcommon in Co. Tipperary and had worked for Owen Owen in the city centre for many years. Bridie was already manning our Reception Desk on a voluntary basis. She left Owen Owen and joined us on a full-time basis.

Croc An Oir was so successful we had to enlarge the shop and we had to create a stock room in the ceiling space. We sold only goods which were made in Ireland with one single exception: we sold a huge number of music records. Some Irish artistes had their records pressed by English companies and we sold them. We regarded that as a service to members. Otherwise everything we sold was made in

Ireland and was of good quality. If an Irish manufacturer was making leprechauns, we excluded them from the products we bought from that company. Among the goods available were newspapers including every Irish Provincial.

Greetings cards were huge sellers including Brian O'Higgins until they became unobtainable. Glassware from Waterford Crystal and cheaper souvenir glasses. Pottery from Achill and Youghal and dinner services from Arklow and Carrigaline. Jewellery, especially gold and silver Claddagh rings, earrings and pendants were huge sellers. Tara brooches and Book of Kells inspired pendants and brooches were always in demand. Records and subsequently cassettes and eventually videos, books in both Irish and English were always available. People came from all over the north of England to buy Aran sweaters and cardigans. We dealt with a lot of actual knitters as well as wholesalers.

If memory serves me right, we were selling about 150 Ireland's Own every week.

I did believe at the time that we probably had the best selection of Irish goods in the world. Certainly through my contacts with all the suppliers, we weren't aware of anyone else, stocking our range.

We were buying big quantities of Rosaries and other religious goods from CBC in Cuper Street in Belfast. Their owner Cyril Woods and representative Roy McKee were so familiar with us, they could make their own cup of tea! In later years, they were forced out of their premises in the Falls Road and moved to Newry, Co. Down.

St. Michael's Irish Centre now deals with them.

Bridie knew everyone by their newspaper if she didn't know their names. If we were trying to tell of good news or bad news regarding a regular customer and we said, 'every Saturday night or Sunday lunchtime'. 'Tall or Short'. 'Husband and Wife'. Bridie would say, 'Oh, you mean

Longford Leader and *Southern Star*!'

While we were buying from the big suppliers in Ireland such as Waterford Crystal, we were also dealing with small companies who didn't have a 'phone. I often think the manual phone with the handle for turning gave a service the modern computerised service can't give.

I was buying several thousand sprays of shamrock every year from a lady in Rosscarbery Co. Cork who wasn't on the 'phone. I would ring Roscarbery Post Office and say I needed to talk to her. The lady in the Post Office would say, "She'll be at 9.00am Mass tomorrow morning and she'll go into her sisters for a cup of tea. I'll ring her there". The following morning about 9.30am, the Post Office would ring me and put Kitty on to me. "Don't worry about the shamrock. You'll have it." I always did.

We bought a lot of thick woollen socks, with the toe, heel and top in natural wool and the rest in dark brown. Men came from all over the North West and bought six pairs at a time. A small firm in Ballinrobe, Co. Mayo supplied us and they weren't on the phone. Again I'd ring the Post Office. "They bring in the parcels about 4.30pm. Ring then and I'll put them on to you."

I was passing through Ballinrobe one day and called into the Post Office to thank them.

The policy of selling Irish products was carried out throughout the Centre. If people asked for Whiskey, Gin or Vodka, they were given Irish Distillers products. If they wanted Scotch or Gin other than Cork Dry Gin, they would be expected to specify.

One of the big differences the opening of the Irish Centre made to the Irish Community was that the big name Irish Artistes who had previously by-passed Liverpool were now appearing here. Bands like Larry Cunningham, Johnny McEvoy and Richard Fitzgerald, and solo artistes like

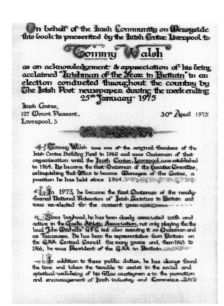

On behalf of the Irish Community on Merseyside this book is presented by the Irish Centre Liverpool to

Tommy Walsh

as an acknowledgement & appreciation of his being acclaimed "Irishman of the Year in Britain" in an election conducted throughout the country by The Irish Post newspaper during the week ending 25th January 1975

Irish Centre,
127 Mount Pleasant,   30th April 1975
Liverpool, 3

Tommy Walsh was one of the original founders of the Irish Centre Building Fund in 1960 and was Chairman of that organisation until the Irish Centre, Liverpool, was established in 1964. He became the first Chairman of its Executive Committee, relinquishing that office to become Manager of the Centre, a position he has held since 1964.

In 1973, he became the first Chairman of the newly-formed National Federation of Irish Societies in Britain and was re-elected for the current year.

Since boyhood, he has been closely associated with and active in the Gaelic Athletic Association, not only playing for the local "John Mitchells" GFC but also serving it as Chairman and as Treasurer. He has been the representative from Britain on the GAA Central Council for many years and, from 1965 to 1966, he was President of the GAA in Britain.

In addition to these public duties, he has always found the time and taken the trouble to assist in the social and spiritual well-being of his fellow countrymen & in the promotion and encouragement of Irish industry and Commerce.

The Irish Centre Liverpool responded to the "Irishman of the Year" announcement by having a big night in the Centre. I was presented with a 'Limited Edition' of the Book of Kells. This page was an insert.

Eileen Donaghy and Bridie Gallagher appeared regularly.

No other band caused as much fuss as Big Tom. The first time he came, the queue was down to the traffic lights at Rodney Street. We were besieged with ticket requests. Jim Butler said, "The history of the Irish Centre will fall into the two periods, 'Before Big Tom and After Big Tom'".

Buying such a high grade Listed Building brought all kinds of problems we weren't aware of. We needed permission to carry out the smallest alteration. When we applied to the planners for permission to build our extension we had Lady Sefton, in her capacity as Chairperson of the Georgian Society, inspecting the place. We always made the case that we had brought the place to life. The building was too lovely not to be used to its full capacity. I did become fascinated by the history of such a beautiful building and have given talks on the Wellington Rooms to groups like the Liverpool History Society.

In 1967, we paid a lot of money to have the stone exterior cleaned only to find that the stone wasn't as attractive as we had anticipated. The roof was the biggest worry. It consists of four separate slated roofs and a circular roof over the foyer. It needed frequent inspections, slate repairs and the removal of dead pigeons from the gutters where two slated roofs met. The neglect of this work since the Irish Centre closed is the reason that the building is now in such a dire state.

NOTES FROM MOUNT PLEASANT: THE 60s AND 70s
• In 1967, Britain was hit by a dreadful outbreak of Foot and Mouth disease. Ireland went to extraordinary lengths to keep it out of the country. Disinfectant baths were installed at car ferries and airports. Many products were not allowed into Ireland. Irish people in Britain were asked not to go to Ireland.

As Christmas approached, the situation got worse.

Pat Eddery

Terry Wogan

Johnny Giles

Paddy O'Connor

Donall
Mac Amhlaigh

Val Doonican

IRISHMAN OF THE YEAR

Tom Walsh—chairman of the Federation of Irish Societies and first British-born winner of Award

Tom Walsh, the chairman of the Federation of Irish Societies and manager of the Irish Centre, Liverpool, is the 'Irishman of the Year in Britain' for 1974.

In the highest poll since we initiated this annual award five years ago, readers voted him 240 votes clear of the next contender, champion jockey, Pat Eddery.

Tom Walsh becomes the first British-born recipient of this Award. Born in Liverpool of Irish parents, he has all his life been involved in Irish community activities. One of the founders of the distinctly successful Liverpool Irish Centre, he has been its manager since it opened a decade ago. For many years he has been Britain's representative on the Central Council of the GAA and was for a period vice-president of the Association. He has also long connections with the Gaelic League.

A year ago he became chairman of the Federation of Irish Societies and is recognised as having given that nationwide organisation a new dimension. Tom Walsh was 7th in last year's poll.

A total of 9,136 readers participated in our poll and in all 162 Irish men and women in Britain were nominated. The voting was as follows:

1. Tom Walsh (chairman of the Federation of Irish Societies) 822.
2. Pat Eddery (champion jockey) 582.
3. Terry Wogan (radio and television personality) 529.
4. Johnny Giles (footballer and Irish team manager) 410.
5. Ald. Paddy O'Connor (Labour member of the Greater London Council) 286.
6. Donall Mac Amhlaigh (author and columnist) 234.
7. Val Doonican (singer) 227.
8. Dr. Barrie Hoare (new chairman Irish Club, London) 210.
9. Danny La Rue (entertainer) 208.
10. Don Givens (footballer) 182.

Despite having regularly pointed out that nobody connected with The Irish Post is eligible for nomination, our columnist **Frank Dolan** has as usual received sufficient votes to have placed him well up in the Top Ten.

Seven others received over 100 votes — **Dana** (singer), **Dave Allen** (television personality), **Bill Halley** (secretary Federation of Irish Societies), **Fr. Michael Connolly** (the Wolverhampton parish priest), **Edna O'Brien** (novelist), **Eamonn Andrews** (television personality) and **Willie**

John McBride (rugby star). Both the latter were ineligible as they do not live in Britain (Eamonn Andrews commutes) and cannot therefore be described as members of the Irish community in this country.

Others to poll particularly well were: **Richard Harris** (actor), **James Burke** (television commentator), **Michael O'Halloran** (Labour MP), **Dr. Donal O'Sullivan** (Irish Ambassador and last year's winner), **Gilbert O'Sullivan** (singer and composer), **Michael Gaughan** (the young Mayoman who died on hunger strike during 1974) and **Lord Longford**.

Among the other well known people to be nominated were: **John Reilly** (whose two sons were killed in the Birmingham bombings), **Charles Kennedy** (Irish Heritage group), **David Brazil** (the young London-based Irish Press journalist), **Joe Gormley** (the NUM president), the **Bachelors** (entertainers), **Joe Molloy** (chairman of ICRA in Birmingham), **Sir Charles Curran** (director general of the BBC), **Brendan Duffy** (secretary Slough Irish Society), **Fr. Jim McManus** (the Shrewsbury-based Redemptorist), **Fr. Patrick Mee** (director Irish Centre, London), **Brendan Magill** (the Republican spokesman), **Tom O'Gorman** (president of the Council of Irish County Associations), **Michael Hipkiss** (the traditional singer), **Margaret O'Brien** (secretary of ICRA, London),

Tom Walsh — first British-born 'Man of the Year'.

Dana

Eamonn Andrews

Bill Halley

Richard Harris

This was the announcement by the Irish Post that I had been elected Irishman of the Year by the readers.

Traditionally, single Irish people went home for Christmas. The Irish Farmers Association asked Irish Centres in Britain to provide Christmas dinner for people who didn't go home and who would be alone.

The IFA made a national collection, to pay for the meals for the people who would stay here. We, in Liverpool, opened two lists of names. One of people who would like dinner on Christmas Day. The second list was of families who would welcome single people to share their family meal. The second list turned out to be the bigger list, and everyone wanting to accept an invitation was accommodated. This attracted a lot of media attention and the Daily Mirror had a famous headline: "Take an Irishman Home for Christmas". As a result, the Irish Centre Liverpool sent its share of the IFA collection, about £400, to our friend Fr. Paul Byrne OMI in the Irish Centre Birmingham, to help them with their costs.

• In 1970, Sister Jane Frances invited the children who attended the regular Children's Corner to her convent in Bidston. My memory of Children's Corner is of Sister Jane Frances in her full habit and veil sitting with all the children on the floor teaching them to sing Ó RÓ MO BHAIDÍN, and 'rowing the boat' while they sang.

• Maírín Bolger passed, with special commendation, her exams to be a Registered Adjudicator in Irish Dancing. A nun in Dublin wrote to the Centre. She had visited with a group of children. She said the visit awakened in them (and her) an awareness of their Irish heritage.

• The disappearance of the old 6d pieces has caused a drop in the use of the fruit machines. The machines will be adjusted to take the new 2p coin.

Vera and Chris Johnston, and Joe and Anne McCabe pictured with Art McMillen after his release from Long Kesh internment camp.

• Michael Murray died on 6th December 1970. He had been Registrar since the Centre opened. An extremely busy post. A former headmaster, he was a legend in Irish Liverpool. He was one of four Murray brothers, all of whom were headmasters in Liverpool schools.

• Kathleen Clarke, the widow of Tom Clarke – the first signatory of The Proclamation, died on the on 29th September 1972. She had been Lord Mayor of Dublin on several occasions. She was living in Liverpool with her son Dr. Emmet and his wife Helen when she died. She was a regular visitor to the Centre, and although in her 90's, enjoyed a good conversation. I really enjoyed her company and missed her greatly. She was given a State Funeral and Chris Johnston and myself were invited to her funeral by her family.

117

On Sunday, January 24th, 1979, the 50th Anniversary of the death of the Irish songwriter, Percy French, was remembered at the great man's grave in St. Luke's, Formby. The best interpreter of such songs as *Come Back Paddy Reilly* and The *Mountains of Mourne*, Brendan O'Dowda, unveiled a commemorative plinth on the grave. It was Mourne granite and read:

JANUARY 24th 1970

THIS PLINTH OF MOURNE GRANITE WAS ERECTED BY THE IRISH CENTRE, LIVERPOOL ON BEHALF OF A GRATEFUL IRISH NATION TO THE IMMORTAL MEMORY OF A GREAT IRISH SONG WRITER AND ENTERTAINER AR DEIS DE GO RAIBH A ANAM. AMEN

• On 3rd January, Anna McGoldrick phoned. She was doing a series of televised shows for RTE. They had suggested doing one from the London Irish Centre. Anna said the only Irish Centre in England she felt at home at was Liverpool. She would only do it there. The notice was short. Very little publicity. 500 people turned up.

Anna was a regular visitor at the Centre. Apart from her concert appearances she and her husband, Mike, always called in on their way to the boat on a Sunday night. On those occasions, everyone who saw her asked her to give a song and she always went on stage, as she was, and sang.

• At twenty minutes past one a.m. on 19/7/74 a man was seen, wearing only his socks, running down Mount Pleasant outside the Centre. I know who he was!! Streaking was just starting to happen.

• Fr. Seán O'Connor left for South America in September 1979. As we all know, he came back, and says our Mass of St. Patrick every year. He also comes in on Sundays for the hurling on T.V.

• The Centre wrote to Cardinal O'Fiaich to congratulate the Irish Church on the success of the Pope's visit to Ireland. We sent £100 towards the cost. The Centre also wrote to the BBC to thank them for the excellence of their T.V. coverage of the visit.

• The major event each year, for many people, was the Anniversary Dinner on the Feast of St. Brigid, 1st February. The Archbishop of Tuam, Dr. Cunnane, was there in 1974. I greatly admired him and saw him often when I attended meetings, in Dublin, of the Emigrant Chaplains,

Mass of St. Patrick was a very popular event in the Irish Centre. Principal concelebrant on this occasion was Bishop Kevin O'Connor.

and the Irish Commission for Prisoners Overseas. Bishop Cathal Daly and Tim Pat Coogan were others who spoke at the Anniversary Dinner. Tim Pat Coogan was then Editor of the Irish Press and has since written many books including the blockbuster *Wherever Green is Worn*.

• In 1969, Harry McHugh resigned after five years in the chair. Jim Butler was elected in his place. Fr. Paddy Spain, the great inspiration of all that was good in the Irish Community, died on 19th July 1969. His example to the Irish Community was impossible to express. He it was whose policy was: 'if you need a premises for a function, go out and find one. If you need a pitch for hurling or gaelic football, go out and find one – and don't come back till you have one'. The Irish Community raised funds and installed a stained glass window in his church, Mother of God, Kirkby.

• The great songwriter, Percy French, is buried at St. Luke's Churchyard in Formby. He was visiting his

The Finn Harps team for a cup final in 1977/78.

Back Row: Danny Britt, Sean Loughran, Danny Doherty, Kevin Ryan, Ged Burke, Colum Walsh, Bobby Touhey, Martin Rafter, Terry Ryan, Sean Murphy, Wilf O'Reilly.

Front Row: Paul Brennan, Stephen McAteer, Paddy Dudley, Des Hanna, Tommy Collister, Brian Bennett, Bernie Ryan.

cousin who was Canon Richardson in the parish, when he died on 24th January 1920. Brendan O'Dowda suggested to the Irish Centre that we should insert a plinth of Mourne granite (Mourne granite because Mountains of Mourne was one of his great songs) in his headstone to commemorate the 50th Anniversary of his death. It was a great day and it was attended by Percy French's two daughters.

There was a concert in the Irish Centre that night, and Brendan O'Dowda was joined by Teresa Duffy and Birdy Sweeney.

• In 1977, the new Finn Harps soccer team reported on their first year in existence. They had been founded by Sean Loughran, Sean Murphy and Colum Walsh. In their first year, they were awarded the Michael McKenna Cup for being the best at punctuality, good attendance at league meetings and general conduct on the pitch (The same Michael McKenna was to offer St. Michael's Centre to the Irish Community many years later).

They had also been invited to Dublin by Fr. Michael Cleary who was a regular visitor to the Irish Centre. Finn Harps team members attended Croke Park for the National

League Final, Kerry v Dublin.

As far as I am aware, Finn Harps were the first ever soccer team in the Irish Community in Liverpool. They took their name from the League of Ireland team in Donegal. Over 30 years on, Sean Loughran (Junior) is still running a very successful Finn Harps Soccer Club for over 100 children and young people.

• Michael Quinlan reported on the Pool Knockout Competition.

People who were Chair of the Irish Centre from 1965-1984 included: H.J. McHugh, Jim Butler, Chris Johnston, Joe England, Sadie Redmond and Seán McNamara.

• In 1976, Sister Mary of the Holy Child, Prioress of the enclosed Carmelite Monastery, Skelmersdale, in her acknowledgement for a cheque said (of the Irish Centre), "We pray for all the work you undertake in quite a remarkable way according to accounts that even penetrate our enclosure."

• In 1978, the Centre was awarded an Irish Post Community Award. The Annual Mass of St. Patrick in 1978 was held in the Cathedral. Archbishop Worlock was principal concelebrant, and was joined by a number of Irish priests. Father Michael Cleary came over from Dublin to give the homily.

BLOODY SUNDAY AND AFTERMATH

What have became known as 'The Troubles' had an enormous effect on the Irish Centre, and the Irish people in Liverpool. We were all involved emotionally and the period affected everybody here. Of course not at all compared to the people in places like the Bogside in Derry and the Falls Road in Belfast.

Kathleen Clarke was a member of the Centre. She is on the right and Mrs. Mackey on the left. Kathleen Clarke was Lord Mayor of Dublin on several occasions, and she was the author of *Revolutionary Woman*. Emmet Clarke, Kathleen's son, was also a member of the centre. Emmet's father, Kathleen's husband, Thomas J Clarke who was executed, was the first signatory of the Proclamation of the Irish Republic in 1916.

In my entire life in Irish Community affairs, I have never experienced a reaction such as there was on the night of what became known as Bloody Sunday in Derry 30 January 1972. On that evening, we opened as usual but there was no music or entertainment. Attendance was higher than usual and everyone said the same thing: they had to come in to the Centre to be among Irish people. There was plenty of talk and plenty of silence.

It was decided that we should invite everyone who wished to, to send a telegram to their own MP expressing their feelings. 176 telegrams were sent. People wrote their message on paper distributed and the name of their MP. All the telegrams were sent from Mount Pleasant Post Office on the Monday morning.

The messages ranged from, 'Blessed Are The Peacemakers' to 'How much Irish blood do you want?' Most were 'Get out of Ireland' or similar. One telegram was signed by 20 nurses from a local hospital.

It was decided to have an 'All Night Vigil' in the Irish Centre from 12th to 13th February 'To Think about DERRY, To Talk about DERRY, To Pray for DERRY and its people.'

'A night of fasting and praying in memory of those who died in Derry on Sunday 30th January.'

The night consisted of a panel dealing with 'Any Questions', a silent room, and various other activities. It ended with many of those present walking up in procession to first Mass in the Cathedral.

A fund was set up at a very early stage, and was called the Innocent Dependants' Fund. The money was sent mostly to Canon Padraig Murphy, the Parish Priest at St. John's, Falls Road, Belfast who ensured the funds all went to assist people in real need.

The families of men detained in Long Kesh Internment Camp were the main beneficiaries of our fund. A man

named Art McMillen, a native of Belfast, who still lives there, wrote to me at the Centre regularly from Long Kesh. I re-produced parts of his letters in our monthly newsletters and, as a result, money from our community in Liverpool poured in. All sorts of fundraising events were held but the bulk of the money was as a result of our members simply giving cash weekly and monthly. Painted handkerchiefs, wallets and purses, wooden crosses were among the items made by the men in Long Kesh for their families and for people like ourselves to raffle to raise funds.

The Newsletter of January 1972 records that a vanload of clothing had been sent to Dublin for refugees who had fled their homes in Belfast. 14 bales of bedding and clothing had been sent to Belfast. A further 28 bales of bedding and clothing were sent a few months later. Many refugees from Belfast came into Liverpool and Sister Rose, our welfare worker, attended to them and found accommodation, clothing and general assistance.

Father Padraig Murphy was invited to be our guest of honour at our Annual Dinner on the Feast of St. Brigid, 1972. After the Dinner, Fr. Godfrey Carney wrote a tribute to Fr. Murphy and his speech on the occasion. As always, Fr. Carney's words were articulate and inspirational. We

A very popular annual event was on the eve of the Grand National. The legendary Michael O'Hehir came every year and many other famous jockeys and trainers came too. Here (left to right) Tommy Walsh, Michael O'Hehir, Pat Taaffe (best known as Arkle's jockey) and Jim Butler. The highlight of the evening was when the huge crowd standing in the hall shouted questions and the guests answered.

When the situation in Ireland improved and Long Kesh closed, Art McMillen came over to thank the regular donors to the 'Innocent Dependants' Fund' personally. Art is seen here.

Amongst ohers in the line-up on the back row: Phyllis Kirwan, Emmet Clarke, Mrs Kanigan, Bernie Cunningham, Tim Murphy, Sadie Redmond, Maureen McMillen (Art's wife), Helen and Michael Walsh, Joe O'Connor, Pat Rooney. Des Faulkener, Mrs. Fogarty, Kevin Cunningham, Tommy Walsh, Anne (Corrigan) McCabe, Vera and Chris Johnston, Pat Cafferry.

Front row (left to right): Kathleen Cafferrey, Ted Lanigan, Phil Farrelly, Jim Butler, Seán and Margaret Murphy, Paul Murphy, Art McMillen, Des Hanna, Seán Walsh and Jim Heneghan

had often staged his plays in the Irish Centre. This is what he wrote:

ST. BRIGID'S NIGHT IN THE IRISH CENTRE

Snow was freezing in the Liverpool streets, but inside the ancient and lovely building on Mount Pleasant, warmth and brilliance greeted eye and heart. In the high hall, the splendidly embossed and patterned ceiling held my attention for a moment, as it always does. The classical frieze which adjoins it all the way round – delicate white figures against a delicate blue – insists with dignified aloofness on other times and other modes, remote and long ago.

Seated for their annual formal dinner, the throng was colourful, voluble and alive with laughter. On my right was a curate from Formby, beyond him, a pair of actors from the Irish Playgoers, on my left was a representative of the Irish Tourist Board, opposite me was a house decorator and his wife, and two nuns from a Nursing Home. Some I had met before, others I had never seen, but all were my friends immediately. Nobody was out of place; no strangers here.

The meal went along on its convivial way, the wine was poured and sampled. The talk was gay, and sometimes a little grave, in keeping with the flag of the Republic which hung before us, an unprecedented strip of black dividing its bright tricolour down the middle. For there was mourning in the air. Two days since 'Bloody Sunday' in the Bogside.

Then came the toasts and the speeches. Father Paul Byrne of 'Shelter' praised the Centre, for its contribution to the cultural and social life of the people, and especially for its assistance to the cause of his heart – the homeless. Father John Gavin, the first life-member, thanked him on behalf of all. Bishop Gray genially proposed a toast to the guests of honour.

Mr. Phelan, a representative of the Irish Embassy, regretted the absence of the Ambassador who, for reasons

124

painfully well known, had been unable to keep his dinner date.

Then the guest of the evening approached the microphones, a clerical giant in his fifties, massive, stooped in shoulder, of broad, wise, patient face, Canon Padraig Murphy of St. John's in the Falls Road. This was the one we had been waiting to hear, the man who for three years has lived and moved in a battleground, the father of a people shocked and shaken day and night by fire and bombs and bullets. A patient pursuer of peace and reconciliation, pleading, restraining, consoling, protesting, encouraging – an unshakeable rock of sanity in a mad sea.

He talked to us quietly with the heart eloquence of one who has something very real to say. He told us about a famous section of his parish – Ballymurphy – and of its twelve thousand inhabitants thrown together in a newly and badly constructed ghetto, without amenities social or industrial. Forty-six per cent of the men are unemployed.

I hate and condemn violence and I tell them this continually, but can't you see how difficult it is for me to go to these caged and frustrated thousands, and tell them, with any sort of conviction, not to throw stones? Journalists come to me from all over, and ask me, 'Father, what is the cause of

*this upheaval, the guns, the bombs, the killings?' I answer –
The cause? why it's simply a case of the privileged ruling for
years over the non-privileged. The Unionists and those who
hope to gain privilege from them, holding power and making
sure of holding power for ever and ever! And the tragedy is
that it could all have been prevented.*

*It could have been prevented years ago, if the Westminster
Government had only bothered to realise that they were
supporting by their military and financial might, this
privileged arrogant junta, supporting them in their
suppression and intimidation of the people whom I represent.*

*I welcomed the British Army as peacekeepers, impartial
and fair. I did my best to co-operate with them in keeping the
peace, and to persuade the people to co-operate with them in
this. But it has long since become clear to me that the
Westminster Government has allowed the Army to be used as a
tool by the privileged, to keep these people in their hopeless
state of subjection. Reforms were promised and arranged for,
but have not been implemented in any real way. How could
they, when the business of producing reform was put into the
hands of the very people who needed to be reformed? Now, I
and my people are convinced by the pressure of wearisome
experience, that Stormont and all it stands for means nothing
to us any more, that to hope for a solution from Westminster is
to hope in vain, that the solution can only come from some
higher intervention of an international nature, and that before
they perpetrate any further blunders in Ireland, which involve
the misery of thousands of its people, the maiming and deaths
of innocent civilians, the bereavements of the families of young
British soldiers in England, Scotland and Wales, before any
more such blunders of policy, I say that the Westminster
Government should simply get out of Ireland. Violence is the
result of injustice, and justice is the only means by which
violence can be ended.*

126

The famous Artane Boys Band from Dublin on stage in the Irish Centre. The band played in Croke Park at every All-Ireland Final.

I stood to join in the ovation given to this gallant and humble parish priest. A cheque for £500 was given to him by the Chairman, Mr. Jim Butler, towards the mothers, wives and children of those interned without trial by the Stormont regime.

The dinner party dispersed to the lounge, the tables were cleared away, dancing began, and the dances tunes from the Shannon Star Ceili Band were stirring and nostalgic. I chatted with many friends, Brother Ryan of St. Edward's, Dan Murray, Mary Earley, Eddie Burke, Jim Butler, and that tireless young man – Tommy Walsh, the Manager.

On the stage, Leo Harris, a winning character from Dublin, with a crippled leg and a golden tenor voice, sang with heart piercing sweetness the old songs – 'Little Town in the old County Down', 'Mother Machree', 'Kathleen Mavourneen', and the 'Ave Maria' of Gounod. The Latin was flawlessly pronounced.

A glib-tongued and most proficient dancer from Limerick – McNamara by name – entertained me with delectable conversation.

At last, congratulating and thanking all within earshot, I went out into the snow. It was ten minutes short of midnight. The picture of Padraig Murphy was in my mind as I drove home – that great, bowed figure, the humorous kindly face, a man caught in a ludicrous clash of extremes, a patient drudge, slaving at an impossible task. But how his

Two people who played a huge part in the Irish Centre were Jim Butler and Father Oliver Brady. Here Jim presents a Waterford Cyrstal Mass Set to Fr. Oliver on the occasion of his Silver Jubilee.

people must love him! How fiercely they must cling to the comfort of his love for them!

Rev G Carney.

Happier times were to follow. When Art McMillen was eventually released, we invited him and his wife Maureen over to a night of enjoyment in Mount Pleasant. It was a great night. Anyone who had contributed to the Innocent Dependants' Fund was invited to meet the man whose words had inspired them to make regular contributions. He took the opportunity to thank everyone there. As a matter of interest, I am still in touch with Art. Sadly, Maureen died some time ago.

What is known simply as the 'Birmingham Bombing' was another single incident during The Troubles which changed our lives at the time. It was on 21/11/74.

Because I was the Chairman of the Federation of Irish Societies in Britain at the time, I had a role to play nationally as well as locally. I appeared on the main BBC news programme, Midweek, representing the Irish Community in Britain.

Immediately after the bombing, the Chief Constable of Liverpool placed a policeman on duty outside the Centre on a 24 hour basis. The policemen who carried out the duties were very courteous and very thorough. On a number of occasions, we were looking for car owners to check parcels on display. The car owners usually turned out to be in one of the nearby hotels.

The occasion was Seán Murphy's finest hour. I deputed him to be in charge of security. All deliveries and every bag coming in were checked. Instrument cases, bags and sometimes individuals were searched. Throughout the period nobody lost their temper with Seán. As a matter of policy, while I was involved with national media and Irish media as a result of my Federation position, I refused to do any interviews with local media on the premise that this was not an issue involving the Irish in Liverpool.

All our functions were badly hit. We lost about a third of every anticipated attendance. Functions in Manchester, Leeds and St. Helens (the Geraldo Club) were cancelled. There were several petrol bomb incidents at the Irish Centre, Birmingham.

THE 80S
My view of the Irish Centre from 1980 onwards will be written from a slightly different perspective as I resigned my position as manager in 1980. The committee appointed Phil Farrelly as manager. Phil had been Assistant Manager for some years so there was minimal disruption.

I still meet people who think there was some big secret reason why I resigned at the time. There wasn't. I had spent day and night there, from the birth of the Irish Centre Building Fund, 20 years before and I had certainly neglected my family.

A year or so before I left, I resolved that I would take one day a week off. It would be Monday, but I invariably agreed to see someone on Monday (for a few minutes) to discuss some very important subject.

So I decided that as my last attempt to cut my hours and see something of my wife and four children, had failed, I had no option but to leave. To resign.

There's never a right time, but it was as good a time as

Sister Rose Cashman from
Cork was the social worker
from 1976 to 1980.

any. The Irish Centre was in really good shape. The dream
had come true. A couple of years before, I had arranged
with Tony O'Neill who was a decorator by trade and who
loved the Irish Centre, that he would work five days a week
for his boss, and work every Saturday in the Centre. He
took a room at a time and transformed them. All the small
rooms and passageways, the foyer, the two lounges, the All
Ireland Bar, and the Claddagh Room, and, believe it or not,
the ballroom. Yes, on his own! The place was looking
beautiful, the furniture was all good. We had a surplus of
almost £11,000 assets over liabilities. There was enough in
the current account to pay all our regular accounts. The
business on paper, was unrecognisable from 15 years before.
I was very proud of what had been achieved. 1,000 people
were attending the ballroom every weekend. 500 on
Fridays, 350 on Saturdays and 150 on Sundays. My target
was to make £10,000 per year on 'non-bar' business. The
bar was taking a lot of money and consistently making a
40% gross profit.

On May 31st that year, 1981, the Sliabh gCua Set
Dancers were over from Dungarvan. They are still coming
over on a regular basis and 100 of them were here in
Liverpool in 2008.

Sister Rose Cashman who had been our social worker
for several years, left us when she was transferred by the
Irish Sisters of Charity to Hammersmith. By coincidence,
she and I left the Centre on the same day. On Sunday,
September 14th, Fr. Seán O'Connor who was home on
leave from Ecuador, was presented with £2,000 for his
work on the missions. The money had been raised by the
members of the Centre. The sad news was that Fr. Oliver
Brady died. He had been involved in the Centre since it
opened and had served as Treasurer. The Chairperson,
Sadie Redmond, represented the Centre at his funeral in

Mullahoran, Co. Cavan. In February 1981, many of the most popular artistes ever to appear in the Centre, appeared. Leo McCaffrey was always extremely popular. On the occasion he brought young singers, dancers and musicians from Moneyglass, Co. Antrim. Dermot O'Brien was there. He had been a childhood friend of Chris Johnston's and they had played for St. Mary's Gaelic Football Club in Ardee, Co. Louth together. They always got together for a chat when Dermot was over. Johnny McEvoy was there. Perhaps the nicest man in show business. I liked him. He liked the Liverpool venue. He liked to send the band home after a tour and appear on his own, with guitar in a concert setting. He sang songs he couldn't sing at dances. Brendan Shine and Dermot Hegarty were also there.

In 1982, I was elected onto the Executive Committee so was again involved in the Centre. In 1983 the speakers at the Annual Dinner were Bishop E. Daly of Derry and Peter Barry, the Minister of External Affairs. These were two quite exceptional speakers. Bishop 'Ned' Daly was a very popular and prominent figure because of his difficult role in Derry and, in particular, because of his high profile on Bloody Sunday in Derry.

The Irish Centre Youth Section won the North West heat of the Federation of Irish Societies' *It's A Knockout* and went on to the national final in Leeds. It's interesting to see the names of the youth team and realise how many are still actively involved in our affairs. It is, I believe, the secret of our success as a Community. The family structure is what we are built on. The team: Maíre McNamara (captain), Tricia McNamara, Eileen Kirwan, Marie Loughran, Norah Quinlan, Marian Fletcher, Michael and John Coyne, Tony Quinlan, Michael Rynne, Peter Dickinson and Paul Loughran. The Team Manager was Betty Kirwan. Sadly, we

Teresa Kelly, who was office manager in the Irish centre, with Seamus from Tyrone.

didn't win the final in Leeds. Seán McNamara was the Chairman of the Centre at this time.

1984 was a big year. Bridie Ryan retired after 16 years as Shop Manager. Teresa Kelly took over as Shop Manager. Teresa had served as Manager's secretary before that. Indeed she had been appointed to that position by myself, and had been a great employee. The annual Mass of St. Patrick in 1987 was celebrated on Sunday 15th March at 11am and then at 3pm, the Irish Centre Dancing Class presented a concert starring Seán O'Sé.

When AN TOSTAL was introduced in Ireland in Drumshambo, County Leitrim, the Irish Community in Liverpool also decided to run the festival every year. An Tostal is now being held in St. Michael's Irish Centre each year, keeping up a tradition.

The 90s started happily as 1990 itself was our Silver Jubilee year. A very full programme of events was arranged and an attractive brochure was produced outlining the achievements of the previous 25 years.

I was invited to be Chairman of the Silver Jubilee Committee, Mary McAndrew (of Comhaltas Ceoltoiri Eireann) was Secretary. The Chairman of the Irish Centre at the time was Seán McNamara. Seán had been a leading member of the Centre since it opened, as well as a member of the famous Liverpool Ceili Band. Every aspect of Irish Community life in the Centre was represented on the Silver Jubilee Committee.

The Brochure contained not only the story of the Irish Centre itself but also articles on the formal opening on 1st February 1965 (by Canon Michael O'Connor); the part played by the Centre when the Cathedral of Christ the King opened in 1967 (by Sadie Redmond); Community Care in the Centre (by Joe England); In the Beginning (by Harry McHugh) and the Irish Centre Today (by Phil Farrelly).

Many personalities of the Centre were highlighted and references were made to people who had played a big part in the Centre. Sean Murphy, Seamus Wynne, Nick Redmond, Phil Farrelly and myself of the staff. People who had returned to Ireland like Breda and Mena Duffy, Sarah (Spud) Murphy, Mary O'Toole, Anne Muckian, Finbarr O Muiri, Lanna and John McNamara who had run Irish Language classes before going to live in Donegal. Others who had already died by then were: Martin Foley, Paddy Dunne, Michael Redmond, Steve Kelly and Michael Murray.

People who had played a role in the foyer and who had been 'the face of the Irish Centre' were Denis Gollock (who was famous as a step dancer), Maureen Murray, Peggy Heffernan, Chris Johnston, Peter McPadden, Frank Fox, Jimmy Dever, Colum Walsh and Jim Lynch. Other staff members referred to in the brochure were Sean Dunne, Chrissie Murphy, Pat Dunne, Kathleen Murphy, Pat Murphy, Peggy Murphy and May Dunne.

In the shop, Croc an Oir, Bridie Ryan served for many years, as did Teresa Kelly, Teresa Ryan and Sue Danham (who were the McQuaid sisters of the Shannon Star Band) and Eileen Kelly. Others who served in the Bar were Vincent Murphy, his sister Mary Mullen, Phyllis Crossan, Mary Quinlan and many, many more. Later, Phyllis Crossan transferred to the shop.

A feature of the Irish Centre Bar was the many, many students, usually of Irish Centre families, who worked in the Centre while they were studying, and who went on to become prominent in their various professions.

The Silver Jubilee also listed those who served as Chairperson since the Centre opened. They were myself, Tommy Walsh, Harry McHugh, Jim Butler, Chris Johnston,

Joe England, Sadie Redmond and Seán McNamara. Tom Redmond was to serve as Chairman after the Silver Jubilee.

The Silver Jubilee Brochure has a lot more information about the Centre and there is a copy in the Heritage Room in St. Michael's Irish Centre.

There was great confidence among staff and members. The *Daily Post* headline read, 'Facelift Creates Irish Centre of Excellence'. News that Mary Robinson, President of Ireland, would visit us in December put a spring in everybody's step.

On Sunday, 4 October 1991, Fr. Kevin McNamara MSC said Mass in the Centre. The intention was 'to pray together at a time of uncertainty'. The gifts at the offertory represented the years since the Centre opened.

1. The Charter, signed by Frank Aiken, Minister of External Affairs on Lá le Bhrigid, 1st February 1965, was carried by Harry McHugh.
2. The Irish Post Community Award presented to the Centre in 1977, 'to the Irish Centre for the excellence of everything it does.' 'There is a style, even an elegance about how things are done there.' This was carried by Joe England.
3. The Distinguished Visitors Book, signed by An Taoiseach Jack Lynch, Cardinals Conway and O'Fiaich, most Ministers of the Irish Government, Irish Bishops, Ard Comhairle GAA in Centenary Year 1984 and many, many more. Carried by Sadie Redmond.
4. *The Book of Kells*, presented to the Irish Centre by Uachtarain Mary Robinson. She said it was, 'a tribute to all those Irish people who made their homes in Liverpool since 1847'. Carried by John Coyne. Sadly, the *Book of Kells* was lost in the turmoil of losing the premises some years later. The CHARTER signed by

134

Frank Aiken was stolen from the foyer. John Mitchels GFC presented a replacement.

It is true to say that the Centre was running at a loss for some years before it closed. On 31st August 1991, the audited accounts show that there was a deficit of £32,742. Wisely or otherwise, it was agreed at an Extraordinary General Meeting on 17th April 1991, 'that we borrow up to £250,000 repayable at the best available terms to carry out a major programme of repair and refurbishment to the premises of 127 Mount Pleasant'.

The borrowed money, and more, was spent on bringing the premises up to an acceptable standard. The premises had deteriorated to a level which was not acceptable. At the beginning of 1991, John Coyne was appointed Services Manager. He prepared a Development Plan which was accepted and put into practice.

Bob Parry M.P. was a great friend of the Irish Community in Liverpool. He was always ready to help an Irish Community cause. His wife Marie was also popular with the Irish Community as she worked for years in the legendary '98 Shop in Scotland Place.

The building was transformed. The bar was re-named the John F. Kennedy Bar, the Claddagh Room became the Claddagh Restaurant, Croc an Oir remained, and had a travel shop added. I was invited back as Croc an Oir manager and enjoyed the experience. Teresa Duffy came from Manchester to run the Travel Shop.

The nature of the business was changed. On Sunday 8th September, 1991, the Centre re-opened. It was a spectacular night. Entertainment was provided by The Indians and Dermot Hegarty. The Ballroom was very different with a raised floor at the rear.

Apart from the usual evening opening, there was a lunchtime opening. The lunch facility in the Claddagh Restaurant was hugely popular, with a number of barristers coming up from the Law Courts. Some of them were our own former Irish Dancers!

In November 1991, Tom O'Connor came back to the

Deidre Doran represented the Irish Centre as the Liverpool Rose at the Rose of Tralee Festival. She later married Pat McAndrew of Mayo who she met in the Centre. Deidre is a sister of Pat Doran who, with his wife, Eileen, is a benefactor of all things Irish in Liverpool.

Centre to make an LP record entitled *Live at the Irish Centre in Liverpool*. Tom had decided to come back to the Centre where he had started his stage career, where he and his friend, Brendan O'Sullivan, sang every Sunday evening as Tom and Brennie. They were paid £8 weekly. Tom and Brennie, as they were in 1965, can be seen on stage with our dancers and other artistes in the Heritage Room in St. Michael's Centre.

In 1992, Paddy Reilly – who famously recorded *Fields of Athenry* – appeared at the Centre. A plaque to the memory of 'Big Jim Larkin' was unveiled by Bob Parry MP and was on display in the Centre before being transferred to Combermere Street where he was born.

The 1991 Annual General Meeting was held on 24th November and we were informed that the Centre had made a loss for the third year in succession. After a long and frank discussion, it was decided to set up a Finance Committee which would be 'given all necessary powers to bring the Irish Centre back to profitability'. The Finance Committee would consist of Tom Redmond (a committee member), two of the Trustees (Harry McHugh and myself), and Seán McNamara (the Chairman).

The Chairman thanked all Committee members and staff, and many members for their loyalty and hard work in their efforts to correct the situation. I wrote to the Committee at the time to pay tribute to John Coyne and referred to the superhuman effort he put in, day and night, to put things right.

I also referred to the damage being done by a small group of 'prominent members' who were endangering the Centre by their malicious gossip. I was afraid they were so anxious to be proved right in their forecasts of doom that they actually wanted the Centre to close.

The re-opening of the Centre in September 1991 was, in

itself, successful. Business had increased dramatically. As is often the case in building projects, spending had exceeded the £250,000 borrowed from the bank. When the opportunity of another job for myself arose, I took it and removed myself from the payroll. I assured John Coyne, that on a voluntary basis, I would continue to keep an eye on stock control and ordering. I had enjoyed my brief return to the staff in the Centre and recognised many of my customers as the children of the people involved in the early days of the Centre. The wheel keeps turning and the young people active in St. Michael's Irish Centre are grandchildren and great-grandchildren of the great people who were involved in Mount Pleasant.

On the 4th July, 1992, the dreaded news went around Liverpool and beyond. Allied Irish Bank had appointed Cork Gully as Receivers. There were two unfortunate coincidences: the Receiver was T. Walsh (he was Tim) and the Company had Cork in the name.

Why the Centre closed is a matter of opinion and everyone who saw it happen will have their own view of what happened and why.

In a letter dated 17th August, The Receiver informed us that all interested parties should submit offers during the week ending 28 August 1992.

A Rescue Committee was appointed by the Irish Centre. Its aim was simple: Save the Irish Centre. The Chairman of the Committee was Ben Willoughby. He had been a member of the Centre since his coming to Liverpool as a very young employee of Aer Lingus. Councillor Joe Devaney of Liverpool City Council. His wife, Eileen, was daughter of Michael Masterton, a well-known member of the Irish Community. Pat Jordan of Bank of Ireland and Anne McGowan. They worked hard raising money to boost the Rescue Fund.

The Centre continued to trade, being managed by the Receiver. We were aware of an initial offer made on behalf of the Irish Community of £250,000. Then we were informed that an offer of £295,000 had been made. A member of the Irish Community made an amount available to the Community which we believed should have been enough to secure a deal. We still believed, after the business was concluded, that the Community offer was the highest.

Our solicitor received a letter from the Receivers' Chartered Surveyor dated 14th September saying, "Subject to the best offers that we receive being over £300,000, we propose to accept the highest offer and send out a contract to that party as soon as possible".

As everyone knows, for good or ill, the Irish Community was not the bidder the Receiver and the principal creditor wanted to do business with.

Although the Irish Community bid for the Centre was believed to be the highest, a bid by a city centre publican was accepted. Michael Finnegan's offer had been accepted by Allied Irish Bank and Cork Gully. Of course, there were very different opinions among members of the Irish Community when Mr. Finnegan announced that he was going to call his premises The Irish Centre, and he invited community groups to operate from there. There were many people who were happy to do so. I fully understood that, but I, personally, was not happy about it. Most of the activity groups continued to run their activities from 127 Mount Pleasant.

According to the Constitution of the Irish Centre, it now became necessary 'to dissolve'. Rule 32 of the Irish Centre 1964/1992 outlined how the organisation should dissolve should it become necessary. Tim Walsh of the Cork Gully Company told us that our legal position was as 'a society without premises'. A meeting of the groups using the Centre was addressed by the new owner. He said he had a

138

Constitution 'virtually identical to your own'.

In accordance with Rule 32, the Executive Committee summoned a meeting 'to dissolve' on 26 January 1993. In a remarkable turn of events, we were informed that the new owner had not yet succeeded in obtaining a licence. His solicitor asked that we should not decide 'to dissolve'. As you might expect, the meeting was divided. Reasons for dissolving and not dissolving were presented. The case for dissolving was simple. We no longer exist in our previous format. The Receiver made that quite clear. We have no choice.

The case for not dissolving was equally clear. Since August 1992, about five months, the Irish Centre had operated in Receivership. All of our Irish Community Groups have operated ever since. The Groups were appreciative of the facilities provided thus far and were fearful of what would happen if we dissolved, and 127 Mount Pleasant closed as a result. One person said he didn't care who owned it so long as he could buy a pint.

It seemed to me we were now in the land of make believe. The Licensing Justices had decided they would only give a Licence to 127 Mount Pleasant if it were retained as an Irish Centre. AIB/Cork Gully decided not to do business with the only group representing the Irish Community.

The meeting decided, in its wisdom, not to dissolve. We must now all pretend that the Irish Community runs 127 Mount Pleasant. For how long? What if the new owner doesn't get a licence? Do we, having ceased to exist, continue to pretend that we do exist? For how long?

That is, of course, a very personal view. I am convinced that the Irish Community in Liverpool was heading for Mount Pleasant for over 100 years. Securing it, was the realisation of a dream. Personally, I will never come to terms with the loss.

We must assume that Michael Finnegan did eventually

obtain a licence. I'm not aware of the comings and goings at 127 Mount Pleasant after the period I have outlined. To me, it wasn't run by the Irish Community any more and I wasn't involved. Nor was I a regular attender. I do know, and I greatly appreciate, that some Irish activities continued to be accommodated there.

Michael Finnegan remained owner for approximately two years before going into Receivership. After he went into Receivership, according to a newspaper report, the premises were bought by a London businessman named William Demetriou. Without ever occupying it, he sold it on to the Irish Centre Cultural Society Co-operative Ltd.

Another newspaper report said that Les Ross of Receiver Grant Ross said, "Contracts for the sale of Liverpool Irish Centre were exchanged on Friday 17th March 1995. To the best of my knowledge, the premises will continue to be run as an Irish Centre."

I can't give any first hand opinion about the co-operative as I only attended on one occasion apart from my visits to Irish Community Care Merseyside, which continued to rent rooms there. On the occasion of my only visit I was invited to a 'Groups Meeting' as a delegate of the John Mitchels GAA Club. As soon as I stood to talk, I was asked was I a member of 'the Irish Centre'. I said I was not, I was an invited delegate of the GAA Club. I was told I was not entitled to be present and I was asked to leave which, of course, I did. My fellow delegates from the GAA Club also left.

I must say, I was disappointed that some members of the 'real Irish Community' remained on at the meeting. Although in my opinion the Wellington Rooms had not been the Irish Centre for some time the premises got a huge amount of publicity as 'the Irish Centre' for the next few years.

In 1997, the Co-operative also went into Receivership and decided to occupy the building by a roof-top protest. I

The Taoiseach and his wife, Mairin, visited the Centre in 1967 on the occasion of the opening of the Cathedral. Here they are with Chairman Harry McHugh (left) and Manager Tommy Walsh (right)

don't know the details but there was a lot of newspaper coverage. I was in the building as a member of Irish Community Care Merseyside when I went in by arrangement with the Receiver to remove some of our property from the office which had been rented from the Co-operative.

I was to pay one more visit when I went in as part of the making of a TV programme about the listed building. I was very sad to see the dreadful state which the building had deteriorated to. Large parts of the ballroom ceiling had collapsed, as had much of the ceiling of the lounge.

The neglect of the roof will have caused a lot more damage in the meantime. I read occasionally that the building has been purchased and will open as a hotel or something similar. I really don't believe that any commercial business will operate from there. The investment in the restoration of the beautiful building would be so great that an investor would not get his/her money back. I have read that a Dance Academy could open there. That would be brilliant! With public money it may be possible.

IRISH COMMUNITY CARE MERSEYSIDE

Irish Centre –
Welfare

Irish Community Care Merseyside

FROM THE VERY OUTSET, in 1965, of the Irish Centre, 'welfare' as we called it then, was an integral part of the Irish Centre. Every Irish group, including the GAA and, indeed, commercial halls like the Shamrock Club, had been involved in welfare automatically. Helping new arrivals from Ireland to find digs and jobs came naturally. A small group of people in the Irish Centre established the Welfare Service shortly after it opened. Joe England who is a leading figure in the Irish Community wrote about it in the Silver Jubilee Brochure in 1990. "The Welfare Service was particularly dear to me as my own introduction to the Irish Centre by Canon Michael O'Connor, had been through the Welfare Committee."

Joe was speaking when the Irish Centre was given an Irish Post Community Award. "As I went to London on that April Day in 1978, I remembered so many of those who had, over the years, given time and energy to help their fellow Irish in Liverpool. Some who came to mind were Maria Duffy, Miss Moylan, Terry Moorhead, Frances Joyce, Paddy Joe McKiernan, Dan Earley, Vin Jackson, Mary Mooney, Winnie Eacope, Joe O'Connor and Anne O'Malley who is now my wife."

Joe England continued: "In 1968, the Welfare Service had been taken over by Sister Jane Frances of the Irish Sisters of Charity, and she was ably assisted by Joe Sullivan and Winnie Eacope. Sister Jane stayed until 1973 when Sister Teresa Harmon took over and she started to move the service out into the Irish Community. 'Home visits' replaced a lot of the office-based work. After three years, Sister Rose Cashman, a native of Cork city, arrived and took over Sister Teresa's good work.

The Irish Post Community Award which I received from His Excellency the Irish Ambassador, Mr. Paul Keating, was a tribute to everyone who contributed to the Irish Centre,

Sister Rose Casman from Cork City with Seamus from Tyrone.

and to the Welfare Service in particular, which had been started by volunteers, and was so ably continued by the Irish Sisters of Charity."

Jim Butler, a former Chairman of the Centre, had been instrumental in getting Sister Jane Frances into the Centre as our first Welfare Officer. Jim had no less than three sisters who were members of the order of the Irish Sisters of Charity. When the Centre was looking for a more professional approach, and when it became obvious that the service was needed during the day rather than at night, Jim approached the Sisters. They had a convent in the Wirral and so we got Sister Jane Frances. For several years, the Sisters were the employees of the Irish Centre.

In 1989, it was considered that the Welfare Section should be independent of the Irish Centre. The Centre had made several attempts to become a Registered Charity but had failed. The major income being from the bar probably didn't help. A Steering Committee was set up and Seán McNamara was chairman while I was Secretary.

In May 1989, we were informed by the Charity Commission that we had become a Registered Charity. Our number was 701796. Our title was Irish Community Care Merseyside. The first Management Meeting was held in the Irish Centre Mount Pleasant on 19 September 1989. I was elected Chairman, Sheilagh Loughran Secretary, and Seán McNamara Treasurer. The Management Committee consisted of:

- Two Representatives of the Irish Centre.
- One Representative of each of the following:
- John Mitchels GFC
- Comhaltas Ceoltoiri Eireann
- Finn Harps FC
- Pioneer Total Abstinence Association
- Irish Centre Dancing Class
- Irish Centre Golf Society
- One Representative of Liverpool Social Services (who should be non-voting).
- One Representative of Catholic Social Services (later Nugent Care Society).

Irish Community Care Merseyside went on to be an extremely well-run organization. It was forced to leave 127 Mount Pleasant when the Centre went into Receivership and was accommodated briefly in Cathedral Buildings before moving to 60 Duke Street, Liverpool.

Its first Community Care lay employees were Breege McDaid amd Mavis O'Connor, both of whom are still employees. Breege is now the Manager of an extremely complex and vibrant organization. Their Annual General Report each year gives details of all of their services. Two of its founders, Seán McNamara and Chris Johnston are still Committee members.

TRIAL BY MEDIA

How police leaks, Press smears and a British Minister convicted the Winchester Three

In November 1988 a woman who had served as a member of the Ulster Defence Regiment in Northern Ireland - the locally recruited section of the British army - was found guilty of handing over information on the movement of military and RUC vehicles to the loyalist UDA, an organisation whose members have in the past been linked with many crimes of violence. She received a six-month jail sentence.

On 2 February 1989 three English police officers and a num[ber] of civilians were tried at Winchester Crown Court, accused [of] tapping the national police computer and obtaining secret information concerning the owners of particular car registration numbers. They were found guilty of conspira[cy] under the Official Secrets Act. Their punishment? Suspen[ded] jail sentences.

In early October 1988 three young Irish people were brou[ght] before the same Winchester court on the basis of a list of [names] and car registration numbers found while they were camp[ing] in the West of England. They were not charged with gath[ering] information or any offence connected with invasion of pri[vacy] they were charged with plotting to kill somebody. And a j[ury] in one of the most controversial trials in recent legal hist[ory] convicted them, without seeing or hearing a shred of substantive evidence that any such conspiracy had ever [existed] and despite the fact that no weapon, bomb or explosive [of any] kind was found. In their case the penalty handed out wa[s a] prison sentence of twenty-five years each.

Finbar Cullen   Martina Shanahan   John M[cCann]

VICTIMS OF INJUSTICE

The Birmingham Six
The Guildford Four
The Maguire Seven

Billy Power was dragged into a darkened room. "The officer who had me by the hair with my head pulled downwards let go and from all sides I was being punched, hit and kicked. I doubled up and slid down the wall... I was dragged up by the hair and again punched systematically".

A voice shouted, "Stretch his balls." Another shouted, "You'll never have sex with your wife again." Power fouled his trousers. Then he signed a statement admitting he had planted one of two IRA pub bombs that killed 21 people in Birmingham, England, on November 21, 1974 ——

... anyone else.

Letters to the Editor
Sunday Press
Burgh Quay
DUBLIN.

Your Editorial of Sunday 30.10.88 "The Winchester verdi[ct]
belive an accurate assessment of the situation in Winche[ster]
Shanahan, Finbar Cullen and John McCann were sentenced [to]

It is true that "there was an air of foreboding and that [it made no]
difference what was said in court, they were going to be [found guilty at that]
time". Without doubt, as you said, "in most other coun[tries the trial would]
have been aborted" when Mr. King made his announcement [which could only be inter]
preted as silence equals guilt.

You were too kind to the Judge however. As you said he [...]
but on the Friday morning he denied that he had criticis[ed ...]
had deserted him.

Having been to Winchester, for part of the jury's delib[erations I agree with]
you entirely that they, the jury, were in a dilemma in [that they were being asked]
to find the three guilty on a lesser charge.

many commentators have agreed with your view that it i[s one of those]
cases which have made Anglo Irish relations even wor[se ...]
Personally I feel it is much more serious than that.

Irish
Prisoners

IFIRST GOT INVOLVED with prisoners around 1969. While I am not in the 'hang 'em and flog 'em brigade', nor do I consider myself to be a 'do-gooder'.

What I can say is that having visited hundreds of prisoners, I don't think I particularly disliked any of them. The circle of people involved in prisoner care was very small at that time, and we tended to know one another.

Nowadays, the Irish Community Care groups in Liverpool and elsewhere, are much more professional and include prisoner care in their client services.

In the years I was most involved, the 1970s, and into the 80s, Irish prisoners were mainly what we called 'politically motivated'.

Authorities, both British and Irish, would not use the term 'political prisoner' as it implied the person was in jail because of their political beliefs, and they wouldn't have that. While I understand that, I am certain that the people I thought of as political prisoners would not have been in prison, were it not for the political situation of the day.

For me, it started when Rita Mullen of the Association for Legal Justice in Belfast started phoning me about people who were detained in the Port of Liverpool. I had been active for some years in the Irish Chaplaincy in Britain and the Irish Commission for Prisoners Overseas (ICPO) was part of that. If there was an Irish person in a police station or prison in the North West of England, the ICPO, which had been set up by the Bishops of Ireland, would ask me to pay the prisoner a visit and report back on their conditions, with messages for ICPO or the family.

When the situation deteriorated in Belfast, and people were being burned out of their homes, the Association for Legal Justice was at the heart of affairs.

Internment without trial and the application of repressive legislation such as the Special Powers Act and the Prevention of Terrorism Act dramatically increased the number of people being detained and imprisoned.

In the early days of 'the troubles' and when the Prevention of Terrorism Act was imposed after the 'Birmingham Bombs', many, many Irish people were detained. As Liverpool was where the Belfast and Dublin boats stopped, more people were detained here, under the PTA than anywhere else.

This made Liverpool a very busy place with regard to Irish prisoners and detainees. Under the PTA, Special Branch police could detain people and were not obliged to confirm they were holding them.

Rita Mullen in Belfast would contact me on behalf of a Belfast family looking for a son or daughter who had sailed on the Liverpool boat and had not arrived at their destination. Phoning the police at Cheapside was no use. The police on duty didn't know the names of anyone detained under the PTA, nor even if anyone was detained. The Special Branch officers would neither confirm nor deny they were holding anyone. The first I usually knew was when I was told 'he/she has been served with an Exclusion Order'. The person then was placed on the Belfast boat to be returned. They could not re-enter England as long as the Exclusion Order was in place.

I must say my relationship with the police was usually very good. Just as I understood they had a job to do, they understood my role. Most of the police believed they were dealing with 'terrorism' and the end justified the means.

I was never aware of any detainee being physically ill-treated while in Liverpool. One prisoner made very public accusations but, frankly, I didn't believe her. The vast majority of those detained were never charged with an offence, let alone found guilty.

Cardinal Tomás O Fiaich took a personal interest in the welfare of Irish prisoners in Britain and we spent many hours on the phone discussing particular prisoners and their families. Father Gerry McFlynn became the ICPO chaplain in Britain and served for many years.

Sister Catherine Fitzgerald, who was a native of Kerry, served in Liverpool for many years and became involved in the welfare of prisoners. When she retired , she went to Dublin and worked full-time for ICPO there for a number of years before she died. Nuala Kelly was the full-time Administrator of ICPO in Dublin for much of the time of my involvement. She inspired me and many others and was a truly great woman while she was there, and no doubt since!

How it happens, we're never really sure but once you're involved, you tend to stay involved, and we formed a group always in touch, but working alone. I was the only person in Liverpool filling my role and most of my colleagues were the same. The big campaigns like the Birmingham 6, Guildford 4, Winchester 3, are much publicised and bring on board large numbers of people who are, rightly, horrified by the thought of innocent people being locked up for long terms.

When these cases are concluded, many people have no further interest in the subject of prisoners. My own view is that if it really matters whether a person is guilty or not, you shouldn't get involved.

Perhaps the most dreadful case I experienced was that of Annie Maguire and family. The only apparent reason for their imprisonment was that they were related to one of the Guildford Four who, himself, was eventually released as an innocent man.

One of the people I visited became a very dear friend, as did her family, and I spent a very happy day at her wedding recently, and met a number of old friends that day.

Tommy Walsh, one of the best known Irish personalities in Britain. As P.R.O. of the Federation of Irish Societies, he has done outstanding work for his fellow exiles. In this picture, taken at a meeting of the Federation, his sister is seated beside him. She is Mrs. Sadie Redmond of Liverpool who has been hon. treasurer for years.

Federation of Irish Societies

W E WERE ONLY OPEN in the Irish Centre for a few years when we felt we should look further afield. The objective of the Irish Centre in Mount Pleasant was to provide opportunities for Irish people to retain their unique identity and to promote sales of Irish goods and Irish tourism, to enable young Irish people to stay at home.

So we thought why stop in Liverpool. Many Irish communities in Britain were very insular. Only a very small proportion of Irish people are inclined to look beyond their own community. Perhaps my own involvement with the GAA at a national level and Harry McHugh's role in the Anti-Partition of Ireland League pushed us to look beyond Liverpool.

We contacted other Irish Centres in Leeds and Manchester and formed the Federation of Irish Societies Northern Region. The Southern Region had been up and running for some years. Portsmouth was at the heart of the Southern Region; they were primarily a social organization. Each affiliated Centre ran an Annual Dinner or Ball, and they all supported one another. We, in the North, were more interested in promoting Irish tourism and discussing problems common to Irish people in the various locations. Dennis O'Connell, the manager of the Irish Tourist Board in the North of England, was the Secretary. Our own Harry McHugh was Chairman, Mick Rooney of Leeds was the Vice-Chairman.

Contacts had been made with the Southern Federation and a National Meeting at which the two Regions would merge was arranged to be held in the Irish Centre, Camden Square, London.

The last meeting of the Northern Federation was held in Rugby on 31st March 1973. Represented were: Birmingham, Corby, Edinburgh, Liverpool, Leamington, Leeds, Northhampton, Rugby, Peterborough and Leicester.

Tom's involvement to the Federation of Irish Societies was of tremendous importance to the Irish Community in Britain.

At the first joint North/South meeting, I was elected to be the first National Chairman. I think this was probably a surprise as the other three nominees were better known in the South of England. Bill Halley of Portsmouth was elected Secretary. Bill – together with Jack Griffin and Bill Kirby – were the founders of the Portsmouth Irish Club, one of the first in the country and of the Federation Southern Region. Kevin Cahill of Rugby Irish Club was elected Vice-Chairman. Sadie Redmond, Liverpool, was elected Treasurer. It was remarkable that two of the first national officers were not only from the same Centre, but from the same family (Sadie and I are brother and sister).

There were also a President and Vice-President in those days. These positions had been observed in the old Southern Federation and were retained for 10 years. They were discontinued from 1983. The President used a chain of office; I never made any secret of the fact that I did not like the chain of office.

Michael Hogan of Watford followed me as Chairman and retained the post for seven years. Seamus McGarry followed, then Gearoid Ó'Mearchair followed by Seamus McCormack. Seamus was from Mayo and returned home shortly after. By coincidence, I know both of his brothers quite separately. John McCormack came to Liverpool as a young man. He was at a Seminary training to be a missionary priest and came to the Irish Centre in Liverpool several summers and worked in the bar: I attended his ordination in Newry. Another brother, Pat McCormack, lives in Manchester and I got to know all three brothers all separately. I have had the pleasure of meeting Seamus and John on visits to Mayo in recent years, while I meet Pat, usually at funerals.

Mary Tilki has been Chairperson of the Federation in recent years, while Eithne Rynne was Chief Executive until she resigned in 2008. Ann Gould has been an administrator for a number of years. Perhaps the most significant achievement of the Federation was to secure annual grants from the Irish Government for the Community Care units of

Federation affiliates.

The Federation succeeded in getting the first grant in 1979.The grant was shared out among the various Irish Community Care Units. Taoiseach Charles J Haughey was very generous and doubled the grant while he was in office. The Department of Labour administered the fund for several years and the then Minister of Labour, Bertie Ahern, became a very familiar figure to the Irish Community in Britain. The other Irish political figure who showed great interest in, and concern for us, was Peter Barry while Minister for External Affairs. In recent years, after an Irish Government Task Force report, DION grants were extended to Irish Cultural and Community Groups and our Irish Centre at St. Michael's in Liverpool has benefited greatly.

As part of the 2008 Capital of Culture programme, the Federation of Irish Societies had their Annual Congress in Liverpool in the Liverpool Echo Arena. One of the projects the Federation involved itself in was: Getting an 'Irish' box in the Census form.

Fr. Paddy Sheridan and Fr. Frank Ryan (both OMI priests) and myself took the *Daily Express* to the Press Council and won. The *Express* had carried a report (by Michael O'Flaherty) alleging that Irish men and women were operating a racket in which tax-payers' money was helping the Provisional IRA, 'through a multi-million pound social security scandal'. We protested and got a lot of support from Bob Parry M.P. and others in the House of Commons. Eventually, the Press Council adjudication was in our favour. The Press Council said, "the *Daily Express* should have published the denial. The complaint is upheld".

One of the subjects which caused much difference of opinion was the question of 'politics'. According to the Constitution, the F.I.S. was 'non-sectarian and non-political'. My term as Chairman coincided with the most 'political' period. I had absolutely no doubt that 'non-political' meant that a person should not be barred regardless of his or her politics.

Some Member Societies were afraid that the Chair (me) 'might move away from the position, long held, of not involving itself in any matter which borders politics'. The 'long held' position referred to the Southern Federation, before the two regions merged.

The Federation had grown from strength to strength .

There have been people who have served faithfully and remained on 'the floor' without ever standing for office. There have been others who have served briefly as officers and then disappeared.

Bill Aulsberry has represented Haringey for most of the Federation's life. He had made a contribution to just about every discussion and decision. His contribution to the Federation is priceless. He has the gift of not giving way and standing his ground, yet raising a laugh. Jim Waters, who sadly died before his time, was the manager of the South London (Wimbledon) Irish Centre and was an active member of F.I.S. One of the nicest people I met in the F.I.S., Jim Moss from County Meath, was known to me as a Herts GAA man before he became Treasurer of the F.I.S.

Sister Joan Kane was a very active Community Care representative for a number of years.

Ros Scanlon was the Cultural representative and represented the Hammersmith Irish Centre. Ros is a person I still like to see when we meet at events occasionally.

Sally Mulready and I had much in common as she was involved in the campaign for the Birmingham Six. She now devotes her time to caring for the elderly.

Seamus McGarry has been the most prominent Federation member for a very long time. Like myself, he started out as a GAA man. Tipperary, London and, eventually, Hertfordshire. Seamus and his wife Annette became good friends and I have stayed in their home in Stevenage. He served as a very efficient Chair and persuaded me to return to the Federation as Secretary long after I had been Chair and P.R.O. He has served the Irish Government well as a member of DION for a number of years.

Michael Forde was Vice Chair of the Federation for several years. He would surely have been elected Chair had he allowed his name to go forward. Michael has dedicated himself to the Manchester Irish Centre for many years, as a very active Chair.

The Oblate Fathers have played a major role in the affairs of the Federation because of their association with the Irish Centres in Camden and Birmingham. Fathers Paddy Mee, Paddy Sheridan, Paul Byrne and Joe Taafe became very close friends. I consider it an honour to have worked with them.

I met Fathers Paddy Sheridan and Paul Byrne on a recent visit to Mayo. We covered a lot of ground!

Others were Fathers Frank Ryan and Butler who raised huge amounts of money by sponsored cycle rides in Ireland.

Father Bobby Gilmore, a Columban father, played a huge part in the Irish Community in London. I had the pleasure of meeting him recently when I visited my dear old friend Father Owen O'Leary in Dalgan Park, County Meath.

Owen O'Neill and I became very good friends when he was Vice-Chairman of the Federation while he represented the London Irish Community. He then went on to Gloucester and became a very dynamic Chairman. His was yet another funeral I attended, when he died too soon.

Mark Kelly was the first full time member of staff to serve the Federation. I was Secretary at the time so we were in regular contact. He was a young man full of vitality and humour. We were all shocked when he died suddenly at a very young age.

Cumann Luthchleas Gael

The GAA
Gaelic Athletic Association

THE GAA has always played a big part in the lives of Irish people in Liverpool, and all over the world. It is not merely a sports organisation involving young people, and is far more than a game of football or hurling. It was founded in Ireland at the end of the nineteenth century, in 1884 to combat the games of the British Garrison which were being imposed on the people. These games were rugby, hockey, cricket and soccer. It was the policy of the British Empire to include games in the indoctrination of the people wherever they were in the world. They were particularly successful with cricket in India.

The GAA was founded by a group of people who were anxious to retain an 'Irish Ireland' way of life. Membership of the GAA indicated a national outlook. This was probably most obvious in the six counties (Derry, Antrim, Armagh, Fermanagh, Down and Tyrone) after the partition of Ireland. Membership of the GAA was a statement of identity. The organisation became established in every parish in Ireland, so it follows that Irish people who came to Liverpool, or to anywhere else in the world, were well aware of it and frequently wanted to maintain their membership of it.

In fact, hurling is not played equally in every part of Ireland, whereas Gaelic Football is. So, it follows that it is much more likely that Irish communities around the world will field more Gaelic Football teams than hurling teams. Although at times in the past, hurling was much stronger in Liverpool than football, in more recent years, the GAA team plays only football.

The Gaelic Football team is the John Mitchels Gaelic Football Club. It is affiliated to the Lancashire County Board and plays its club competitions there. If it wins the Lancashire Championship, which it has done for the past two years, it goes into the All-Britain Championship. If it wins the All-Britain Championship which, it has done for the past

Some of the outstanding men in the history of Liverpool GAA are here. Two of the founders of the Provincial Council of Britain are on the front row, Jim Ryan on the left and Seán McInerney on the right. The great Father Paddy Spain who was very recently ordained, is centre having been captain of the Lancashire team which won the Provincial Championship of Britain and the O'Connor Cup which was played for annually by London and Lancashire (1940). With Gerry Mulholland and P. O'Neill behind.

The Liverpool Eire Og Hurling Team. The earliest team of the present John Mitchels Club which became St. Patrick's in 1940 and John Mitchels in 1949.

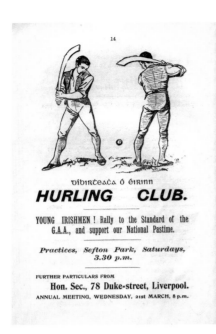

An early advertising programme for hurling practices in Sefton Park every Saturday.

The earliest evidence of GAA activity in Liverpool. A hurling medal dated 1902, and awarded to C. Segrue.

two years, it goes into the All-Ireland Junior Championship. (Junior in Ireland is not age related, it is, in simple terms, second best. Top clubs play in the Senior Championship.)

In 2008/2009, having won in Britain, they went on to beat the Leinster champions, Moynalvey in Navan and the Connacht champions, Killala in Carrick on Shannon. In the All-Ireland Championship Final, they lost by a single point to Skellig of Kerry. 0-10 to 0-9

Although the GAA was founded in 1884, Gaelic games were no doubt played in Ireland and in England and abroad much earlier. The organisation's task was to administer the games, not to invent them.

Seán McInerney was one of the pillars of the GAA in Liverpool, his father being from Clare. In a written article he said: 'older gaels remember games being played in Greenwich Park in Aintree in 1906'. As far as I can ascertain, Greenwich Park was in the Melling Road area and was most likely where the racecourse is now. The first hurling match recorded was, in fact, in 1901, In 1906, both hurling and camogie (ladies) were played. Liverpool Young Ireland's defeated Manchester Martyrs. About 300 spectators, including Special Branch, were in attendance.

The Liverpool Hurling team of the time is the forerunner of the present team which plays only Gaelic Football. At some stage, Young Irelands changed to the Irish language of the name Eire Óg, probably as a result of the influence of the Gaelic league. The Club changed its name to St. Patrick's in 1940.

In 1924, a new GAA ground was in use at Dingle Brook

Farm in West Derby, where Gaelic Football was being played as well as hurling and camogie. Although there are no written records of games before then, it is likely that some of the people who came over at the time of the potato famine would have played games after they settled down. We know that the Fenian movement was strong in Liverpool, from the Fenian memorial in Ford Cemetery, and it is very likely they would have played their games there.

On August 4th, 1912, Liverpool lost to Kilkenny in the All-Ireland Senior Hurling Championship Semi-Final. The score was Kilkenny 4-3 Liverpool 1-3. The venue is not recorded except that it was in Liverpool.

The Provincial Council of Britain was founded in 1926 and at first only Liverpool and London County Boards were affiliated. London and Liverpool played hurling and football matches annually, for the P.J. O'Connor Cup and the Sam Maguire Cup respectively.

P.J. O'Connor of Liverpool donated the hurling cup which Liverpool won quite frequently, and Sam Maguire, a member of the London GAA, presented the football cup which was usually won by London. Sam Maguire also presented the cup for the All-Ireland Senior Football Championship. These annual games were played long before the Provincial Council was founded.

I have a Minute Book covering the 1926/27 period and from that I can include some of the personalities and teams of the time. Of course, no one is alive who can help.

In 1926, Father Park was the Chairman of the Liverpool County Board. This was before the Lancashire County Board was formed. Fr. Park secured a new agreement for the use of Thingwall Hall in Broadgreen. This was usually known as St. Edward's Orphanage. The rent was to be £40 a year. Fr. Park said if there was any fighting, we would lose the field. Mr. Blackhurst said if there was any more crossing of the

LANCASHIRE IRISH HURLING TEAM · CROKE PARK 1929

The Lancashire Hurling Team which played in Croke Park in 1929. I can only identify four of the men. Seán McInerney is second right on the back row. Michael Redmond, Sim Donoghue and Jim Ryan are third, fifth and sixth from the left in the centre row. Michael Redmond is Kathleen Cunningham's grandfather and Jim Ryan is the Rabbette family's grandfather.

railway line, he would lose his farm.

There were two railway lines at the time: one which now runs parallel with the M62 motorway and one which ran near the gate of Thingwall Hall and under the road near the gate of Broadgreen Hospital. I'm assuming that Mr. Blackhurst had his farm there at the time, probably near what is now Broadgreen Station.

Also in 1926, the Ancient Order of Hibernians affiliated to the County Board and fielded a team for games.

On 12th July, 1927, Seán McInerney proposed that the Baseball Park in Lower Breck Road should be hired for the match against London to be played on August Monday. It was agreed 10,000 handbills were to be printed, and Fr. Park promised to talk to Mr. Priestley to arrange posters in tramcars.

About the same time, the Irish National Foresters asked for particulars about affiliating a team.

Fr. Park said he would like the GAA to give £10 towards the proposed new cathedral on the site of the old workhouse

160

(this would have been for the Cathedral which was not built because of World War II).

Brother Hilarian of Sutton Monastery, St. Helens, asked for an exhibition hurling match between Liverpool and Manchester on 17th July. It was agreed and they were told if they wanted a football match as well, Liverpool would play Earlestown.

In 1927, Fr. Park was re-elected as Chairman and two men who were to give many years of service at every level, Club, County and Province, were also elected. Seán McInerney as Treasurer and Jim Ryan as Secretary.

Among the teams fulfilling fixtures in the 1926/27 season were: Granuaile who were based in Southport and were usually referred to as 'Southport'.

Eire Og were the Club based in Liverpool, whose successors, John Mitchels GFC are still the Club representing Liverpool. They have always provided players for Lancashire teams and officers for the County Board. As I have been a member since 1947, I, naturally, have a strong feeling for the club.

An interesting fact about Eire Og / St. Patrick's / John Mitchels is that only two men born outside Ireland have ever been President of the GAA in Britain. They were both members of the same club, they were Seán McInerney and myself.

Other clubs in 1926/27 were Exiles, Gaels, Thomas Ashe, and Terence McSwineys. Camogie teams were Kathleen ní Houlihans who represented the Gaelic League and St. Brigid's of Manchester. A football team from Earlestown and listed as Earlestown GFC also affiliated. The County Board Secretary's Report say five Hurling, two Football and two Camogie teams affiliated.

On February 10th 1928, the Annual Convention was called off due to the death of the Patron Archbishop Keating of Liverpool. Other names appearing as Club delegates were Bernard O'Rourke, Sim Donoghue, Harry Gilligan, John McDonald, Sean Crowley of Exiles and Messrs Eade and McBride of Thomas Ashe.

At the Convention, the Treasurer Mr. Kirwan said we would supply boys with hurleys. (Mr. Dunleavy of St. Anthony's was teaching hurling to his boys.)

Meeting venues were given as St. Martin's Hall and the address on the Minute Book as 65 Derby Lane. This was the home address of Michael Redmond of Eire Og. It was the address where I was to meet my wife Kathleen Redmond who was his daughter. My sister, Sadie, who played camogie for the club married Tom Redmond of the same address.

In 1927, a 'stop watch competition' was held to raise money. The minutes read, 'The Stop Watch stopped at one hour 18 minutes, nine seconds. The winner was M. Larkin 68, Watford Road, Anfield'.

When Central Council in Dublin set up the Provincial Council of Britain, and Liverpool and London were the two member counties, Central Council said they couldn't give them any money to start up, but they would send two top county teams over to play Exhibition Games at Whit weekend and Liverpool and London could keep the gate.

At a meeting on 16th April, 1928, it was agreed that Liverpool should accept the offer. After ascertaining that the pitch at Broadgreen could be closed in so that every person entering on the day could be charged admission it was agreed that the game should be played there. However, a meeting on 25th May, heard a letter from Waterloo Football Ground, confirming that the game would be played there. The game was played there on May 26th, 1928.

Faughs Hurling Club of Dublin played the Liverpool County team in Liverpool at Easter 1927. Admission charge was 6d and it was recorded that Faughs would play Liverpool

on Easter Sunday and Manchester on Easter Monday.

In 1932, an All-Britain team consisting of Liverpool and London players took part in the Tailteann Games and drew against South Africa. An All-Britain camogie team also took part in the Tailteann Games, and the Captain of the team was Annie Hennessy. Many years on, Annie was a dear friend of mine and she told me that the Liverpool club provided six players in the 1928 and 1932 games. She was also known as Annie Mulholland which was her maiden name. She eventually went home to Newry to live, but kept in touch with all Irish activities in Liverpool. Whenever there was a good cause in the Irish Community, Annie's was always one of the first donations to arrive.

In 1935, the 1916 Memorial Cup (camogie) was won by the Caitlin Ni hUilachain team, captained by Sally Murphy.

In November, 1937, the Eire Og GAA Club affiliated to the Liverpool Council of Irish Societies. All the actions were to be directed towards 'the realisation of complete independence for all Ireland and the furtherance of Gaelic games, pastimes, culture and the Irish language'. It should be noted that almost every delegate from the affiliates, was born in Liverpool.

The Lancashire Camogie Team in Lurgan, County Armagh at Easter 1950. Sadie Walsh (later Redmond), is second left on the back row and the great Kathleen Cody of Dublin is sixth from the left on the back row. She was a guest player with Lancashire. Most of the players are from Manchester and Altrincham. Kathleen Cody won many All-Ireland camogie titles.

The 1937 GAA Liverpool and District County Board Meeting was held in Islington Hall, 22A Islington. The Liverpool clubs present were Eire Og, Sean O'Donovans and Patrick Pearses.

1937 and 1938 were relatively successful but there does appear to have been a feeling of dread about the future and the state of European politics. Some people were going home despite the fact that there was little work to go to. The clubs in Lancashire were Eire Og and Sean O'Donovan (H and F), Patrick Pearse (F) and Kevin Barry (F).

Liverpool County / Lancashire County changed its name several times, and registered black and amber as the County colours. They were the jerseys of Patrick Pearse Club.

Officers were T. Morgan, Michael Redmond, Seán McInerney, Jim Brennan, Jack Brennan, Jim Ryan, Jerry Mulholland, and delegates were Pat Crossey, Pearse McNamara, Tim O'Keeffe and John Tynan. Barney Keble usually represented Manchester at County Board meetings. These meetings were usually held in Islington Hall at 22a Islington or Wood Street (Gaelic League) while games were at Thingwall Hall and at Bootle Stadium (Liverpool Feis Venue).

In 1938, the balance in hand at the Convention was 14 shillings 6d. Liabilities (if pressed) about £18.

At a County Board meeting on May 4th, 1939, there was a letter from Paddy Costello (London) who was Secretary of Provincial Council, on the subject of conscription (into the British Army). Paddy, who was a good friend of mine and of the Irish in Liverpool, had interviewed the 'High Commissioner for Eire' (forerunner of the Irish Ambassador) 'regarding the position of Irish citizens in Britain'.

A meeting was held on 21st January, 1940 in the Islington Hall which was given its full title 'United Irish Social and Athletic Club Rooms'. Seán McInerney reported back from a recent Provincial Council meeting, World War II now being in progress. He said London County Board was hoping to continue operating but probably with less clubs. Birmingham were also hoping to continue, as was Oxford. There was no report from Keighley (who, although in Yorkshire, was affiliated to Lancashire County Board).

Seán McInerney informed the Provincial Council there was, 'little likelihood of Lancashire functioning as all last year's clubs were breaking up'. He hoped there might be better news at the Annual Convention. Barney Keble said there was little hope of Manchester functioning, 'as the few members were scattered'.

The meeting concluded with the delegates sharing the opinion of the Chairman, with regard to the futility of trying to function. The chair closed the meeting by saying that the Convention would be re-convened if the situation improved. The Chairman Jim Ryan was supported by Seán McInerney of the Provincial Council in his decision.

Two months later on 24th March, 1940, the re-convened Convention was held in Widnes, where the one and only Father Paddy Spain had arrived on the scene. He spent a short while in St. Patrick's Parish, Widnes. Fr. Paddy was asked to be Chairman for the day at the re-convened meeting, with Seán McInerney acting as Secretary. Eire Og and Kevin Barrys were represented and about 16 men turned up to represent the new St. Patrick's Club. After the meeting, Jim Ryan resumed his position as Chairman of the County Board. Some of the new members were recently identified as Widnes Rugby League players.

Lancashire were drawn against Warwickshire in the Provincial Championships. The games were played in Widnes on Whit Sunday, 12th May, 1940. The referee of the football match was Frank Short who served as President of the Provincial Council. He was a member of a famous Crossmaglen family and was on the national executive of

J.P .Mannion of Wigan, Seán McInerney and Tommy Walsh. Two elderly men who greatly influenced Tommy not only in GAA affairs but in all things Irish.

the Anti-Partition of Ireland League. His daughter Clare, was a Minister in several Labour Governments. Clare wrote a moving tribute to her father in my book *A History of the GAA in Britain*.

Meetings in Liverpool were often held in St. Anne Street Club after that time, where Mr. Pat Lawlor owned the Dance Hall, as well as one in Islington which was run by Mrs. Lawlor.

Seán McInerney took over the Presidency of the Provincial Council in 1946 (from Frank Short).

Fr. Spain succeeded in obtaining the ICI grounds in Widnes for Lancashire's matches.

In July, 1940, Jim Ryan resigned as Chairman. He said that as Fr. Spain was now based in Liverpool, he thought it was the right thing to do. Fr. Paddy was now based in St. Michael's, West Derby Road. Now there's a coincidence!

The GAA stayed alive during World War II. The clubs in Liverpool had good spells and bad, and a club had formed in Wigan named Young Irelands. The representative for the Wigan club was usually J.P. Mannion. He was an Alderman in Wigan and was a native of Roundstone in Galway. He was a great man and he and I became close friends.

The next Minute Book I have access to is for the 1945 – 1948 period, which happens to be the period in which I became involved. Seán McInerney, of course, remains involved. He was ever-present, from 1926 and maybe earlier, until he died in 1962.

Many of the people who were involved were young people of my own generation (I was 17 in 1947) and, of course, there were many older men. The 'second diaspora' was just getting under way and young men were pouring into Liverpool, and England generally.

A group of young people who were Liverpool born were

also very involved in the St. Patrick's Hurling and Football Club which was the name of our club at the time. It was quite normal for Tom, Nick and Eddie Redmond (who were to become my brothers-in-law) to attend club meetings as did Vin Boyle who had been my friend at school, and myself. The Redmond brothers were the sons of Michael Redmond who had been an officer of the club for 20 years or so. His home in Derby Lane, Old Swan, had been the venue for club meetings and hurleys and sliothars had been repaired in the cellar.

Vin Boyle and myself, under the wing of Seán McInerney, had gone on to be involved in County and Province, while all of us remained involved in the club for the rest of our lives.

The active members in 1945, apart from Seán McInerney, Fr. Spain and Michael Redmond, were John Tynan, Michael O'Sullivan, Tim O'Keefe, Michael (Mick) Battles, Frank Molloy, Liam Phelan. Eddie O'Reilly had arrived in Liverpool from his home in Killorglin, Co. Kerry and became very involved as a player and an officer. In later years he, together with Mick Gill of Galway, who was a hurler with the club, opened the Shamrock Club in Lime Street. Meetings were usually in St. Anne Street Club in 1945 and 1946.

In 1946, Eddie O'Reilly ran some functions in a hall in Green Lane to raise funds. Eddie Fox's name appeared in October, 1946. He became very involved with the hurling team and was captain as well as Club Chairman.

A ceili was held in Acacia House, Everton Brow in December, 1946.

At a meeting in January, 1947, Irish Sweep tickets were available for sale. £1 to go to Club funds for every book sold.

The list of players for 1947 included myself and my brother Colum, Mick Festy and Billy Walsh who were living in Shaw Street. Tommy Hunt, Father Dinny Ryan and

Seán Floyd and John Harrington have travelled from Chester to Liverpool for games for over 50 years. Sean is from Tullyallen, Co. Louth and John from Castletownbere, Co. Cork. John is an uncle of the famous golfer Padraig Harrington.

Joe Cahill of the Oisin Club, Manchester, joined John Mitchels in all their sad and happy occasions since he came over from County Kildare in 1948. Here he is in the Irish Centre with Fr. Michael O'Connor on the left and Chris Johnston on the right, with Sean Floyd and Tommy Walsh at the back.

Father Jack Bergin, Jim Coady who was also a member of the Shannon Star Band, Connie O'Leary.

In 1947, a Concert was held in the Picton Hall in William Brown Street, proceeds to the Club. Fr. Spain, was, of course, the driving force.

Fr. Spain informed the meeting in October 1947 that a pitch was available at Rimmers Field, Bridge Farm, Ball O'Ditton, Widnes.

It was agreed that Eddie Redmond would represent the club at the Comhgail Cois Mersi meetings.

At a meeting in March 1948, it was agreed that as the Irish Association of Merseyside (Cois Mersi) was including items which were contrary to the rules of the GAA, the GAA could not continue to be affiliated members.

What had happened was that dances other than ceili dances had been included in the evening. At the time, Rule 29 GAA Official Guide said "Clubs shall not organise any entertainment at which foreign dances are permitted". If the Club had remained as affiliates, it could have been suspended "for not less than four weeks".

The incident was to affect the formation of the Irish Centre Building Fund Committee about 15 years later, of which I have written elsewhere.

Between 1948 and 1950, the John Mitchels Gaelic Football Club was founded. It was affiliated to the County

Board as part of the Craobh Seán Mhisteil of the Gaelic League. They didn't succeed in attracting the young Irish men who were coming into the city at the time and after a short period, they were dissolved into the St. Patrick's Club and became the St. Patrick's Hurling and John Mitchels Gaelic Football Club. Peter Delaney had been one of the founders of the John Mitchels Club and he became Secretary of the larger club.

Club meetings in 1950 were held in Sim Donoghue's house in Lindale Road, Fairfield or the Walsh household in Edge Lane Drive, as well as the Redmonds' in Derby Lane. When the club decided to buy 12 hurleys, it was arranged that they would be brought over by one of the teams crossing to London to play exhibition games at Whit. They would be collected in London and brought back by some of the members going to London for the games.

The name Jim Butler appears in the Minutes in 1950. Jim was to become Chairman of the Lancashire County Board and, indeed, to be Chairman of the Irish Centre, Mount Pleasant. Danny Lynch's name is there too. Danny and Jim were great friends.

The meeting of January 1951 was held in the Shamrock Club, Lime Street.

At the meeting, it was proposed that Liverpool form their own County Board and break away from Manchester. Vin Boyle and I opposed it and the meeting agreed to stay as they were.

Four doctors, Bernie Murphy, Mick Herlihy, Mick Desmond and Jim O'Reilly were playing and attending meetings about now. They were all at Providence Hospital, St. Helens and were all from Cork. Dick Wright had also appeared on the scene. He was full back on the hurling team and was Chairman of the club and the County Board. He had a distinguished appearance with a splendid moustache.

In 1952, meetings were being held in Cathedral Buildings, Brownlow Hill. This was the last remaining building of the old workhouse. In Liverpool you are never far from history. In March of that year, there was a discussion about where the best hurleys could be bought at the cheapest price. Dick Wright will write to Mr. Fogarty of Ballinure and get a price. Bernard Bradley, a lifelong friend of mine, was attending meetings about that time. The football team was congratulated on winning the County Final.

The minutes of the meeting in February 1953 were written in the familiar handwriting of Seán McNamara, better known as a fiddle player with the Liverpool Ceili Band, but a very loyal and active GAA member too.

Between 1953 and 1956, there were very many changes in officers. More young people were arriving from Ireland and were willing to stand for office. Seán McNamara, Jim Butler, Tom, Nick and Eddie Redmond, Bernard Bradley, Tom Sheils, Michael O'Donoghue. Sean Floyd who lived in Chester travelled regularly for meetings as well as games.

Cuchullains were a new football team based in Preston and Tom Chambers, Paddy Donnelly and Aidan McGarrigle were involved and became active in the County Board. Aidan McGarrigle of Donegal became Secretary and surprised me one evening on the way back from a Provincial Council Meeting in Birmingham when he told me he was going to be a priest. He did and, eventually, served in South America.

In 1953, Paddy Dunne who was not a member but who was my brother-in-law, brought 12 hurleys from M. Heffernan in Tipperary. Paddy was a seaman!

All the games then were being played at Yew Tree field.

In 1953, Lancashire won the Provincial Championship of Britain, beat Glasgow in the All-Ireland Junior Semi-Final and lost to Cork in the All-Ireland Final.

On the Lancashire team were Tom Shiel, Joe McCabe,

The John Mitchels team pose for the post-match photo Back Row: Seán McInerney, Bob Tinneny. Tommy Walsh, Eddie Redmond, John Harrington, Michael Donoghue, Tony ___, Joe Begley, Kevin Fullen, Patsy Donnelly, Tom McNeice, _____, Tim O'Keefe

Front Row: Tommy Sheil, Fr. Michael O'Connor, Johnnie Guirk, Chris Johnston, Joe McCabe, Nick Redmond, _____, Charlie Taylor, Seán Floyd

Sean Keane, Chris Johnston, Johnnie Guirk, Joe O'Malley, Sean Floyd and Michael Donoghue. I was Secretary of the Lancashire County Board and Seán McInerney was also an officer of the Board. There were 10 representatives of John Mitchels Club in the party.

A number of club members went to the boat on the Friday night to see the team off. Shortly after this, Fr. Michael O'Connor was active in the club and played on the Lancashire County team for many years. He became Canon O'Connor and served in St. Christopher's, Speke, the Isle of Man, Christ the King, Childwall and as Administrator of the Cathedral of Christ the King before a spell at St. Monica's, Bootle from where he retired to return home to County Kerry.

In 1954, the joint presidents were Fathers Paddy Spain and Michael O'Connor. The Chairman was Tom Redmond.

(Dr.) Bernie Murphy was captain of St. Patrick's Hurlers while I was John Mitchels (football) captain.

In December that year, we were trying to raise money for a new set of jerseys. Father Tom Lynch said he would ask the Roscommon County Board for a set of used jerseys. The offer was accepted but I don't remember wearing a Roscommon jersey.

At the end of that year, we lost the use of the two pitches at Yew Tree Lane which had been our home for many years. The cemetery was to be extended across 'the top pitch' while houses were built on the bottom pitch, opposite Yew Tree Golf Club.

In 1955, Chris Johnston became Vice-Chairman having

arrived in Liverpool from Ardee, County Louth three years earlier. He has been an officer of the club ever since. Joe McCabe arrived from County Meath about the same time, became a close friend of Chris and remained a member until he died.

We were playing our games in Thingwall Hall (St. Edward's Orphanage) in 1955.

A hurley repairing session was held in Derby Lane on November 4th of that year. 16 jerseys were ordered from Clerys, Dublin at a cost of £1.2s.6d. each. Doctor Bernie Murphy had returned to Ireland after a number of years here and he sent a gift of 4 hurleys to the club. Bernard Bradley also donated hurleys to the club.

The Lancashire County Convention of 1956 was held in the Stork Hotel, Liverpool. Gerry O'Connor and Tommy Ryan frequently travelled to County Board meetings in Liverpool and Manchester from their homes in Ellesmere Port. Gerry was a member of the club for more than 60 years when he died in 2009. In 2008, he had his leg amputated but still made it to the hurling final in Croke Park.

The Club Convention (AGM) of 1956 was held in the Bradford Hotel, Tithebarn Street. The attendance reads like a list of the men who kept the GAA flag flying for so long: Seán McInerney, Tim O'Keefe, Chris Johnston, Fr. Paddy Spain, Jim Butler, Joe McCabe, Gerry O'Connor, Michael Connolly, Nick, Tom and Eddie Redmond and their father Michael, Sean Floyd, John Harrington, Pat and Aidan Kirwan, Gerry O'Brien, Seán McNamara, Chris Johnston, Dick Wright, Michael Donoghue, Bernard Bradley, Joe England, Jimmy O'Reilly, Vin Boyle and myself.

In 1957, the Marian Players were asked to put on a play to raise funds. St. Alphonsus Hall was available (Father Michael Colman was always co-operative). Tickets would be 1/6d and 2/6d. A row of seats would be reserved for clergy, and tickets would be on sale at the 98 Shop. Steve McKeon of the Irish Playgoers would provide a fireplace for the play. In April that year, it was decided to send 200 cigarettes to Fr. Lynch who was convalescing at home.

Seán McInerney had purchased six jerseys for the club at Clerys, Dublin. He got the price reduced as they were shop soiled. Games at this time were being played at Sefton Rugby Club, West Derby.

Fr. Spain asked club members to 'give a hand' with an Irish Concert in the Philharmonic Hall in aid of his new school in Kirkby. Club members acted as stewards at a very successful event.

Bernard Bradley, as Secretary, reported that the football team played 14 matches plus three friendlies. We played in three finals and won the Wolfe Tone Cup.

Pat and Aidan Kirwan were both congratulated on their weddings to Phyllis and Mary.

In 1958, Chris Johnston and Joe McCabe were captain and vice-captain of the football team and Pat Kirwan and Gerry O'Brien of the hurlers.

Speaking as the President, Father Michael O'Connor outlined the history of the club praised Seán McInerney, Michael Redmond, Sim Donoghue and Jim Ryan for having been involved for so long. He said he had enjoyed every minute of his six years membership and he praised his fellow players for their self-control with regard to temper and language.

Later that year, a trip to London was arranged to coincide with the games at Wembley. We attended the games on Saturday and played Shamrocks of London at New Eltham on the Sunday. A number of such trips were made and we were usually a few players short. As a result, some of the great players of the time 'guested' for us. The great Dan and James McCartan of Down and Derry players played for us having played at Wembley the day before.

The estimated cost of train fare, hotel and Wembley ticket was £7.15.0d. We left Lime Street at 8.10am on Saturday and departed Euston on Monday at 5.30pm. At night, we visited the famous Galtymore Ballroom.

It is interesting to note that the club, on several occasions, discussed the possible use of the dressing rooms at Sefton Rugby Club. Sefton didn't actually refuse the use of the dressing rooms, but they did fix a charge and demanded responsibility for the care of the premises including the bar. Whenever the matter was discussed, the committee decided not to avail of the use of the facilities, feeling that accepting responsibility for the care of the premises by both teams was too much of a worry. We continued to change in cars and behind the stand.

In 1960, Chris Johnston reported that the footballers played 19 matches and won the Wolfe Tone Cup for the third year in succession. The hurlers reached the league final. Joe Begley and Charlie Taylor had become very involved.

Gerry O'Connor and Liam Doyle were thanked for manning the gate throughout the year. After Income and Expenditure for the year, we had a balance of £1.

In those days, annual meetings always concluded with the De Profundis for deceased members. Tommy McNiece was to the fore in the running of the hurling team about this time. Seán Floyd and John Harrington, our Chester contingent, had been joined by John's brothers, Tadhg, Brendan, Raymond and Aidan. Their older brother, Paddy, was golfer Padraig Harrington's father.

In his Chairman's address, Joe McCabe criticised some players who didn't turn up for club games but who were always available for county games. He also said he had been in Liverpool for 10 years and being Chairman of the club was an honour he could never have dreamed of.

Jim Sherry arrived from Ireland and became a very loyal

174

club member. After a few years, he returned to live in County Cavan but to this day he regularly presents a new O'Neills football to the club.

Nick Redmond was thanked for using his car to carry the flags to line the pitch every match day.

In his Secretary's report, Chris Johnston referred to the formation of the Irish Centre Building Fund and urged everyone to support the venture.

A bit of bad news was that the rent for the Sefton Rugby Club was to be increased to £100.

The 1962 AGM was the first after the death of Seán McInerney. Joe McCabe's Chairman's address was very emotional. He said "There will be an empty seat at every GAA unit in Britain, but ours is a special loss. He was our club man". Father Paddy Sheridan OMI had arrived in Liverpool and was in Holy Cross Parish. He was a Cavan man and was larger than life. He went on to be Director of the Irish Centres of Birmingham and London.

In 1963, Harry Walsh and Jimmy Mallen joined our ranks as players when they arrived from Laois and Louth respectively. Both were psychiatric nurses. They were dedicated club members until they returned to Ireland some years later. Harry and Jimmy turned up in Navan and Croke Park to see the John Mitchels team in 2009.

Harry Walsh, Raymond Harrington and Michael O'Donoghue were on the Lancashire team which won the Provincial Championship of Britain and played against Kerry in the All-Ireland Junior Final in Manchester.

Off the playing pitch in 1964, I had become President of the Provincial Council of Britain and our club provided four members to the Lancashire County Board.

In the same year, Sim Donoghue and his wife returned to Wexford after 40 years in Liverpool.

The footballers reached the county final for the third

year in succession – and lost again.

In 1965, Michael Redmond expressed sadness that we were not able to field a hurling team. The Eire Og team, which had become St. Patrick's, had been formed in 1920/21, having previously been Young Irelands. We lost the use of Sefton Rugby Club and Chris Johnston and Eddie Fox went to see Simon Mahon MP hoping to get a pitch from Bootle Council.

The club AGM referred to the opening of the Irish Centre, Mount Pleasant. All the meetings and fundraising events from now on would be held there. The existence of the Irish Centre dramatically affected every aspect of Irish life in Liverpool.

In 1966, Father Patsy Carolan OMI was a footballer and the Chairman and the good news was that the footballers won the Lancashire County Championship. They went to Dunleer, Co. Louth at Easter and played Tullyallen (also County Louth) on Easter Monday. Tullyallen was Seán Floyds home club.

We entertained St. Eunan's of Glasgow in Liverpool and played St. Finbarr's of Coventry in the club championship of Britain. The game was played at Bootle Stadium. Joe England said we fielded 15 players for every hurling match in the year. He also put forward that the hurleys be sold to hurlers for ten shillings. This was a subsidised charge and he suggested that if the hurley was broken in a game the club would replace it. Joe was having a major influence on the hurling team which had been struggling.

About this time, a team from Roscrea, Tipperary (Antigen Ltd) spent a weekend in Liverpool and played one or two games. The Wolfe Tone Hurling Club from Drogheda also visited us for a match.

In 1968, the footballers won the Wolfe Tone Cup and had therefore won at least one trophy every year since 1963.

The 1970s and 80s were very different in the Irish Community in Liverpool and elsewhere in Britain. The

176

A group of under age John Mitchels footballers with parents. John Hegarty underage manager on the left. The group is in Newsham Park in the 1970s.

'second diaspora' was over. The situation in Ireland was good and improving and the influx of people coming over looking for work was over. The situation in Ireland was so good that there was a strong trickle of people returning home, usually with work assured.

As usual, the GAA accurately recorded the financial situation at home, and new players from Ireland were few and far between. Although the underage scene had its best ever decade or so in Liverpool, there weren't enough players coming through to keep the adult team supplied with players. My son Colum Walsh was ahead of most of the youngsters and played not only for John Mitchels but for Lancashire too. Bernie McGovern was another player born here with Seán and Paul Loughran, Paul, James and Edward Moriarty and Aidan, Eddie and John Kirwan close behind. Michael Coyne and Sean Floyd Junior were others who came through our under-age system into the adult team.

Two of our players, John McCormack and Liam Campbell were now priests in Liberia and the club kept in touch (Fr. John is now home in Mayo and still in touch).

John Hegarty arrived from Cork and was responsible for our best ever under-age spell.

In 1978, there were 40 under-age games played at Newsham Park. A very strong group of families were active,

which included: Sheilagh and Sean Loughran, Joan and
Peter McPadden, Josie and Jimmy Morrin, Kathleen and
Henry Owens, Nora and Pat Lynch, Seamus Sloyan and
P. Collister who went to live in the Isle of Man, Steve Yim,
Tony Grimes, Mary and Donie (Chalkie) Whelton and their
sons, Chris and Anthony.

In 1972, both Michael Redmond and Eddie Fox passed
away having both given a lifetime's service to the club. The
club presented the Redmond / Fox Trophy to the Lancashire
County Board.

In 1973, Cormac Lally had arrived in Liverpool as
manager of the newly opened Bank of Ireland and was soon
involved in every aspect of GAA life. He became Chairman of
the club and of the County Board and refereed frequently.
When Cormac returned to Ireland, he was appointed as a
referee by the Croke Park authorities and frequently served
at national level. He too was in Croke Park to see John
Mitchels in 2009.

In 1974, Phyllis and Pat Kirwan went home to Wexford
with their son and daughter. No man had given greater service
than Pat. Tim O'Keefe who had spent a lifetime always in the
background became President. He was a gentle man who did
anything that needed doing. Also in the 1970s, Chris Johnston
became Chairman, after 15 years as Secretary. Francie
McMahon – a model player in every respect – returned home
and was soon playing senior for the Armagh County team.
Around this time, another Armagh player Brian Campbell
(known to all as 'Soupie'), was playing wonderful football with
us. Larry Lynch was helping John Hegarty with the under-age
players before he left for New York. Larry welcomed any of our
players who went to New York including giving my own son
Nick, a bed for the first crucial weeks.

In 1980, numerous clubs visited our under-age teams
from Dublin, including Kilmacud Crokes, Matt Talbots,

John Mitchells 1- 10
Moynalvey   1- 8
Pairc Tailteann 11/01/2009

All-Ireland Junior Quarter Final, Navan 2009. John Mitchels v Moynalvey. Back Row: Jimmy Biggane (over from Liverpool), Peter Gallagher (from Donegal), Jimmy Morrin. Middle Row: Tommy Walsh and his cousin Padraic Allen (a Connemara man living in Meath). Front Row: Jimmy Mallen (Louth), Harry Walsh (Laois) Jimmy and Harry played for Mitchels before returning home. Chris Jonston is a lifelong member of Mitchels.

O'Connell Boys and St. Anne's (Tallaght). David Griffin of Dublin was involved in all these activities and still retains an interest in the GAA and Irish scene in Liverpool.

Our Under 16s played New Haven, Connecticut in Croke Park, arranged by Brendan Crawley.

In 1982, Peter Gallagher was a very efficient Secretary. He produced the first comprehensive fixture list for Lancashire. He also remembered to thank the ladies who washed the jerseys in a very comprehensive Secretary's Report. Also that year, Bernie McGovern, Colum Walsh, Kieran Daly, Brian Campbell and Jim O'Connor played on the Lancashire Team and Sean Loughran and Eddie Kirwan played on the County U21 team.

Sadly, the 1980s saw hurling peter out. We simply couldn't field a team. Mick Larkin and Joe England had to travel to Manchester to keep playing hurling. After a great 10 years or so, the under-age teams went the same way. Children's football was greatly affected by the closure of the Irish Centre in Mount Pleasant, as under-age football was very much a community activity unlike adult football.

As John Mitchels found it harder to field a team, a young man named Barry Morris came from the famed Enniskillen Gaels Club in County Fermanagh. He played with us until we could no longer field a team. None of us could have guessed how much Barry's games in that team would affect the future of the club. A few years later in 2006, John Mitchels re-formed and affiliated to Lancashire County

Back row: Paddy Brandt, John Spencer, Dennis Dunne, Brendan Rabbette, Steve Yim, Kevin Ronan, Paul Cooney, Tony Grimes, Chris Whelton, Kieran Doyle.
Front row: Tony Murphy, Anthony Whelton, Kevin Spencer, ? Ash, Peter Owens, James Moriarty, John Morrin, ?
Possibly the best team of Liverpool-born players ever to play for John Mitchels G.F.C. Many were selected to play for Lancashire, approx 1981.

Board. Due to Barry's games with John Mitchels, the newly affiliated club became the 'new John Mitchels' and didn't form a completely new club.

Barry was quickly joined by Danny McDonagh from Ballina, County Mayo, Conor Kelly, Conal Doherty, Conal Cunningham, Ronan McBride and so many players that the Club are now fielding Senior and Junior teams. As a further example of how strong the GAA is in Liverpool, there is now a Ladies' team, also named John Mitchels.

The good work is developing further in that Paul Melanophy and John Fitzpatrick who are players and teachers, are introducing boys in several schools to gaelic football.

The outstanding memory for myself and many others was the appearance in Croke Park in the All-Ireland Junior Football Final 2008/09.

Former John Mitchels members came from all over Ireland and all over the world. Unfortunately, the team lost by a single point, but it didn't take away from the immense pride that all of us felt in the current team.

The team won games against Moynalvey, the Leinster champions and Killala, the Connacht champions before the final in Croke Park. Among the former John Mitchels players were Cormac Lally, a former Club and County Board Chairman, Jim Sherry from Cavan, Harry Walsh from Laois, Jimmy Mallon from Louth, Peter Gallagher from Donegal, Sheilagh and Seán Loughran from Newry, Eileen and Colum Walsh from Cork, Vincent Murphy and Seamus Sloyan. To my great surprise, my son Nick Walsh from New York strolled into the hotel on the Sunday morning, and came too.

Among our greatest supporters was Barry Morris's family from Enniskillen. They never missed a game in Ireland. There was Barry's brother Mark who also played for John Mitchels in the past, together with Colette, Dermot, Eithne, Clodagh, Seán and Liz.

Phil Duddy's mother and father were also regulars and Gerry McNamee's mother and father who came from Cavan for the games.

Sadly, the jubilation among the players was subdued by the fact that there were several bereavements during the series of games. There were one or two hundred John Mitchels supporters at the earlier games and several thousand at Croke Park. The extent of the travelling by John Mitchels supporters was remarkable.

Barry Morris and Danny McDonagh made every preparation you could think of for the games and a few you would never dream of.

Another former player who was involved at every stage was Brian Finlay. Brian had played for John Mitchels for years. He is now a professional physiotherapist and gave his services freely to the team. By happy coincidence, his native club was Navan so he was 'at home' for the All-Ireland Semi-Final.

Barry Morris said during the period, "In 2006, we didn't have any money to buy goal posts and now we're in the All-Ireland Final. The Club now has an excellent pitch and is fully prepared for every home game".

It has not been my intention to give a kick-by-kick report on games, but to give an overall picture about how the John Mitchels Club ticks, what it means to those involved and, above all, its role in the Irish Community in Liverpool.

Irish Centre

6 Boundary Lane, West Derby Road, Liverpool, L6 5JG. Tel: 0151 263 1808

Registered Charity No. 1089059

St. MICHAELS CENTRE

St. MICHAELS CENTRE

" The Home of the Irish Community on Merseyside "

Objective: To provide and maintain a community centre for the promotion of cultural and social activities for the Irish Community on Merseyside

St. Michael's Irish Centre

THE LOSS OF THE IRISH CENTRE, Mount Pleasant, was a huge blow to the Irish Community in Liverpool. Would the community get over it? Probably not! Very few clubs or centres in Britain have closed and been successfully re-born. By 1999, most of the Irish Community activity groups had found an alternative home. Máirín Bolger's Irish Dancing Class had been in Holy Cross Parish Centre for a while before moving to the Eldonian Centre, Vauxhall. They joined Comhaltas Ceoltoiri Eireann, who had been having music classes there for some time. The Irish Community Care Merseyside Tuesday Club had settled in St. Oswald's, Old Swan before moving to Our Lady's, Wavertree, where they still meet every Tuesday.

The James Larkin Band met in Holy Cross Church hall and kept their flag flying.

Fr. Jennings and some other 25 card players including Bernard Bradley, Jimmy Morrin and Jimmy O'Connor continued to meet for a game in Our Lady of Mount Carmel Club in High Park Street.

Early in 1999, I got a phone call from Mgr Michael McKenna saying that the Archdiocese of Liverpool intended to close the St. Michael's Parish Centre. He offered it to the Irish Community for use "as an Irish Centre". Father Seán O'Connor was at Our Lady of Queen of Martyrs, Croxteth, and he was the first person I spoke to. Fr. Seán invited a group of us to meet in his house and Mgr. McKenna was there too.

We decided to call a meeting of Irish people in Liverpool, to be held in St. Michael's Centre. It was on 14th April and incredibly 140 people turned up. This remarkable turn-out was despite the fact that there was no Irish community structure at the time, and no mailing list. The telephones in Liverpool were busy, and old friends were called. The overwhelming feeling was that the absence of an

The first illustrated brochure¬ produced by St Michael's Irish Centre, Liverpool.

A group of the very earliest members on a cleaning session in St. Michael's Irish Centre.

Irish Centre in Liverpool was a matter of great concern and sadness to the Irish people in the city.

There was an obvious demand that we should give these premises a try. A one year trial period was agreed.

A Steering Committee was set up immediately and they were asked to negotiate with the Archdiocese. The meeting was held on 12th May 1999.

The members of the Steering Committee were: Myself, Seán Loughran, Siobhán Whelton, Stephen Spencer, Maureen Morrison and Bernadette Adderley. We soon asked Seán McNamara and Joe England to help us.

Each had filled the post of Chairman in Mount Pleasant and had much to give. Joe England immediately started working on a Constitution. He drew heavily from the Constitution of the Irish Centre, Mount Pleasant as it was when it was owned and run by the Irish Community.

A General Meeting was held on 1st December 1999. This was an interim meeting to review the situation half-way through the trial year.

Many cleaning sessions were held as there was no

money for paid staff. Furniture was repaired. Grass was cut. Curtains were made. Flooring was patched and made safe. This was no committee just for committee meetings. Committee members brought their whole families to cleaning sessions. They brought their own brushes and mop buckets. Eileen Burke, a Wexford woman, was very involved in St. Michael's parish. Either she adopted us or we adopted her, but Eileen has been involved in every single aspect of life in St. Michael's Irish Centre ever since.

The Irish Community in Liverpool left the Committee in no doubt, this was to be our new home. We were an Irish Centre again. Maírin Bolger and her dancers were again, as she was in Mount Pleasant 35 years before, the first activity group to move in, closely followed by Comhaltas Ceoltoiri Eireann with their weekly music classes.

In May 2001, about two years after we took our first tentative steps in our new home, we were honoured by a visit by His Excellency, Mr. Ted Barrington, the Irish Ambassador in Britain.

We had already been welcomed back into the Federation of Irish Societies, who kindly waived the membership fees. It seemed that the whole Irish Community in Britain were delighted for us. The Irish Post and Irish World newspapers said 'Liverpool Are Back'.

The Steering Committee invited Mary Biggane, Joe England, Peter Gallagher and Pat Lynch to join us on the first St. Michael's Irish Centre Committee. All accepted.

We now had a 20-year lease with the Archdiocese. While they still own the premises, we pay our way and are completely independent. The Constitution confirmed our new name 'St. Michael's Irish Centre'.

We believed that to call it *The Irish Centre* would be confusing as our people still referred to 127 Mount Pleasant as 'The Irish Centre' even though it had not filled that role for some years. It was, of course, necessary to experiment and to consult, to discover the requirements of the Irish Community of the day. For several years, we ran a regular Sunday evening function. The M.C. was Frank O'Grady and he included visiting artists and bands, and Play Your Cards Right, as well as a regular sing-song.

Ten years hardly calls for a detailed history of 'the new Irish Centre'. However, a tribute must be paid to the committee for a remarkable success. The committee and other volunteer helpers, as well as the staff, have worked tirelessly to give the Irish people in Liverpool a home to be proud of.

Right from the outset, it was agreed by all concerned that the objective was 'A Home for the Irish on Merseyside' and that the objective was 'To provide and maintain a community centre for the promotion of cultural and social activities for the Irish Community'.

When the word went out that there was a new Irish Centre in Liverpool being run by and for the Irish people, messages came in from all over. Margaret and Seán Murphy in Killybegs sent good wishes. Seán O'Sé in Cork said "Great to hear the good news. I want to offer to sing, free of charge, to raise money for the new Irish Centre". Dermot Hegarty made a similar offer. Monnie Hallahan and the Sliabh gCua Set Dancers from Dungarvan couldn't wait to come over. Paul Moriarty provided signs. Eileen and Paddy Doran paid for the Setanta signal so that we could show Gaelic games.

After a few months, the committee decided it didn't need to wait a year to confirm that we now knew that we had found our new home.

On September 10th, 1999, a formal opening was held. The whole weekend was a party. Dermot Hegarty performed on the Friday. On Saturday, the Lord Mayor and Lady Mayoress of Liverpool attended and became our first members. It was a very happy coincidence that Joe and Eileen Devaney, two of 'our own' were holding the office that year. Eileen's dad, Martin Masterson of County Mayo, was a much loved member in Mount Pleasant.

To our amazement, the Ireland Fund of Great Britain gave us £3,000 towards our expenses improving the premises. It made up for the disappointment at not getting a penny from the local authority in Liverpool.

The links with Mount Pleasant were inevitable. Everyone involved in St. Michael's had a Mount Pleasant connection, either direct or through parents. Some of the regular activities which had become traditions, were resurrected in our new home.

The Mass of St. Patrick on the Sunday before St. Patrick's Day is one. Father Seán O'Connor puts his own distinctive stamp on it. His homilies are tailor made for the Irish Community and, invariably, 'hit the spot'. Irish dancing and music have their part and are part of our 'offertory'. The attendance is consistently the highest attendance of the year.

The collection goes to an agreed charity. One year it went to Fr. Tim Redmond for the Kiltegan Fathers in Kenya. It has also gone to cancer charities as a token of our gratitude for the care extended to members of our community. Alder Hey Hospital and Claire House Hospice have also been recipients .

An Tostal. When An Tostal spread throughout Ireland from its birthplace in County Leitrim. Liverpool established it in Mount Pleasant. We run it every year as a fun day for the family. Non-stop entertainment and such things as tug-o-war and 'picking spuds' are regular features. *Crib Sunday* is held on the Sunday before Christmas. The tradition started in 1983 again in Mount Pleasant. We have always had a live baby in the lead role. Our baby Jesus has been played by baby girls and twins as well as boys. Again, we mix in Irish traditional music and dancing and every year so far we have had a very special visitor with gifts for the children.

Forty-five years ago, life was simple. What did the Irish people in Liverpool want? A dance hall. A dance hall big enough to be able to bring Big Tom, Larry Cunningham, Brendan Shine and Johnny McEvoy.

Times have changed. Social habits have changed. If 25 was the average age of our community then, it is now much older. Fortunately, the children and grandchildren are now part of our community too. What we need now is a community centre with facilities for older people and young families.

More people now want afternoon events. Any Sunday

The handbill for the first Tea Dance run by the Irish Community Care Merseyside in October 2000. The Tea Dance is still being held every month.

IRISH COMMUNITY CARE MERSEYSIDE

PRESENTS

AFTERNOON SOCIAL

AT

ST MICHAEL'S CENTRE
BOUNDARY LANE, WEST DERBY ROAD
LIVERPOOL

THURSDAY 5TH OCTOBER 2000

1.00PM — 3.30PM

(AND THE FIRST THURSDAY OF EVERY MONTH THEREAFTER)

ENTERTAINMENT THIS MONTH:
MICHAEL COYNE

COME ALONG AND ENJOY GOOD MUSIC,
REFRESHMENTS, DANCING, BINGO
ADMISSION: 50P

WE LOOK FORWARD TO SEEING YOU

*FURTHER INFORMATION PLEASE CONTACT
IRISH COMMUNITY CARE : 707 4302
ST MICHAEL'S CENTRE: 263 1808*

*BUSES FORM THE CITY CENTRE:
STAND NUMBER 6 QUEENS SQUARE: 11,12 & 18*

afternoon social occasion now automatically fills the hall. Afternoon events in the early days in Mount Pleasant were unheard of. The average community centre, Irish or otherwise, has two roles to fill. One is to provide for the cultural and social needs of its community. The other is to provide bar facilities.

St. Michael's Irish Centre has concentrated on the former role, with great success. We have very efficiently run the bar facility, but have not set out to run a pub. The bar is run for the convenience of our community. When we took over, we undertook to provide facilities for any St. Michael's

Parish event and for parish families. We have honoured that promise. Apart from Parish events, we have provided for families when they have needed facilities for funerals.

It's an ill-wind that blows no good. The Irish Centre Mount Pleasant never succeeded in obtaining Registered Charity status primarily because all the profits came from the bar and the dance hall. Shortly after our move into St. Michael's, Joe England and I negotiated with the Charity Commission and succeeded in having us declared a Registered Charity.

This was vital as it is virtually impossible to get grant funding without charity status. We have been blessed by having people who have given themselves very generously to maintain and continuously improve our centre. The Committee policy is to be an 'umbrella' and not to run the activities themselves. This had also been the policy in Mount Pleasant and served us well.

The centre accommodates the activity groups and encourages them to retain their independence. *Comhaltas Ceoltoiri Eireann* run Irish music classes for most instruments. Comhaltas also runs a monthly Seisún and occasional events.

The Irish Patriots, Formerly The James Larkin Flute Band have been based in the centre since we opened. *The Bolger Cunningham School of Irish Dancing.* Since we moved in, Máirín Bolger has gone to her eternal reward. Kathleen Cunningham who had been one of her pupils, gained her teacher's qualifications and now runs the Bolger Cunningham School of Irish Dancing. Many of Máirín's dancers are now bringing their children.

John Mitchels GAA Club is based in the Centre and has its meetings there. The Irish Golf Society and St. Michael's Golf Society, as well as the Finn Harps Junior Soccer Club are based there.

There is an Irish Language class weekly and an Irish Language nursery on Saturday mornings. *O.N.E. (Oglaigh Náisunta na nEireann)* meets monthly while the 25 card players meet every Friday and on Thursday evenings there is a quiz. Two Tea Dances for 'seniors' are scheduled every month. Irish Community Care Merseyside run one on the first Thursday of every month. They started these on 5th October 2000. On the third Thursday of every month, St. Michael's Centre itself runs a Tea Dance.

Joanne Gaul brought us into the 21st Century when she created a website and allocated an e-mail address to each of the committee members. From the very latest technology to the mists of time. Joanne also painted, by hand, with her sister's help, the 32 county Coats of Arms on the front edge of the stage. Exactly 32 feet. One for each county. Could anyone doubt that this place was destined to be an Irish Centre?

A few years ago, the Irish Government announced that the DION Fund would be available for Irish Social Centres, as well as Irish Community Care groups. We have successfully applied for funding. The DION funding has dramatically changed our entire operation. It has enabled us to employ two full time staff members. The first employee under the new arrangement was Peter Gallagher. When Peter returned home to Donegal, Phil McQuaid took over and he was subsequently replaced by Stephen Doyle, who is in post now. We were then fortunate enough to get further funding for the appointment of an Administrator, and Maureen Morrison was appointed. Maureen had been totally involved on a voluntary basis since the day we had moved into the Centre. Maureen had all the right experience. She had also been involved in management in Mount Pleasant.

With the combination of DION funding and a very generous community, St. Michael's Irish Centre has been transformed. The hall has a new stage, curtains and lighting and is looking great. The Heritage Room is the talk of the Irish Community in Britain. It tells the story, around the walls, of the Irish Community in Liverpool, since over a million Irish victims of the 'great hunger' came through the gates of Clarence Dock.

Through a series of pictures, the story of Irish Dancing, Music, Games and Language in the City of Liverpool is told. The Irish Centre in Mount Pleasant is remembered. There is a great stock of books of Irish interest.

As the Heritage Room neared completion, His Excellency, the Irish Ambassador Mr. David Cooney expressed a willingness to formally open it. We were indeed honoured. It was one of his first engagements since his appointment. It has proved to be an ideal venue for meetings and lectures, and Dr. Ian McKeane of the Institute of Irish Studies at the University of Liverpool gave the first series of talks on Irish history, with particular attention to Liverpool.

The children's playground with its safe, soft surface is said to be the only one in an Irish Centre in the world. Maureen Morrison's expertise in fund raising has also enabled St. Michael's to take its senior members on coach outings and to provide dinner at Christmas and St. Patrick's Day.

Mary Biggane, who happens to be our Vice-Chairperson, performs miracles by providing beautiful full dinner meals in our tiny kitchen. These lovely occasions include gifts and wonderful entertainment usually provided by Michael Coyne. Some of those attending are called up by Michael to give a song.

St. Michael's Irish Centre played its part in Liverpool's Capital of Culture in 2008. We staged *From Skibbereen to Scotland Road* in St. George's Hall and repeated it, by public demand, in the Centre. We were also hosts to the Federation of Irish Societies Annual Congress which was one of the first events in the new Liverpool Arena. It was generally agreed that the 'delegates night' in St. Michael's Centre on the night before Congress was a highlight of the weekend.

Also in Liverpool's Capital of Culture Year, we were honoured by a visit of Uachtarain na hEireann, Mary McAleese. She visited us in our home, St. Michael's Irish Centre, and invited most of us to be her guests at a concert in St. George's Hall.

During an extremely high profile year, when St. Michael's Irish Centre was so busy with local and national events, we were fortunate in having Carmel Robinson in the position of Chairperson. She filled the role with finesse and dignity.

In recent years, the Rose of Tralee Festival has returned to Liverpool. Since St. Michael's Irish Centre became a Festival venue, Grace Kelly, Fiona McConnell and Maeve Gallagher have been chosen as 'Liverpool Rose'.

President Mary McAleese's visit to St Michaels Irish Centre in 2008, with her husband Martin, and the then Irish ambassador to britain David Cooney with his wife Geraldine, pictured with various members of the committee.

The people who have served St. Michael's Irish Centre in various roles are:

Chairperson Tommy Walsh, Carmel Robinson, Pat Lynch
Vice Chair Joe England, Mary Biggane
Secretary Maureen Morrison, Joe England, Patrick Gaul, Carmel Robinson
Treasurer Siobhan Whelton (Walsh), Patrick Gaul, Dennis Campbell

Apart from the above, the following people have served as committee members: Seán Loughran, Peter Gallagher, Andy Colhoun, Philip Doyle, Stephen Doyle, Angela Billing, Patrick Morrison, Kevin Ronan, Stephen Spencer and Bernadette Adderley.
Managers Peter Gallagher, Philip McQuaid, Stephen Doyle
Administrator Maureen Morrison

The Irish Centre

To view the world in its present state,
would fill you full of fear.
Society has lost the plot
Or so it would appear.
People have become consumed
with themselves and what they own.
On having more than the guy next door.
It's a total 'Me First Zone'
Neighbours are redundant,
communities bereft
Oneupmanship is the Golden Rule
And forget whoever's left.
Yet somehow here feels different.
An oasis trapped in time.
Of days gone by, though I don't know why,
things were more sublime.
People here are willing,
to share the simple things.
To lend a hand if needed,
To laugh and dance and sing.
The age groups know no boundaries,
where else would you see,
babies in arms, kids and teens,
spending time with you and me?
It's important for the future
that the kids all see the light.
Maintain the culture and traditions.
With God's help we'll get it right
And so what brings them to gather
and unite in Celtic Band?
Simply a love of life, a love of fun,
and a love of Ireland.

Written by Bill Parry, who with his wife Pat and children Bernadette and Michael are members and regular attenders at St. Michael's. Bill, who is ever ready to give a song, was inspired by his admiration for the young people in St. Michael's Irish Centre, to write this poem about it.

193

Families of the Irish Community in Liverpool

I N THIS BOOK, *Being Irish in Liverpool*, I have given my opinion about how the Irish Community in Liverpool ticks. It is all about families.

When the 'second diaspora' occurred after World War II, the Irish people coming into Liverpool might have become good English people, not seeking one another's company and could have been swallowed up without a trace.

Because of the various venues which attracted Irish people, they sought out other Irish people; they met and married in large numbers. Some families have married within our community into the second and third generation. All our cultural activities benefit from this. I have taken children into the St. Michael's Irish Centre Heritage Room to show them pictures of their grandparent and even great grandparents, in the various G.A.A. teams, and dancing and music groups.

The sample of 'Family Stories' is just to tell the story of how it is in the Irish Community in Liverpool. During the interviews there were lots of laughs, and just as many tears. Someone should write a book 'The Irish Families of Liverpool'. It would make a huge contribution to the folklore of the city we call home. It would also be a best-seller.

Broderick / Hughes

Liam Broderick and Joan Hughes are both from County Galway, just a few miles apart. Joan is from Mountbellow and Liam from Menlough.

They met at school in Mountbellow and came to Liverpool on 12th January 1973. Liam's brother and Joan's sister were already in Liverpool. Joan and Liam were married in 1975 at home in Galway, and came to Liverpool intending to stay for six months. When Martin Broderick went home, Joan and Liam went to live in the house in Aigburth and have lived there ever since.

They danced in the Irish Centre, Mount Pleasant every night there was dancing of any kind, from ceili to show-band. In time they took their two children John and Siobhan to every activity in the Centre. They were very involved in music and having played with Comhaltas as children, they went on to play in the Blackthorn Ceili Band. They danced in Mairin Bolger's Dancing Class, although John never liked wearing the kilt. John played gaelic football with John Mitchels as his uncle Martin had done. The children went to Mountbellow every year on their holidays and Siobhan always came back with an Irish accent.

Their grandmother Mrs Broderick was a frequent visitor to the Irish Centre when she was in Liverpool. Liam worked in construction and plant hire while Joan was always a home-maker.

The whole family were an integral part of the Irish Centre. Liam was on the committees of the Irish Centre and Irish Community Care Merseyside and Joan was a volunteer helper with all the activities, and, after all those years, she is still a voluntary helper with the Tea Dances for the elderly in St. Michael's.

Joan's brother Johnnie Hughes was a great footballer and played for Mountbellow and for the great All-Ireland winning Galway team. He also won All Star Awards.

Joan and Liam say they enjoyed every minute of their life in Liverpool, and they believe their children are what they are because of their life in the Irish Community.

Callaghan / O'Shea

Eugene Callaghan was born in Breaffy, County Mayo in 1921 and came to Liverpool in the early 1950s. Eileen O'Shea was born in St. Elizabeth's parish, Litherland in 1922. Her mother was Esther Curran from near Dundalk, County Louth and her father Thomas was born in Liverpool but his father was from Fethard, County Tipperary.

Esther had come to Liverpool with her sister Bridget (Biddy) when she was 17 years old. She married Tom O'Shea in 1921. Tom was 92 when he died while Esther was 95. In her 95th year, Esther would recite a poem about the Titanic she had learned at school in Ireland. She would have been 12 years old when the Titanic sank.

Eileen's father Tom had lived with his aunt in Moyra Castle, County Louth after his mother died when he was a child. Tom's father was interned in Mountjoy Jail, Dublin for a while and when he came out, they reluctantly moved to Liverpool (after several false starts when 'Oh we just missed the boat' was the excuse for why they hadn't gone). Tom cried all night the night he left Ireland. He spent most of his working life as a warehouseman for the Co-op.

Eileen was evacuated with her sister Doreen to an aunt in Forkhill at the outbreak of World War II but returned to live through the Blitz in Bootle (though they were bombed out of their home). She and Doreen were taught Irish Dancing by the legendary Mr. McNally in Bootle.

Eugene met Eileen O'Shea in the Shamrock Club and they were married in St. Robert Bellarmine's church in 1953.

Eugene was a pub manager for the famous Liverpool brewery, Walkers (later Tetley Walker). He managed The Dryden, Scotland Road as well

as The Earl Marshall, The Oyster and The
Grapes in Thornton. He then went to work for
Father Denis Meehan as Steward of the Holy
Rosary Parish Club. Eileen had worked alongside
Eugene at all of these licensed premises and she
became Steward of the Holy Ghost Parish Club
working for the renowned Kerryman Father
Doney (Donal) Coffey.

Eileen and Eugene had two children Thomas
and Moira. Thomas is the manager of a
psychiatric social work unit in Wigan. Moira is
an administrator in the Liverpool Everyman and
Playhouse theatres in Liverpool. She attended
Irish Dancing classes with Ann Willoughby. She
has travelled widely in her career and always
makes a point of making contact with Irish
people in the various theatres and theatrical
groups. Irish people gathered at the pubs and
clubs which Eileen and Eugene ran and they
were Irish Centres in their own right.

Holidays were spent in the West, Dundalk and
Clare while their home was a first point of call for
family and friends 'off the boat' from Ireland.

Eileen and Sheila Goodwin who were well
known in the Gaelic League and The Irish
Playgoers were connected to the Callaghans by
Eileen's marriage to a cousin of Eugene's, Jimmy
Callaghan, Moira's Godfather. Eileen and Moira
attend many of the regular activities at St.
Michael's Irish Centre. Moira played a major part
in the presentation of the 'Skibbereen to Scotland
Road' concert in St. George's Hall and has also
been of invaluable help, together with Maureen
Morrison in the production of this book.

Gibbons / Coyne

John Gibbons was from Louisburgh, Co. Mayo,
he worked for many years on the docks in
Liverpool. He met and married Frances Hughes,
her parents originating from Drumintee, Co.
Armagh. They lived all their married lives in
St. Monica's Parish in Bootle.

They had four sons John, Austin, Peter and
Desmond and six daughters, Nora, Maureen,
Joan, Eileen, Rosaleen and Bernadette. Maureen
sadly died of diphtheria at five years of age. The
rest of the girls went on to marry Irishmen that
they met at various Irish venues in Liverpool.
They were regular visitors to the Shamrock Club,
St. Anne Street, Lawlors, St. Marie's in Southport
and Mount Pleasant.

Nora married Des Mc Ginnity of Killean,
South Armagh. They had four sons and one
daughter. Des regularly brought the boys to play
for John Mitchels in Newsham Park and was
always ever ready to give a hand. Sadly Norah
died in 2009.

Eileen married Patsy Mc Veigh who is
Longford's best supporter in Liverpool, and is a
regular at GAA games on TV in St. Michael's

Irish Centre. They had three children Sean played with the Irish Centre Pipe Band in Mount Pleasant, Moira and Bernadette danced with Mairin Bolger.

Rosaleen married Archie Fallon from Co. Galway. They had six sons one of whom is Nicholas a famous Irish dancer, having won the World Championships on two occasions and travelled the world with Lord of the Dance, he is now teaching Irish dancing.

Bernadette married Danny Cooney from Kilkenny. They had four daughters and a son. All the girls were Irish Dancers.

Joan married Paddy Coyne who was from Louisburgh, Co. Mayo the same place as her father. They met many times as children when the Gibbons family would go home on holiday, they also attended school in Killadoon, Louisburgh for a while when Joan and some of her sisters and brothers were evacuated there during the war. Paddy worked first on farms in Nelson and in Southport with his brother Jim and then settled in Liverpool working for Murphy's, Wimpey's and Cubits over the years. Joan remembers them meeting in the Shamrock Club, Paddy would always be standing in the corner at the back never saying a word to anyone, the quiet man!

Joan and Paddy were married in St. Monica's Church on 17th March 1956 and moved into their home in St. Joan of Arc Parish. Over the years they had regular lodgers who arrived in Liverpool, from Mayo, Pat's sister Gretta stayed for a few years before she moved onto London and Joan's cousins Austin and John Gibbons both of whom played for John Mitchels in Liverpool. Sadly Paddy died when I was writing this book.

They had three children Maureen, Michael and John all of whom have been involved in the Irish community. All three danced with Mairin Bolger and played music with Liverpool Comhaltas. Not that John lasted long with

either. Both Michael and John played for John Mitchels GFC and took part in 'It's a Knockout'. All three, along with Joan, were regular bar staff in Mount Pleasant and Maureen and John were both part of the Management team in Mount Pleasant. Maureen is now the Administrator at St. Michael's and has been involved since the beginning. Michael is one the most popular entertainers in the UK, he was also in the Liverpool Junior Ceili Band that won three All-Ireland's back in the 70s, and was in the winning Liverpool Plearacha in Ennis.

Maureen has two children Patrick is a Development Officer with Comhaltas Ceoltoiri Eireann, and also a committee member of St. Michael's Irish Centre. He was also involved as a dancer with Mairin Bolger and took part in many of her Choreographies his most famous one being Crooked Pat in Phil the Fluters Ball. Siobhan is in her final year at university studying medicine. She has been an Irish dancer and musician all her life. Both have been involved in St. Michael's Irish Centre since 1999.

Michael married Marian Fletcher and they have three daughters Clare, Christina and Louise all of whom have been involved in Irish Dancing and music all their life.

Marian Coyne said: "I know little about my mother's side (the Tierney family) but because my dad was passionate about his family history, and because they left a family bible, I know a lot about the Smiths and Raffertys".

Despite this Marian did discover recently that her maternal great grandmother was also Irish and that she died aged 24, in extreme poverty in Liverpool in the year 1889.

Mary Rafferty and Patrick Smith were Marian's great, great grand parents, probably from Bray in County Wicklow. They married in St. Peter's, Seel Street on 26th May 1850. Mary was a headstrong woman, while Patrick was a quiet, hardworking, gentle man. Mary, pining for Ireland, was inclined to 'drown her sorrows' in the local pub. One Sunday while she was 'under the influence' her husband refused to kneel beside her in church. She never drank again. They lived in Eldon Street, and in 1880 were living in Roderick Street. Their daughter Annie was Marian's great grandmother, like her mother she was a strong woman. She was born in 1856; she had a lovely singing voice. In 1880 she was married in St. Francis Xaviour's church, and the priest was the famous Jesuit poet Gerard Manley Hopkins.

Annie's husband was neither Irish nor Catholic but she was determined to keep her faith and her culture. She named her first son; Marian's grandfather, Leo Patrick Smith Fletcher. Leo was the pope at the time, Patrick was her father's name and she kept her maiden name because she thought Fletcher was a protestant name.

Marian says her great aunt told her that the naming was to 'rub salt into the wounds' of her protestant in-laws. Marian's dad (also Leo) was a good singer and was taught to play the piano by his aunt. He played all the old Irish songs and taught Marian to play *Believe me if all those endearing young charms* and T*he Rose of Mooncoin*. Marian and her husband Michael Coyne have three daughters, all of whom have music, singing and dancing talents. While Michael is a great singer and musician, it's not only from one side they get their talents. Marian says she'd like to think they have inherited something from her Irish ancestors too.

Unlike Michael, Marian was not brought up in the Irish community in Liverpool, but her family did hold on to their Irish music and heritage and to their catholic faith. She is glad that her daughters have been brought up in the Irish community and hope they will carry it forward to the next generation.

Curran / Billing

Peggy Curran and her sister Mamie came from Sean Pobail (Old Parish), part of the Ring Gaeltacht in County Waterford. Peggy came in 1953 and Mamie came two years before. They both became nurses in Liverpool, Mamie in the Womens Hospital on Catherine Street, and Peggy for a brief while in the Stanley Hospital near the Rotunda in Scotland Road, before going to Mill Road Maternity Hospital where she spent the next 35 years.

Ted Robinson came to visit his mother in Sefton General Hospital, met Mamie Curran, her nurse, and they were eventually married, in Mamie's parish church near Dungarvan. They had two children Angela and Kevin, who are well known to the Irish Community in Liverpool. Angela is a committee member of St. Michael's and she and her children Richard, Ellen and Niall are involved in every aspect of Irish Community life. Richard was captain of the Lancashire Gaelic Football underage team, Ellen

learned Irish dancing and music in the Centre, and is now to be found in the shop on Sundays.

Looking back to her days nursing, Peggy remembers very happy days with the other Irish girls in the nurse's home in Mill Road and visits to the Irish Centre in Mount Pleasant. She has fond memories of Sarah (Spud) Murphy of County Tyrone who was Sister Tutor at Mill Road and who was a volunteer receptionist in the Irish Centre.

Peggy went to a World Cup game at Goodison Park in 1966 with her brother-in-law Ted Robinson and became an Everton supporter. She has been a season ticket holder ever since. She went to the games with Ted until his death.

Peggy regularly attends the Tea Dances at St. Michael's as well as most other events there.

She says her earliest impression of Liverpool was bricks, bricks and more bricks – and smog.

I asked Angela for her feelings about Ireland and St. Michael's Irish Centre. She said, "As children, we spent summer holidays with family in Ireland. I remember crying at the sight of the coastline of Ireland and I cried even more when I left. The fields and cows on the journey from Dublin to Waterford delighted me, but the return journey was absolutely black. A dark cloud descended on me. It would stay with me for the next few weeks. One day about nine years ago, I stepped into St. Michael's Irish Centre and knew I had found something very special. I wanted to be part of it. I wanted my children to belong here. I didn't realise then what a huge part of our lives St. Michael's would become. Among all the wonderful times I have enjoyed in St. Michael's, I think my happiest hours are on Sunday afternoons in the company of the funny, intelligent gentlemen on the 'Top Table'. They are storytellers and ballad singers too. Every Sunday is an education.

I leave the centre a wiser person. The rich broad curriculum can range from which colour cows give the creamiest milk to the Dublin lockout in 1913/14. The Irish language flows as freely as the Guinness – perhaps we should apply for a AN GAELTACHT sign.

Many others are like me, passionate about our Community. St. Michael's means so much to so many people, for so many different reasons. Go raibh mile maith agaibh to the few people who met in Father Sean O'Connor's kitchen and had the courage and foresight to see beyond the ripped wallpaper and worn carpet in the shabby building in Boundary Lane to create our little piece of Ireland in the middle of West Derby Road.

Eileen & Paddy Doran

Eileen Ruane arrived from Mayo in 1954 and Paddy Doran, one of a family of twelve children arrived from Loughinisland, County Down in 1959. They met in the Shamrock Club in Lime Street and attended the Irish Centre, Mount Pleasant from the time it opened.

Eileen and Paddy were married in St. Ambrose Church in Speke in 1962. They became Life Members of the Irish Centre and remained so until it closed.

Many Irish Cultural organisations have been financially supported by Eileen and Paddy particularly Bolger Cunningham School of Irish Dancing and John Mitchels Gaelic Football Club.

Deirdre & Pat McAndrew

Deirdre and Paddy Doran are brother and sister. Deirdre arrived from County Down in 1968 to become a nurse at Sefton General Hospital. Pat McAndrew came from his home in Rossport County Mayo also in 1968. They met at a Friday night showband night in the Irish Centre in June 1972, and married in 1974. They have three children Siobhan, Patrick and Kieron.

In 1969 Deirde was selected as the Liverpool Rose to represent the Irish Centre in the Rose of Tralee Festival. Since then she has frequently

been asked to be a judge at the Liverpool Rose Selection. Deirdre and Pat said it was great experience, the security, help and Irish Culture at the Centre, and they remember Sean Murphy with great pleasure. They said "he always made us so welcome".

Gallagher Family

Margaret (Daly) and Maurice (Mossy) Gallagher came to Liverpool with seven children in 1964. One girl, Rosemary, was in London. They came from their home in Bansha, County Tipperary.

Margaret was originally from Tipperary town, and she is quite famous in that she was the first secretary to Canon Hayes when he founded the remarkable Irish countrywide organisation Muintir na Tire. In that capacity she met the then Taoioseach at the 50th anniversary of the organisation.

The Gallagher's lived briefly in St. Charles parish, Aigburth Road, before settling down in St. Clare's parish Sefton Park. The eldest daughter Rosemary was still in London and Myra, Robert, Patrick (Patsy), Maurice (Mossy), Jeremiah (Jerry), Noel and Margaret were in the family home.

It was there that Fr. Sean O'Connor first met the Gallagher's, and he still enjoys their company in St. Michael's Irish Centre on a Sunday afternoon, especially when Tipperary are playing Cork.

Mr & Mrs Gallagher returned to Bansha in 1992. Margaret went with them, while Myra, Patsy, Jerry, Mossie, Robert and Noel stayed in Liverpool. Some of the lads played in the Irish Centre pipe band and Con Doyle arranged Mossy's first job interview. Mossie remembers Denis Gollocks ceili classes on a Tuesday night and his daughter went to Mairin Bolgers dancing class. He also remembers hearing Irish Showbands like Big Tom on Paschal Mooneys Radio Eireann programme and then going to see them in the Irish Centre.

Mossie has fond memories of Sean Murphy, Peter Mc Padden and especially John Mc Cormack in the foyer. The Gallagher brothers are regular attenders at St. Michael's Irish Centre, particularly on Sunday for gaelic games on T.V. Mossie is a member of the committee and is closely involved in every aspect of the centre. Jerry is always available when willing hands are needed. Mossy and Jerry enjoy the quiz on a Thursday night and Mossy gives a song, and Jerry a tune on the tin whistle, whenever there's a 'session'. After a big Sunday event Patsy does the rounds with the mike, getting people to give a song.

N.B. Canon Hayes, the founder of Muintir na Tire, briefly served as a young priest in a Liverpool parish.

Garrigan

Tony Garrigan's parents, Patrick and Margaret were born in Liverpool and their origins were Virginia County Cavan and Waterford. They lived in St. Joan of Arc Parish, Bootle, where they married in 1938. The influence of the local Irish population was strong and they attended ceilis in St. Joans, St. Augustines and St. James.

Tony was taken to his first ceili at Bootle Town Hall to hear the Lally Brothers Ceili Band. There was much music and song in the home and Tony remembers his father playing his small accordion and singing. He also danced a step of the hornpipe using the kitchen table and the corner of the dresser for support as the legs weakened.

His mother had a lovely singing voice. A highlight of Tony's young life was when Eamonn Coyne visited the house and played his fiddle, Tony said it was heaven. After the Bootle bombing the family moved to Waterloo.

Paddy Garrigan's Irish interests were many. He was secretary of the Anti Partition of Ireland League and was an active member of the old IRA and Cumman na mBan group. He attended the Easter Sunday commemoration ceremony for many years. This included Mass in the cathedral, reading the Proclamation on the steps of the Irish Centre in Mount Pleasant, then, in the afternoon a visit to the Fenian Memorial in Ford Cemetery.

Tony says his parents loved the Irish Centre and always enjoyed their visits. Tony himself became a noted musician with his own ceili band. He played all over Britain and Ireland and frequently on Ceili House on R.T.E. and on the new Telefis Eireann in the 1980s. He was Sean O'Se's favourite accompanist and played for Sean in Cork as well as in Liverpool. Tony's brother and sister Mary and Gerard were also musicians in ceili bands.

Gaul-Furlong

The picture is at an Irish Dancing event in Liverpool. 3rd from left is Breda Norris, 4th from left is Evelyn Stockdale who also became an Irish dancing teacher and next to her is Kathleen. Also in the picture is Pat Clarke who was a very well known Irish Dancer in Liverpool.

Kathleen Gaul (nee Furlong) has an interesting story to tell. It includes a tragic and historic event. Her mother's parents come from Moygannon near Rostrevor, County Down, and settled in Liverpool in the early 1900s. They made regular trips home for holidays and family occasions.

Sadly Kathleen's grandfather, and one of his daughters, Lily, lost their lives in the terrible Carlingford Lough disaster on November 3rd 1916. 94 people died when there was a collision between the S.S. Connemara and the S.S. Retriever. Most of those who died were passengers on the S.S. Connemara which was en route from Greenore to Holyhead.

Kathleen was one of eight children. She had three brothers and four sisters. She remembers that they all listened to Radio Athlone (RTE) every evening until the National Anthem was played. They also had a gramophone and records of John Mc Cormack, Cavan O'Connor and Delia Murphy, among others.

Kathleen attended Irish dancing classes run by the Misses Kelly (Mary and Sarah) in St. Theresa's Parish Hall, Norris Green. It was a very popular dancing class at the time and hundreds of children were taught over many years. The dancers were asked to perform at numerous events all over the city, including the Adelphi Hotel and the Picton Hall. On one occasion at the Picton Hall the compere was Rinty Monaghan, the singing champion boxer. When she was a bit older she started going to evening classes for ceili dancing, as distinct from step dancing. These classes were also run by the Misses Kelly.

She enjoyed going to the weekly ceili in the John Mitchels branch of the Gaelic League in Burlington Street, off Scotland Road. She also went to ceili's in a number of parish halls, such as, St. Alphonsus, Holy Cross, St. Robert Bellarmine's, St. Peter and Paul's, St. Dominic's, Christ the King, St. Oswald's and a very special memory was when Fr. O'Mahoney brought the Gallowglass Ceili Band over from Ireland to play.

Kathleen has happy memories of the many Irish priests in Liverpool at the time. She remembers doing the devotion of the seven churches between Dale Street and St. Anthony's, Scotland Road.

Another place she loved to visit was the '98 Shop in Scotland Place. All the Irish papers and other Irish goods were there. It had a lovely Irish atmosphere.

Because of the ceili dance classes, she and her friends knew all the ceili dances. Her particular friend was Breda Norris. They went everywhere together. In 1954 Kathleen married Bob Gaul at St. Cecilia's; Bob was a friend of her brother. His grandfather was from Belfast. They had six children Cecilia, Danny, Kevin, Marie, Peter and Patrick. As the children were growing up they took advantage of Ryanair and Easyjets routes to various destinations in Ireland and spent many holidays all over the country.

Kathleen's first love in Irish Culture is dancing, and she is delighted that her two daughters and three granddaughters followed in that tradition. She particularly enjoyed the big St. Patrick's week events in Liverpool, especially the concerts in the major halls including the Picton and the Philharmonic Halls, and later the Irish Centre. She loved the Irish Centre and was very sad to see it close. She is delighted to see that St. Michael's Irish Centre is keeping all the old traditions alive.

Her son Peter played gaelic football for John Mitchels and he won a pool competition in Mount Pleasant. Patrick and Peter, and son-in-law Tam have played in St. Michael's as 'The Hoops' while Patrick and Peter play and sing regularly at the Sunday night Ballad Night.

Kathleen and Breda have a remarkable memory of 127 Mount Pleasant. Before the Irish community bought the building it was used by Rodney Youth Centre. Kathleen taught ceili dancing to the children in the cellar there.

Other memories are of great ceili's in Bootle Town Hall, her favourites bands being the Shannon Star and the Brian Boru, along with The Irish Playgoers and Vera Furlong for her great monologues at Irish Concerts. Kathleen went to all their productions in the Crane Theatre, Christ the King Hall and later, the Irish Centre.

Kathleen's husband Bob made a unique contribution to the Irish Community in Liverpool. When we bought the premises in Mount Pleasant and applied to the Licensing Justices for a license, the committee were told – off the record – they hadn't a chance. Bob Gaul handled the application in his capacity as legal executive for Solicitor John Cowper. After a long drawn out case, including many court appearances, the Centre did get a license. It was a 'Justices On License – With Conditions'.

Sadly Bob died in 2002. Kathleen's son Patrick plays a big part in the St. Michael's Irish Centre. He is a member of the Committee and has filled the posts of Treasurer and Secretary. He runs the Sunday night Ballad Night and the Monday night Book Club. Patrick's wife Joanne is responsible for the 32 County Coats of Arms painted by hand on the edge of the stage in the hall. She was assisted by her sister Andrea.

Richard & Josephine Grainger

Josephine McIntyre was born in Donegal, and arrived in Liverpool in 1958. With many other Irish girls she trained as a nurse in Walton Hospital. Richard Grainger, born in Dublin, came to Liverpool to teach in 1961.

A stranger in Liverpool he found a new family among the Irish community, and became involved with the GAA and was a founder member of the Irish Centre Building Fund.

Josephine and Richard were both parishioners of Blessed Sacrament Parish, Aintree, and in 1962 they met through mutual parochial friends, and socialised within the Irish Community. They found success in nursing and teaching and for a period Richard was a part-time politician and councillor.

They were married in Ireland in 1964 and have two daughters, Josephine is married to John Greene, also of Irish descent (Mayo and Roscommon), they have three daughters who have attended Irish dancing classes. Frances married Steve Hilton, they have three sons. All the family visit Ireland, particularly their ancestral roots in Dublin, Donegal, Mayo and Roscommon.

Anne & Joe England

Anne and Joe met when they were both members of the Welfare Committee at the Irish Centre in Mount Pleasant. They were married in 1970 and held their Reception at the Centre. They have two children Celine who is a nurse in Seattle in the USA and Keiran who is married and lives in Crosby. Joe has been involved in Irish affairs in Liverpool since 1964 and had the honour of being the Chair of the Executive Committee when the Irish Centre was presented with the Irish Post Community Award for excellence in 1977. He came to England in 1963 from Roscrea, in Tipperary. There was no work in Ireland at that time but there was plenty here. He joined the Irish Centre in Mount Pleasant soon after it opened and served on various committees during the lifetime of the Centre. He also played hurling for Shamrocks in Birkenhead and St. Patrick's in Liverpool. Joe had various jobs on building sites, in Fords Factory in Halewood and as a van driver, before becoming a Probation Officer in 1970. He retired in 2002.

Anne's father, William O'Malley was born in Devlin, Louisburgh, County Mayo and first came to England when he was 16 years old. Like many of his generation he worked on farms in Lancashire, then on the roads and later as a docker in Liverpool. In 1937 he married Annie Mc Namara in Killeen Church near Louisburgh and they set up home, first in Bootle and later in Crosby. They had five children Joan, Anne, John, Nora and Kathleen.

Soon after the Irish Centre opened in Mount Pleasant, Anne helped out in the Coffee Bar and became a member of the Irish Centre Welfare Committee. She was employed as a clerical officer with Sefton Youth Service until her retirement in 2007.

Kennedy / White / Doolin

Maura White came from her home in Ennis County Clare to work in Southport and Tommy Kennedy came from Oldcastle Co Meath in 1960/61. Tommy was the eldest of 11 children and was only 15 years of age when he started working in the construction industry in Liverpool. His purpose was to send money home to help his family.

Maura and Tommy met at a dance in The Shamrock Club, and they married in St. James Bootle in 1963. They had four children, three girls and a boy. The whole family were into Irish music and dancing. Maura senior had been a champion step dancer at home in Ennis. She remembers losing her navy blue knickers in the middle of a feis, she kicked them off and won the competition. Tommy played the mouth organ and danced 'sean nos' at home in Meath, and sang his

favourite song Dan O'Hara. They lived briefly in a flat in Bootle before settling in their present home in Worcester Road. The children were Maire, John, Michelle and Judith. Maire and John went to Mairin Bolger to dancing classes, where John was King of the Fairies in one of Mairin's choreographies. Maura senior formed the Green Velvet Ceili band in which Maire and John took part. Apart from playing in Liverpool they also played a big part in the regular visits to Dungarvan. The family were a big part of the Liverpool Comhaltas Ceoiltoiri Eireann and Maire Junior became Regional Secretary.

They played a big part in the Plearacha group which won the All-Ireland Final in Ennis at Fleadh Nua. Maire and Tommy Walsh were partners in the Set Dance and Maura danced solo. The family were regular attenders at the Irish Centre, Mount Pleasant from show-band to ceili. They also ran ceilis in their home 'Around the house and mind the dresser'. Canon Michael O'Connor who was a founder of the Irish Centre and was then Parish Priest of St. Monica's was a regular visitor.

Kennedy / Doolin

Maire Kennedy met Neil Doolin in 1991 in the Irish Centre, at a karaoke night. Neil sang that night. Phyllis Crossan who worked in the shop 'Croc and Oir' in the Centre kind of matched them. She told each of them they would be great together. They agreed. They married in 1994 in St. Monica's. Canon O'Connor was celebrant. They have three lads Ciaron played football with Finn Harps under Sean Loughran's guidance, Feidhelm and Declan danced with the Bolger Cunningham School of Irish Dancing and Feidhelm now dances with Nicholas Fallon. Feidhelm had a lot of success qualifying for the World Championships several times.

Apart from their cultural activities Maire and Neil have played a major role in administration in

Irish life in the city of Liverpool. Maire was Regional Secretary of Comhaltas and is now a committee member of St. Michael's Irish Centre. Neil was a member of IBRG (Irish in Britain Representation Group) both locally and nationally. He formed the James Larkin Flute Band which is now known as the Liverpool Irish Patriots Band. He and Jeff O'Carroll take the band to venues all over England, Ireland, Scotland and Wales. Neil was secretary of Irish Community Care Merseyside for three years.

Paddy and Olive Doolin, Neil's parent moved back to Dublin in 1996 having lived in Liverpool for some years. Paddy teaches children in The Liberties in Dublin, to play fiddle. Paddy and Olive still come to Liverpool to visit their family and they were delighted to be asked to 'let the 2010 New Year in' at St. Michael's Irish Centre.

Neil's brother David is also a member of the Irish Patriots band and he and his partner Leanne are very much part of the Irish Centre, as are their children Siobhan and Shea, who have both attended the Bolger Cunningham Irish Dancing class.

Dave brought a group of Lithuanian friends from the Liverpool One site to the annual An Tostal. They formed a team and won the tug of war final. One of the Lituanian's said that they enjoyed the family atmosphere. It reminded them of home.

Kirwan / Scahill

Aidan, John and Pat Kirwan came to Liverpool from their home in Kilmuckridge, County Wexford in the early 1950s. Aidan and Pat became very involved in GAA life in Liverpool, while John returned home after a few years.

Mary, Norah, Kathleen and Rose Scahill came from Carramore, near Croagh Patrick, County Mayo also in the 50s. There were seven children and their father died when he was only 39 years old. Their mother lived until she was 97 years old. All of them found work in Liverpool and, like so many other young Irish people attended the Shamrock Club in Lime Street.

Mary met Aidan Kirwan there, and they were married in Liverpool in 1957. They lived at first in St. Bernard's parish, and, for most of their lives in St. Charles parish. Sadly Aidan died in 2005. Norah met and married Gerry O'Brien who was also a hurler with St. Patrick's GAA club. Kathleen married Charlie Towey who had come over from County Roscommon. The fourth sister of the Scahill family, Rose, married her neighbour Danny Hastings, at home in County Mayo, before they, too settled in Liverpool.

Pat Kirwan and his wife Phyllis, who was from County Tipperary, returned to Ireland with their children to settle in County Wexford, while Norah and Gerry O'Brien and their family also returned to Ireland to live in County Westmeath.

Aidan and Mary Kirwan had six children, Aidan, John, Eddie, Eileen, Betty and Maria, 12 grandchildren and a great grandchild.

The whole family were an integral part of the Irish Centre, Mount Pleasant, and were involved in every aspect of Irish life in Liverpool. The Kirwan's are unique in the Liverpool GAA. Three members of two generation played a vital part in the local club. The first generations were all hurlers, while the next generation Aidan's sons, Aidan, John and Eddie were footballers with the John Mitchels Gaelic Football Club and with Lancashire. A third generation of Kirwan's became John Mitchels Gaelic footballers when Aidan's sons Daniel and Sean played under-age, Eddie's son Michael played for Manchester Metropolitan University Gaelic Football Team.

Apart from the GAA connection, all the family were involved in every activity in the Irish Community in Liverpool, including music, dancing and 'It's a Knockout'.

Mary said they all enjoyed going to the Irish Centre where they all made good friends. "Being in Liverpool is home from home"

Loughran – Hannaway

Sean Loughran is from Killeavy, County Armagh. He left home at 18 years of age to go to his father who was working in Macclesfield.

Sheilagh was the first daughter of Josie and Peter Hannaway. Josie's real name is Mary but she has always been known as Josie. There were nine Hannaway children one of whom died in infancy. Their father Peter Hannaway was from County Armagh. Sheilagh Loughran's grandfather, Josie's father, was from Mayo and he and Josie's mum eloped to Liverpool. They had five children and lived in Everton and Kirkdale. Josie and Peter Hannaway quickly became involved in the Irish life in Liverpool and Sheilagh remembers that they talked about dances in Gay Street and St. Anne Street. Sheilagh herself went to the famous Mr McNally to Irish dancing classes. Every year the family went to Killeavy and Sheilagh met Sean there. They were married in St. Francis de Sales in Liverpool in 1960. They danced in the Shamrock Club and Sean played gaelic football for the Sean Mc Dermott's Club, which was based in the Shamrock Club and in Birkenhead.

They became involved in the Irish Centre, Mount Pleasant and Sean served on the committee. He was a founder member of the Northern Ireland Childrens Holiday Scheme (NICHS) and was involved in raising funds for the Innocent Dependants Fund during internment at Long Kesh.

Sheilagh was the first secretary of Irish Community Care Merseyside and remained in that position until she and Sean returned to live in South Armagh in 2001. Sheilagh and Sean had three children Sean, Paul and Marie and they, like their parents, were involved in every aspect of Irish life in Liverpool.

Sean and Paul played gaelic football for John Mitchels GFC and Lancashire. They played soccer for Finn Harps and were junior members of the Irish Centre pipe band., They remember Con Doyle who was pipe major of the band.

Marie did Irish dancing and they were all involved with events like 'It's a Knockout' which was organised by the Federation of Irish Societies for Irish Centre's all over Britain.

In July '89 Sean Junior married Norah Quinlan a member of a similar Liverpool Irish family to his own. They have one son Thomas and three daughters Rebecca, Megan and Ciara who are well known for their Irish dancing skills. Rebecca was British National Champion and North West Regional Champion on five occasions. Ciara was North West Regional Champion three years in succession. Both Rebecca and Ciara hold All-Ireland and World Championship medals.

Paul married Tara Kelly and their baby Caoimhe was the star of the Crib Sunday Nativity play in St. Michael's Irish Centre in December 2009 when she played the part of baby Jesus.

Marie is now working in London but turns up to Irish Community events in Liverpool. Sheilagh said that their friends in Liverpool were all parents whose children were involved with their own children, at various Irish activities especially gaelic football. She mentioned the Mc Paddens, Morrins Wheltons and Kirwans.

Quinlan / Hurley

Michael Quinlan went to London from his home in Rathcormac, County Cork in 1957, and Mary Hurley also went to London from County Clare when she was 18 years old. They both worked on the buses, Mary as a 'clippie' and Michael as a conductor, which is where they met.

They enjoyed all the Irish dance halls in London, which were open seven nights a week. Their favourite venue was the Galtymore. They were married in 1962, came to Liverpool, and settled off Smithdown Road.

One day Michael was driving in Mount

Pleasant and he saw a girl in Irish dancing costume, on the pavement outside the Irish Centre. He and Mary went back and found the Centre. From then on they were an integral part of everything that happened in the Centre and in Irish life in Liverpool.

Their children Norah, Pauline, William, Tony and John all attended the Centre socially, and the whole family made their friends in the Centre. They were involved in the dancing, music and football. Pauline was a very talented actress and always had a leading role in shows like *Phil the Fluters Ball*, Tony played in the pipe band. Mary worked in the Irish Centre bar for about 20 years, and at the same time she drove a bus taking special needs children to school.

Michael worked on the buses in Liverpool for 28 years. Their happy memories are of Sean Murphy, Martin Foley, Chris Johnston and so many others.

Michael's happy memories included the New Year's Eve when he had to work and could not attend the Centre. After midnight he was passing the Centre on his way to the depot, and saw a crowd outside. He picked them all up and took them home. On another occasion he was watching Finn Harps playing in Walton Hall Park, with the bus parked nearby. An inspector drove the bus back to the depot. That night when he came into the Centre, Sean Murphy had a poster on the wall 'Bus Missing'.

Sean Loughran and Norah Quinlan met in the Centre when they were teenagers. Their story is told separately.

Lynch / Curran

Pat Lynch went from his home in Cappamore, County Limerick to London in 1966 'to find work'. He came to Liverpool in 1967 to attend teacher training college and never left.

Nora Curran left her home near Listowel, County Kerry in 1965 to go to her sister in Barrow-in-Furness, and after training as a nurse in Providence Hospital, St. Helens, ended up in Liverpool.

Nora and Pat met one night in the Irish Centre, Mount Pleasant, and were married in Ireland in 1975. They returned to Liverpool and lived briefly in Grassendale and Broadgreen before settling down in their present home in St. Paul's parish, West Derby. Pat's working life was in teaching while Nora was a nurse.

They have two children Neil and Theresa and the whole family, children and parents, were all involved, like so many other Irish families in Liverpool, in every aspect of Irish Community life. Pat played hurling for St. Patrick's Hurling Club where one of his playing colleagues was Joe England.

When St. Pat's couldn't field a team, Pat went up to Manchester to play for Harp and Shamrock. Mick Larkin was doing the same thing.

As the children grew they attended music and dancing classes in the Irish Centre, and Neil played Gaelic football with John Mitchels and soccer with Finn Harps.

Pat was helping to run the John Mitchels under age team, along with Aidan Kirwan. Neil and Theresa also attended martial arts classes. Theresa is now studying for a Doctorate in Law, having qualified as a barrister. Neil is following in his fathers footsteps and is teaching.

Pat's memories of Mount Pleasant include fond thoughts of Martin Foley, who was always busy giving a hand with anything that needed doing. Another memory is of the 25 card games. Mrs Burke, Eithne McNamara, Father Jennings and Bernard Bradley were always there. At Christmas so many people attended the card game that the ballroom was almost full. He also remembers raising funds with Kathleen Walsh to take children to the next Fleadh in Britain or Ireland to play in their music competitions. Eamon Coyne, Peggy Peakin and Maurice Quinn are fondly remembered too.

Pat has served as chairman of Irish Community Care Merseyside and is, at present, chairman of St. Michael's Irish Centre. Nora is one of the team who provide Tea Dances, in the name of Irish Community Care Merseyside, and St. Michael's Irish Centre, twice a month in St. Michael's.

Mc Donnell / Lavin

Andy McDonnell and Lena Lavin are from Keelogues, Ballavary, County Mayo. They were married in Keelogues in 1945. They had five children, four boys and a girl, all of whom were born in Mayo. Andy came to Liverpool in 1965 and Lena and the children followed in 1966. They lived briefly in St. Philip Neri parish and have lived since in St. Sebastian's parish.

From the beginning they have visited home every year, taking the children with them. When Andy came in 1965 the Irish Centre, Mount Pleasant, opened. He and then Lena and the children used the Centre as their 'home from home' until it closed.

They went to all the concerts and they feel as though they know Sean O'Se. They went to his concerts in Mount Pleasant and they still go to see him in St. Michael's Irish Centre. They enjoy going to St. Michael's and see it as a continuation of Mount Pleasant. They go regularly to the Tea Dances.

They miss the many friends they had in the Irish Community who have died. Their daughter Bridie and son Vincent worked in the bar in Mount Pleasant with the Winter's family and they became friends.

Bridie met Padraig Kelly, of Sligo in Mount Pleasant and they were married, while their son Pat met Anne Boylan who came over regularly from Birkenhead. They also married.

N.B. Lena and Andy were nice enough to say they always enjoyed meeting me in Mount Pleasant, and in St. Michael's, and I must say

the feeling is mutual. I was lucky enough to be invited to Andy's 90th birthday party and I really enjoyed meeting all the family again. T.W.

Mc Namara / Duffy

Brenda Duffy and Sean McNamara were married in 1958. Brenda's grandmother, whose name was Drumm came from Castlebar, County Mayo, and married Brenda's grandfather in Liverpool. They lived in Burlington Street, Scotland Road where they had a shop. Brenda remembers the shop and she also remembers the local wash-house. They moved to St. Theresa's Parish in Norris Green where they were living when Brenda met Sean.

Sean father Peter came from Kilmihill, County Clare and was in London for 10 years, before he moved to Liverpool where he met, and married Molly McLoughlin. They lived at first in St. Bernard's parish, and later in St. Clare's.

Their daughters, Maire, Eithne and Aileen and sons Joe, Pearse and Sean, were all involved in Irish activities. The girls were all Irish Dancers, while the boys all played the fiddle, at ceilis and sessions. Pearse played hurling with Eire Og, and Sean was a very active member of St. Patrick's Hurling and John Mitchels Gaelic Football club, serving on the committee for some years. Sean remembers playing the fiddle for the dancers at the Liverpool Feis when he was 10 years old. He played at ceilis and concerts from about 1945 with musicians and bands all over Liverpool.

Sean and Brenda met at a ceili at the Sean O'Donovan branch of the Gaelic League in Wood Street and they danced there and at ceilis all over Liverpool from then on.

They have three daughters Maire, Trisha and Anne, all of whom attended Irish Dancing classes with Mairin Bolger and Ann Hayes.

Of course being Sean McNamara's daughters they attended music classes too.

Maire married Ray Rooney whose mother is from the Belcoo/Belleek area. They sing Irish songs at venues around Merseyside.

Trisha and Michael Lacey met in the Irish Centre, Mount Pleasant when they were students and both doing holiday work in the bar. Michael's parents Frank and Mary Lacey were very well known in the Irish Centre. Frank was from Connemara and Mary from Cavan.

Trisha is also on the committee of Comhaltas, and as you might expect her and Anne's children are very musical and they have attended dancing classes.

Sean McNamara is of course well known world wide, as a great Irish fiddler. He was a founder member of the famous Liverpool Ceili band who came together in the 1950's and 60's. They are best known as the band who won the All-Ireland championship in 1963 and 1964.

Murphy / Burke

Sister and brother Eileen and Paddy Murphy came to Liverpool from their home in Taghmon County Wexford. Eileen arrived in Liverpool in 1952 having worked in Dublin on the way. She started work in Meccano, Binns Road after two days in Liverpool, and found lodgings with Miss Kennedy in Shaw Street.

Eileen met Mayoman John Burke at a dance in St. Marie's, Southport where Irish people gathered. They were married in July 1955. They had five children. John died in 1993.

Eileen worked briefly in Brougham Terrace before going to work in Mill Road, Oxford Street and the new Woman's Hospital.

After she retired from hospital work she went to help in St. Michael's Presbytery where Christian Brothers and students from St. Edwards College were staying. Among those staying there was Brother O'Grady who was very well known among the Irish Community in Liverpool. Eileen has been involved in every

aspect of parish life in St. Michael's for many years and in St. Michael's Irish Centre since we moved in to the old parish club in 1999.

Murphy / Murphy

Paddy Murphy, Eileen's brother came from their home in Wexford, shortly after Eileen. He was offered a job in a tannery as he arrived in Liverpool, (while he was still on the boat) and worked there briefly before spending the rest of his working life in the construction industry. Paddy met Maureen Murphy (yes, she was a Murphy too) in the Shamrock Club and they married in Sacred Heart church in 1957.

They have three children and six grandchildren and they live in St. Paul's Parish, West Derby. Paddy is a 25 card player every Friday night in St. Michael's and is responsible for the famously perfect beer lines in St. Michael's Irish Centre, which he cleans every Monday. The Guinness Company recently said "Great tasting Guinness served here".

Paddy says he was always treated well by Liverpool people at work and in the parish.

Bourke / Roche

Bridie Roche came from Balla County Mayo. She and her husband Jimmy Bourke had married in Mayo and came to Liverpool in 1959. They lived in St. Sebastian's parish and then in Molyneux Road from 1964 to 1986 before moving to their present home in St. Paul's Parish West Derby in 1986. It was a very happy move and they have had very good neighbours. They had five children and six grandchildren.

Bridie has a remarkable memory of her own little miracle. She had lost her purse with every penny she had. She had no money even for food. The next morning a letter came from her mother in Mayo with £2 in it.

At one time Bridie and Jimmy were living in

one room with their three children. They had no garden, not even a clothes line and, of course, no washing machine.

Bridie was an auxiliary nurse from 1971 to 1995 working three nights a week in the Royal, Mill Road, Oxford Street and the new Woman's Hospital. She also worked in St. Michael's Parish Club from 1971 – 1991 and she came back to St. Michael's Irish Centre when we opened in 1999. She still works at the Tea Dances every second Thursday with Nick Redmond who was Bar Steward in Mount Pleasant.

Bridie says no one in Liverpool ever said a wrong word to her about Irish people. She and Jimmy were happy here – they "couldn't be happier". Sadly Jimmy died in 2004.

N.B. Jim Bourke and John Burke were brothers and spelled their names differently.

Owens / Cahill

Kathleen Cahill and Henry Owens lived only three miles apart in County Wexford, Kathleen in Rathangan, Henry in Kilmore.

Henry went up to Dublin to the All-Ireland Hurling Final in 1956, with Kathleen's brother. Kathleen was working in St. Michael's Hospital Dun Laoghaire and met the lads.

Henry came over to Liverpool and Kathleen came shortly after in September 1957. They went to the Shamrock Club and other Irish dance halls in Liverpool.

They were married in London in 1958 and moved up to settle in Liverpool a few months later. They lived near Henry's brother for a short while. They moved to their present address in Knotty Ash in 1974. They have five children Gerald, Bridie, Francis, Peter and Alan. Peter and Alan played gaelic football for John Mitchels and soccer for Finn Harps. Alan was a good corner back for John Mitchels and is now a consultant doctor.

Francis has been confined to a wheelchair but leads a full life, his main interests being music and sport. He argues with his dad about the horses. His knowledge of Irish songs has always surprised everyone at concerts and events.

N.B One of my happiest moments was being told that "God bless Tommy Walsh" was one of his night prayers.

Patrick and Nora Winters

Pat (Frank) and Nora Winters came to Liverpool in 1956. Pat was born in Gateshead in 1923. The death of his mother meant that his father took his two young sons back to his native Clare Island, Co. Mayo to live. Nora hailed from Limerick Junction, Tipperary.

Pat and Nora met in Rugby in June 1953 on the day of the Queen's coronation and were married in St. Marie's Church in February 1954. The newly weds went to live on Clare Island. However, island life was not for Nora so after almost two years on the island they headed for England. They took the boat from Dublin not sure where they would end up. Pat met an acquaintance on the boat who offered him a job in Liverpool and so they put down roots and stayed. Pat and Nora had five children; Mary, Angela, Patrick, John and Charles.

Pat became well known around Liverpool playing accordion and singing in the many Irish bars in the city. He was known as Frank to many people – this happened because of a mix up with names when he played in the darts team of one of the best known Irish bars in the city 'McGreals' (The Parkside) on Smithdown Road.

Jim and Mary (nee Winters) Biggane

Jim came from near Broadford, Co. Limerick to Liverpool in 1964. and Mary was born in Castlebar, Co. Mayo and spent her early years on Clare Island till her parents came to Liverpool in 1956.

Jim and Mary met in the Irish Centre, Mount Pleasant in 1972 and held their wedding in the

211

Irish Centre in September 1973. They have four children Julie, Patrick, James and Siobhan.

Julie and Patrick enjoyed the good times associated with their age group at The Irish Centre, Mount Pleasant and could be found there with their family every Sunday morning and on many social evenings. James and Siobhan did not experience Mount Pleasant but did enjoy the good times associated with St. Michael's Irish Centre from 1999 onwards. All of the Biggane family have been involved in St. Michael's from the onset.

Duane / Robinson
Carmel Duane (Kerry) met Bob Robinson (Liverpool) whilst on holiday in Tenerife in 1980 and they were married in Cork in July 1981. They decided to make their home in Liverpool as it was easier at the time for Carmel to get a job in Liverpool than for Bob to get a job in Cork/Kerry. The plan was to stay in Liverpool for two years and then to return to live in Ireland. At the time Bob was a heavy goods driver and Carmel found work as a Social Worker with Liverpool City Council.

Almost 30 years on Carmel is still a Social Worker and Bob is now a driving instructor. They have two children Louise and Niamh and they are still living in Liverpool.

Carmel and Bob found that the Irish Centre in Mount Pleasant was reminiscent of rural Ireland and enjoyed some good nights there. Shortly after St. Michael's Irish Centre opened they came in and had a drink sitting in what is now the playground. The first pint of Guinness left them wanting more and they came to a ceili the following Saturday night. The Robinson family fell in love with St. Michael's that night and have never left the place.

Carmel's mother and father, Andrew and Martha Duane were frequent visitors to Liverpool and at one time considered moving over here to live. Andrew is now deceased but Martha continues to visit and loves going to St. Michael's where she is always made to feel welcome. Carmel became so involved in St. Michael's Irish Centre that she joined the Committee and soon became Chairperson. After two years in that position she became Secretary, a position she still holds.

Louise and Niamh are equally involved and attend the Comhaltas music classes which are held in St. Michael's every week. They have been altar servers at the Mass of St. Patrick and Louise is a regular attendee at the Thursday quiz. Bob's area of expertise is running the potato picking and wellie throwing competitions at An Tostal.

Carmel thinks it is important to have an Irish Centre like St. Michael's. It keeps the community in touch with one another and gives them focus. She believes that St. Michael's is a safe place for young people to explore their 'Irishness' as they are with people who understand Irish culture, values and history.

Granny Duane teaches her grandchildren the value of their Irish heritage including the Irish language which is both promoted and supported by St. Michael's Irish Centre.

The Ryans
Everyone in the Irish Community in Liverpool knows, or knows about, the Ryan family. For a couple of generations they have been known for their football and, even more, for their singing.

212

The first Ryan family came to Liverpool with their children from Tramore County Waterford in the 1920s. One of the children was James. He married Winifred in Liverpool in the 1930s and they had one child, Michael. Sadly Winifred died and James married Jenny Murray from Longford.

They had nine children and they, and Michael, are the Ryans we all know. They are Patricia, Jackie, Kevin, Terry, Maureen, Bernard, Alice, Jimmy and Sheila. They were all born in the Anfield area. Mike remembers the Shamrock Club and all the others went to the Irish Centre in Mount Pleasant.

Mike has happy memories of the Irish Centre. He went in every Sunday with his father James, to meet all his friends. In the evenings he went in for the showbands.

Jackie played professional football for Notts County, Luton and Tranmere. With his brothers Kevin and Bernie he played for Finn Harps. Terry was one of Finn Harps best supporters.

They Ryans are great singers, Jackie, Kevin and Bernie sang as the Ryan Brothers. Jackie and his son are still singing in the Wigan area where they live. They also tour Ireland singing. Bernie is now singing as Rebel Heart and can be heard all over Liverpool.

Maureen and her sisters have always supported their brothers, singing and playing football. They have been great supporters of all Irish activities in Liverpool.

Mike's memories of Mount Pleasant included his visits on a Sunday when he and his father came in to meet their friends. Jim's sister was May Stannard who with her husband George were regulars with a group all of whom were very republican in their outlook. Sean and Felix Hannon was always there with copies of An Phoblacht. George Stannard was known as the 'English Republican'. Jim Wynne who is now one of our 'Top Table' in St. Michael's was another member of the group.

Mike's memories of familiar faces in the Irish Centre were the people who made you welcome at the door, like Sean Murphy, Martin Foley and Colum Walsh. Nick Redmond was the welcome face behind the bar. There was always someone you knew. The centre was the people.

Like many others who used the Irish Centre in those days Mike Ryan and his wife Eunice now come regularly to the Tea Dances in St. Michael's. Until Frank Murphy died recently he enjoyed meeting him. Frank and Sally had been members of his group of friends in Mount Pleasant.

Stockley / Dunne / Shaw

The Shaw family was a Liverpool Irish family with its roots in Tralee. Frank Shaw was a well known Liverpool Irish writer. His sister Pauleen Shaw. known as Pal, married Denis Dunne who was from Wexford and was a shopkeeper in Liverpool. Pal was always very involved in Irish affairs in Liverpool and quickly became involved in the new Irish Centre, Mount Pleasant as a staff member as well as using the Centre socially.

Pal's daughter, Pat, married Colman Stockley. Colman Stockley is a native of County Cork, having been born on Bere Island, and lived in Cobh. He sailed into Liverpool as a merchant seaman on board the Irish Larch. He met Pat Dunne as a result of a blind date foursome. Colman and Pat were intended to be 'the other couple' but they were destined to be together. They socialized at Irish dance venues like Blair Hall and the Shamrock Club.

They were married in St. Francis Garston in 1963 and had four children, six grandchildren and one great grandchild. Pat thinks that as their baby was born on 4th March 1965 only 32 days after the Irish Centre opened, it is probably the first baby born to Irish Centre members.

After living briefly in St. Clare's parish they have lived in St. Margaret Mary's Parish for 40 years. Pat has been a member of the UCM in the parish for those same 40 years.

Pat's brother Sean was in charge of the Claddagh room in the Irish Centre when it was named, while his brother Mogue also worked there before going to live in Ireland. Colman has worked in St. Michael's Irish Centre since shortly after we opened and he and Pat attend many events including Patrick Gaul's folk nights. Colman is also a regular 25 card player.

Colman says he loves every minute he spends in St. Michael's and he likes the fact that the church on Bere Island is St. Michael's. Pat says that the Irish Centre, Mount Pleasant and St. Michael's Irish Centre have played a very important and enjoyable part in their lives.

The Top Table

A group of men meet in St. Michael's Irish Centre every Sunday. They sit just by the door into the bar and office. Mossie Gallagher has christened them 'The Top Table'.

TOM HOWLIN came from his home in Murrintown, County Wexford in 1969 to visit his two sisters, and he stayed. In those 40 years he has never been out of work. He remembers going to Mount Pleasant every Sunday. He went to the bar during the day for the session, and to the ballroom for showbands on a Friday and for the ceili on a Sunday night. In those days he was known as Hairy Jack. If you saw him you knew why. Tom met Chris, who was to be his wife in the Grafton Dance Hall. He asked her name and she said "Chris Mayo". He thought she said she was from Mayo! She wasn't! They had three children Samantha, Patrick and Susie who became a great flute player. She attended Comhaltas Ceoltori Eireann classes. She still occasionally plays in St. Michael's Irish Centre. Sadly Chris died before her time.

PAT POWER is from Kilmacthomas, County Waterford. He married Angela Brown a neighbour from home. They came to Liverpool in 1996. Pat says they like it here. He first came to St. Michael's Irish Centre to see the hurling and gaelic football games on RTE, and has been coming in for the GAA games ever since. On big All-Ireland days there's a huge crowd, but on some junior club days the Top Table could be almost on their own. Pat lives for a Waterford All Ireland Hurling Championship win. Although the GAA games are important these men are there for the stories and the devilment too.

PAT DOHERTY is 'a Dub' and proud of it. He is Padraig O Dochartaigh and uses his 'cupla focal' frequently. He is a member of the Sean O'Donovan branch of the Gaelic League. He loves history, especially, but not only, Irish History. Pat came to Liverpool as a seaman in 1950. He married Gertie and settled down in Bootle in 1956. He says his wife was very proud to be 'Bootle Irish'. Her father's family was originally from Wexford. He enjoys Sundays on the Top Table because there's plenty of talking. He laughs when Tom says he supports everyone except Dublin.

BERNARD MORGAN is also a member of the Top Table. He was born in Liverpool, near St. Peter's in the city centre and then lived in Dovecot in St. Margaret Mary's parish. His parents were Henry J. who was from the Cooley Peninsula in County Louth. His mother Rose Ann Murphy was born in Liverpool. Bernard says his mother was very proud of her membership of Cuman na mBan and of her role in the 1916 Rising. In the Irish Centre, Mount Pleasant, he always had copies of the Irish Democrat and he was usually in company with his great friend, the author Desmond Greaves. Bernard says his memories of the Centre are good because the beauty of the building and the cultural nature of the activities lifted the community. Bernard's drink is a cup of tea!

BILLY QUINLAN, a brother of Michael Quinlan was a founder member of the Top Table but sadly died some years ago. His photo is on the wall there, as a permanent reminder.

JIM WYNNE sometimes joins them on the Top Table. His mother came from Belfast to help start a workshop here, having worked for the owner in Belfast. Jim's father was from Sligo. Jim was very involved in the Irish Studies in Mount Pleasant. His cousin Leo who lives in Belfast, is a regular visitor to St. Michael's whenever he is over to visit Jim. Jim's mother told the story of how bunting was being put up for a coronation or similar event, in their street in the southend of Liverpool. The bunting eventually ended on the house next door and started again on the house on the other side.

FATHER SEAN O'CONNOR isn't really a full member of the Top Table but he visits them whenever he's in the Centre for a GAA game. They all enjoy his visits and the craic is always mighty. Father Sean is a Cork man from Ballydesmond. His great love is hurling and above all Cork Hurling. He has been known to watch the Cork footballers too! In the Irish Community in Liverpool he is simply 'Father Sean'. He is at the heart of everything Irish in the City. Every year on the Sunday before St. Patrick's Day he says Mass in the Centre. His homily of the day is eagerly looked forward to each year. The Mass consistently has the biggest attendance of any event of the year. All the rooms are always filled to capacity. Father Sean says "I suppose I am the Spiritual Director of the Top Table".

Conclusion

*B*EING *IRISH IN LIVERPOOL* records my own memories of my life as a member of the Irish Community in Liverpool in particular, and in Britain in general.

I started with my childhood and then wrote about *Liverpool as the first Diaspora found it*. I have always found Liverpool and its history fascinating.

My story, including my interpretation of history, is very much my own opinion. I am well aware that every person who lived through the period I have described will have a totally different view of events. I do hope other people will be encouraged to put their memories into print, particularly if they have a different view.

I have never doubted that the Irish communities in Britain should retain their identity by keeping alive their cultural activities.

I have heard the argument that we should not keep our cultural identity, that we should become totally involved in the host community or that we should "integrate".

In 1964, when we were asking people in Ireland to donate towards the deposit on the Mount Pleasant premises, Father B in Carlow said, "Of course, there is an advantage in an Irish Centre, but is there a danger that such social gatherings prevent Irish people from integrating into the host community?" Father B did enclose a donation.

I believe that if we fail to have an Irish Centre, and fail to keep our Irishness alive, then we sink without trace. That is NOT integration.

If we don't keep our cultural identity alive or retain our Irishness, we will have nothing to give Liverpool.

The culture of Liverpool is made up of the combined cultures of the various nationalities that live here. Our musicians and dancers were included in the major events of Capital of Culture 2008.

After the sad closure of the Irish Centre in Mount Pleasant, our activities were fragmented and scattered. It

The Top Table The group of men who meet in St. Michael's Irish Centre every Sunday. They sit just by the door into the bar and office. Pat Doherty, Jack Murray, Jimmy Murray, Jim Wynne, Mossie Gallagher, Pat Power, Bernard Morgan and Tom Howlin.

Kathleen and Tommy Walsh.

was the opening of St. Michael's Irish Centre which I have described elsewhere that enabled the activities to come together and thrive. Those of us trying to book rooms were told "Not around St. Patrick's Day" or "We close around Christmas time."

Any group of people. Irish or otherwise, can only flourish and thrive by having their own premises. That was Father Paddy Spain's message in the 1950s and 1960s.

Recently, we had a huge Irish weekend, which cannot be achieved by booking various rooms for odd occasions. The Bolger School of Irish dancers had day and evening events on Saturday, filled with children, parents and grandparents. Comhaltas Ceoltoiri Eireann ran an open air Ceili in our garden on the Sunday afternoon in what was a feast of Ceili Dancing and Music. Meanwhile, two GAA Provincial Finals were televised live from Ireland, and were watched by crowds in the hall and bar. Such a weekend could only be staged in our own premises.

The numbers of young parents attending with their children, points to a healthy future. The dreadful events of the early 1990s in Mount Pleasant indicate that we must not take anything for granted. I believe we have teenagers and young adults in the Centre who are full of all that's good in human nature! They are educated to a level we never dreamed of. They have a love of Ireland and of things Irish to equal any of the achievers of the past.

The Irish Community and the Irish Centre are in good hands. Many wonderful people who worked hard to retain our Irish culture have gone to their eternal reward.

The music, dancing, language and games have to be preserved and passed on to the future Irish community , as they passed them on to us.

BREANDÁN MAC LUA.

I would never have written this book but for Breandán Mac Lua. He urged me over a period of years to write it. I told him that as the best writer I knew, he should write about the Irish in Britain. He responded that, as he came to Britain as an adult, he wasn't qualified. I made a start on the book ten years or so ago. I sent my first draft to Breandán in August 1998 but did no more.

After the *GAA Provincial Council of Britain – A History* was published, I asked him what he thought of it. We were standing in that big room in the Irish Embassy. Most people had gone. "It's OK but it's the wrong book."

I told him I would go back to this book, but it was at his funeral in Windsor in January 2009 that I really decided I had to finish it.

I had met Breandán in Croke Park in 1964 and we then met regularly at Central Council Meetings. We met again when he came to the Irish Centre Liverpool to tell me about his plans for the Irish Post.

We remained in close contact ever since. Telephone calls were in hours rather than minutes. In latter years, there were letters enclosing newspaper cuttings "in case you missed it".

He inspired the Irish people in Britain through very difficult times, particularly with the Frank Dolan column, though he never publicly acknowledged that the column was his own. He made one of his few journeys north to attend my wife's funeral, and I attended his beloved Maeve's funeral years later.

After Maeve died, Breandán was never as vibrant and the next funeral in Windsor was his own.

On one occasion he wrote "Your obligation is to provide a context and a dignity for your Liverpool Irish folk". "If you don't do it, it won't be done properly."

"Your telling will lay down a foundation for viewing the Irish Community in Britain, not just Liverpool, for two or three generations."

Since his death, his daughter Sinéad found the correspondence about the book in her father's papers. She has inspired me to finish the work referred to. I hope that this will do Breandán. I wouldn't expect more than 'it's ok'.

KATHLEEN

My wife Kathleen was my life partner until she died in July 1994. She was responsible for the life that I led and, in particular, for the Irish Community life described in the book, and encouraged me in my activities. We were both born in Liverpool, and, as my spiritual home was Carraroe, County Galway, hers was The Ballagh, County Wexford. Kath gave me four wonderful children, who have also inspired me in all that I do. Colum married Eileen O'Riordan of Grenagh, County Cork where they now live. They are very involved in GAA affairs and in every aspect of community life. Mary met and married Paul Nannery of County Cavan. They live with their children Deryn and Caoilin in High Wycombe. Nick is in New York. Many members of the Irish Community in Liverpool call in to Molly's on Third Avenue and are made welcome. Kathleen married Gary Cunningham who, like her, was born in Liverpool of a Galway family. Kathleen runs the Bolger Cunningham School of Irish Dancing. Like many others referred to in my book, they met in the Irish Centre, Mount Pleasant. Their children are Sinéad, Tomás and Seán.

Tomas O'Canainn of Cork, or Tom Canning as many people in Liverpool know him, came over with the Comhaltas Concert Party in 1995. It was his first visit to Liverpool since Kathleen's funeral. This was his tribute.

For Kathleen Walsh

My "Limerick's Lamentation" is for you, Kathleen
Here in Liverpool on my first visit
Since we followed you that July day to Yew Tree.
You would have liked these dancers too -
Happy reminders of other times
In St. George's Hall or in the Centre,
When Milton Avenue was all a bustle
With concert singers from Ireland and Tommy
Was in need of your calm. You were the fulcrum then
Of all the Walshs. You are still.

Tomás Ó Canainn.

Comhaltas Tour of Britain, 1995